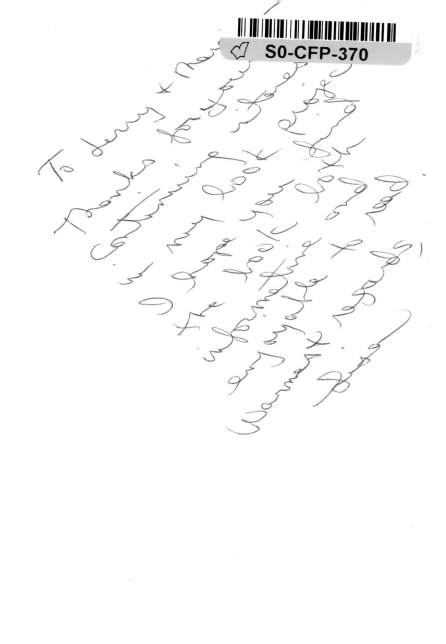

The L.A. Sensation

Armen Antonian, Ph.D.
Lisa H. Iyer, Ph.D.

Copyright © 2004 by Armen Antonian, Ph.D. &
Lisa H. Iyer, Ph.D.

ISBN 0-7414-1809-6

Published by:

PUBLISHING.COM

519 West Lancaster Avenue
Haverford, PA 19041-1413
Info@buybooksontheweb.com
www.buybooksontheweb.com
Toll-free (877) BUY BOOK
Local Phone (610) 520-2500
Fax (610) 519-0261

Printed in the United States of America

Printed on Recycled Paper

Published March 2004

Contents

Part Three
How L.A. Became the Cultural Aspiration of the World

Part Four
L.A. Today

**Part Five
The L.A.-ing of the World**

Acknowledgements

The L.A. Sensation is, unabashedly, an L.A. book that speaks to the notion that Los Angeles is a city that has come of age as a cultural leader. Our commitment to this project results from the need to highlight this "other" L.A., the L.A. that creates cutting-edge modern culture. The "bad-boy" L.A. or the L.A. *noir* image recedes in the face of the rapidly emerging cultural earthquake that is L.A./Hollywood. Without the openness and generosity of the many people who advised, commented, guided and granted us interviews along the way, we certainly would not have completed the project. We especially wish to thank Jody Jacobs for sharing her wealth of knowledge about L.A. Society and for her invaluable guidance as we conducted our interviews. Terry Stanfill was extremely helpful in pointing the way in the interview process at an early stage both with regard to L.A. Society and Hollywood. Agent Toni Loppopolo was the first to direct our writing toward a general audience. Agent Brenda Feigan insisted that we do interviews at a time when we were hesitant to do so. Agents Ken and Vincent Atchity helped us in editing the book and Ken Atchity coined the title, *The L.A. Sensation*. We wish to thank Alan Berliner for his wonderful photos, and Jeff Hyland for providing us with historical images of the Westside. Many thanks also to Frank Gehry for allowing us to use the sketch of Disney Hall, and to the Beverly Hills Hotel for giving us permission to use a photo of the hotel. 2 Rodeo Drive graciously provided us photos of that famous Beverly Hills street. Finally, we are grateful to Ann Claire Van Shaick for her excellent editing and to Ashok Iyer for his many hours of technical assistance on the project.

Foreword

A long-standing debate, decades old, is still being argued back and forth. The feud, if it can be called that, between two cities on opposite coasts—New York and Los Angeles—as to which one deserves the top position socially, economically and culturally—still goes on. Until now!

Two daring writers, Armen Antonian and Lisa Iyer, both West Coast residents, have tackled the subject, and in this book they reveal the truth about Los Angeles, which today is possibly the world's best-kept secret in terms of diversity and cultural wealth. In meticulous fashion they interviewed prominent movers and shakers in L.A. social circles, financial hot spots, in the Hollywood film industry and entertainment circles. They visited showplace homes in Pasadena, Bel-Air, Holmby Hills, and Beverly Hills to gauge how Los Angeles has developed in terms of architecture, style and taste. Their research has been molded into a fun, fascinating read, the title of which indicates their conclusion: The L.A. sensation is a force that is taking America and the world by storm. Los Angeles has grown into a genuine cosmopolis—a city whose artists, intellectuals and philanthropists rival those of great cities like Paris or London.

I met Armen and Lisa at the beginning of their research for *The L.A. Sensation,* and was pleased to serve as a mentor and advisor to them throughout their development of this groundbreaking book. I was impressed at how enthusiastically these two young, bright, highly educated Angelenos took to their task of learning about Los Angeles—as it was, and as it is now. Their professionalism, objective approach and sense of humor make for a lively, informative journey through the socio-cultural landscape of the West Coast.

This book is a must for anyone interested in Los Angeles, and for educated people the world over who are curious about just how Los Angeles has quietly moved into the forefront of world culture. My hope is that these two writers' work will open readers' eyes to the new L.A., and invite more first-rate thinkers and creators to visit Los Angeles or become an integral part of its existence.

Jody Jacobs
L.A. Times Society Editor 1972-1986
Atascadero, CA
December 2003

PART ONE

HOW L.A. DEFINES SUCCESS FOR THE WORLD

CHAPTER ONE

Los Angeles Comes of Age: The Triumph of Hollywood

The only thing worse than being talked
about is not being talked about.

—Oscar Wilde

Taking a Bite Out of the Big Apple

Whether you praise L.A. as cutting edge or criticize it as shallow, in the modern media-driven culture, Los Angeles has definitely upped the stakes on New York in a game of social poker. The top drawer L.A. crowd now sits at the cusp of social and cultural trends. Thank the media and modern culture—or curse them. How Los Angeles came to occupy such an exalted position is the story to be related here, a Hollywood plot made real. A journey through the social, cultural and economic strata of Los Angeles in search of how this once maligned city has, like the tectonic plates that underlie it, shifted to the forefront of world culture reveals that it was not simply financial power or traditional cultural institutions that have catapulted L.A. to the top of the social heap. When all the multi-colored pieces are laid together in a thoroughly modern mosaic, the fierce dreams, luck, passion and economic acumen that have taken the city to heights above and beyond its middle-of-the-road, culturally impoverished past become apparent. Los Angeles has become honestly significant: Trend-setting, surprising, and full of promise. And like a formula rags-to-riches Hollywood movie, the story of how Los Angeles pulled itself out of relative obscurity is rife with dramatic twists and turns.

The determined westward movement of pockets of new wealth and creativity initially set the stage for the birth of glamorous Old Hollywood and the beginning of a fledgling Los Angeles culture. As Angelenos began to marry the area's incredible natural advantages with their own ambitions and talents, Society moved outdoors. The cloistered, inward-looking, Old World New York lifestyle gave way to an expansive, more liberated outlook toward people and projects. The idea that **anything** was possible in the sunshine state was not only the mantra of those who came here to make it big in the movies; it was the unspoken prayer in the hearts of those who stayed to make the place their own. Decade after decade, bright minds answered the call of Los Angeles. European chefs began to create magic in L.A. restaurants and changed the face of American cuisine. Architecture, art, design and fashion quickly followed suit. Notable artists found themselves uniquely positioned to meld the ethos and tenets of Far Eastern culture with the European traditions that had formed the basis of their training. Through these provocative, brilliant new formats and creations, Hollywood and Los Angeles have been able not only to court high society—those elevated jet-setters and global tastemakers—but also to propose marriage to them and have their offer accepted most graciously.

Out of this union has come, among other developments, an increasing philanthropic commitment to the city. How this commitment has played out, and how it continues to shape Los Angeles as a city and as an arbiter of cultural values worldwide—influences beamed to the world by Hollywood—is nothing short of fascinating. Los Angeles now not only has a global reach in terms of style—both haute and hip—it is sending its message of dynamism, hope and infinite possibilities to people around the world. Whether L.A. is fully prepared to lead the modern culture is perhaps the proverbial $64,000 question. Doubters wonder about the robustness and depth of this new "spirit of the city." Is it genuine, or just a façade, like the one-dimensional towns that dot the landscape of Universal Studios?

Amidst an L.A. Westside real estate market in which homes double as rare jewels and often sell for more than the asking price, buyers tear down multimillion dollar houses and erect modernistic Southern California showcases in their place. Bing Crosby's former house wasn't big enough, so T.V. producer Aaron Spelling tore it down to build a 48 million dollar, 123-room estate complete with bowling alley, fishpond and ice-skating rink. Neither did Walt and Lillian Disney's longtime home near UCLA fit its 8.9 million dollar bill. The new owner tore down the Disney home merely to add its 2.6-acre lot to the property he had already purchased next door for a paltry 4.9 million dollars. Is nothing sacred in L.A.? One axiom rings true: Buy Westside real estate and stake your claim to the L.A. upper crust lifestyle.

Herbalife founder Mark Hughes bought the three lots adjacent to his 20,000 square-foot mansion, Greyhall, once leased by legendary actor Douglas Fairbanks, tore down the homes on two of the lots for a backyard and used the third home as a guest house. The youthful-looking Hughes died unexpectedly at age forty-four in a second Westside home he had purchased in Malibu for $25 million. Hughes was awaiting the completion of yet another project—a 45,000 square-foot home on 157 acres in Benedict Canyon overlooking Beverly Hills that he bought from "Jeopardy" and "Wheel of Fortune" king Merv Griffin—a home he will never see. The Mediterranean villa was to cost as much as 50 million dollars and would have been a crowning addition to Hughes' portfolio of homes. As for Griffin, he had earlier sold the rights to his shows for 250 million dollars and promptly bought the Beverly Hilton Hotel.

Even the admittedly jaded high-end realtors privately marvel at home prices on L.A.'s Westside. One such realtor, Jeff Hyland, who sold Hughes the Griffin property, laments that he has had trouble finding a Westside home for his own family that is not ridiculously priced. In Beverly Hills, "entry-level" homes within walking distance of Rodeo Drive exceed one million dollars; an acre in Bel-Air or Holmby Hills has soared to $4 million plus. Meanwhile, Ruth Ryon's popular "Hot Property" column in the *L.A. Times* highlighting high-end homes has expanded to keep up with the goings on. Ms. Ryon's phone rings off the hook.

The buying and selling of prime real estate in L.A.'s most coveted enclaves is more than symbolic. The haute consumption playing out on the now world famous Rodeo Drive in Beverly Hills—a street which was only a bridle path in the 1920s when New York's Café Society was in full swing—is anything but frivolous. The L.A. upper crust eye is carefully trained on haute products, available only at specialty stores on Rodeo Drive and environs. And only haute products will do. Distinctive goods—the couture gown, the designer chair, the custom home—become works of art and architectural models, alluring images transmitted to the middle class in magazines such as *Town and Country* and *Vanity Fair*. This Pandora's Box of haute images, transmitted times ten by television and film, projects a definitive beat throughout the country and the world, etching the good life L.A.-style indelibly on our national psyche and directly influencing middle class buying habits. L.A. is the social cauldron, the hotbed of new trends from chic to ultra-cool.

Another sign in a long series of signs of the new-found L.A. social clout dating back to the 1970s: The traditional, somber *Town and Country* devoted its October 1999 issue to the L.A. upper crust and Hollywood, highlighting the mid-century modernistic home of an L.A. socialite. What has taken place in the last two decades to compel **the** magazine of the American upper class to explore the lives of a "few well chosen Angelenos" and to see how Hollywood really lives now? The magazine exclaims to its select group of readers that mid-century modernism is "all the rage" in L.A. Indeed.

L.A. is finding its modern calling and is a leading influence on design. "The market for modern design has been explosive in the '90s both in America and Europe," says Bruce Wilmer, editor of New York's *Art & Auction* magazine. "It's the reinvention of cool—a hip style that has become high style." L.A. is the place that gives the freest expression to the mid-century design with streamlined fiberglass, molded plywood and polished aluminum furniture, much of it designed in the city itself. The Hollywood movers and shakers want homes and furniture that owe their origins to Charles and Ray Eames, Richard Neutra, Frank Lloyd Wright, R.M. Schindler, and now Frank Gehry and the like, and they are paying more than top dollar to get them. A 1940s molded plywood Charles Eames-designed chair sells at the Los Angeles modern auction for $129,000. The sculptured furniture of another pioneer of the L.A. mid-century modern design, Paul Laszlo, is featured by the Manhattan furniture gallery Donzella. Gallery owner Paul Donzella explains the minimalist approach of the mid-century modernists: "After years of filling their houses with European stuff like Queen Anne design, people were letting go of tradition . . . Southern California was leading the way."

A group of L.A.'s top furniture designers, who generally work out of the Melrose-Robertson corridor on the city's famous Westside, meet for a convention. These designers cater to some of Hollywood's top entertainment executives. Their furniture is laid out like pieces of sculpture in an art show or better yet, a furniture fashion show. This furniture-as-art concept is all the rage at the 2000 Milan International Furniture Fair, where young designers from Pasadena's Art Center College of Design near Los Angeles bring their own modern imprint to the event. Many of the hundreds of furniture and lighting firms will take their "free-flowing" furniture to L.A. for validation, because what sells in L.A. sells worldwide. Meanwhile, a 2003 modernism show in Palm Springs attracts Charles Hollis Jones, known for his work in acrylic furniture. Sylvester Stallone pays $32,000 for a Jones-designed bed with a lighted acrylic base. 700 people meet at the Cinerama Dome in Hollywood to pay tribute to architect Welton Beckect, whose credits include the Cinerama Dome itself along with the Music Center and parts of Century City. Culture has demonstrably gone global, and Los Angeles is at the head of the modernist parade.

L.A. is known for celebrity estates, for stars poured into sleek designer gowns, but for bread? Yes, even bread is an item up for scrutiny and interpretation in the drive for quality. No product escapes this unbridled striving for excellence, first demanded by the L.A. upper crust but now also considered essential by eager-eyed segments of the middle class. Suzanne Dunaway, who began her Buona Forchetta bread company in her West L.A. home, comments on bread and status: "You get people thinking about their bread. Do they really want soft, sliced bread or would they rather have something with a little tooth that makes their day a little nicer? You get a little luxury in your life with your bread." L.A. bread is definitely not Wonder bread. Another L.A. bakery, the LaBrea Bakery, with its olive, rosemary, chocolate sour cherry and fig breads, is now a nationwide concern. From furniture to fashion to bread, middle class Americans are re-discovering quality in the goods around them. They reach out for a quality that comes from craftsmanship, a quality once spirited away from them in the name of progress with the flourishing of the mass market in the 1950s and '60s. And it is the upstart Los Angeles, home of the uncouth, of the whimsical, of Tinseltown, that is leading the cultural revolution in all things fit to buy.

In this latest contest for the social distinction destined to define a new modernism for the new century, no one projects the happening beat the way the Hollywood trendsetters of the L.A. upper crust do. L.A.? Does it even have a distinct upper crust? It does. In L.A., consumption and spectacle join in the Magic Kingdom of Hollywood. No one matches the pizzazz of L.A.'s top social circles, their sleek sophistication, their flair. Dress up, dress down, or turn your head away in disgust—but the center stage of social life, spectacle, is never far away at an L.A. benefit, ball, studio gathering or première. To the dismay of traditionalists, New York's Café Society finds its purest expression over a half-century later in Los Angeles.

Meanwhile, among the skyscrapers of Manhattan, hovering about Fifth and Park Avenues, the Beautiful People, popularized on the pages of Diana Vreeland's *Vogue* in the 1960s, have readily given way to the Nouvelle Society of New York: To the Kravises, the Steinbergs, the

Perelmans, and the Trumps—photographed at Society events, appearing on the watchful pages of *Women's Wear Daily* and of *W*. New players, same game. Their elegant co-ops and penthouses graced by priceless art boast the finest silver and sparkling crystal. Their lifestyles display and define the beauty, elegance, and expensive taste that have served as unique symbols of upper class distinction for over a century. But now the position of elegant, refined New York is being usurped by that rogue on the other coast: L.A.

Los Angeles, that once vulgar upstart, the avant-garde, tinseled pretender to Society, has moved to the forefront of the upper class to share the top honors. From the Westside enclaves of Malibu, Santa Monica, Brentwood, Beverly Hills, Bel-Air and Holmby Hills inland to the more traditional locales of Hancock Park and Pasadena, Angelenos step into the spotlight. The Los Angeles upper crust, imbued with the power of Hollywood's movers and shakers—the movie moguls, behind-the-scenes dealmakers, financiers, super agents and stars that make up the motion picture industry—now creates social distinction in America. Los Angeles becomes the auction block of the modern media-driven culture akin to the Chicago futures market. Yet the vigorous bidding in L.A. is not on wheat and soybeans, but on future lifestyles and trends.

L.A.'s top social circles, led by the ever-expanding cultural power of Hollywood, beam images of the Southern California good life via films and Oscar parties and custom homes and Rodeo Drive. Imperial New Yorkers must bow to the cultural wand of this new empress. Once the crass pretender, L.A. has become the global focal point of haute culture and hip attitudes. East Coasters gawk at passing guests at the Peninsula, the new hotshot hotel of Beverly Hills. As pale guests from the East sit poolside at the classic Beverly Hills Hotel on their visits to Los Angeles, they try to look busy as they watch their new rivals swing their latest movie deal on the cell phone while lounging in a private cabana with a papaya sorbet in hand and a masseuse standing by. What a difference a century makes. Or does it?

Looking back some one hundred years, the old, impenetrable Knickerbocker aristocracy, families such as the Van Rensselaers and Livingstons whose ancestors had founded the Colonies, succumbed also to an upstart class who challenged their supremacy in the social arena. These established families were also ungraciously pushed aside, that time by the families of the industrial robber barons who converged on New York with carriages full of cash, setting new rules and forming the basis of the modern American upper class. Having left their provincial cities, these social pioneers headed East, wanting to erase quickly any traces of their humble origins. Surprisingly, the family names so prominent today—Rockefeller, Vanderbilt, Mellon, Du Pont and others that symbolize upper class heritage and "old money"—once carried no social distinction at all.

The top industrialists—the Goulds, the Fricks, the Vanderbilts et. al.—boasted little charm, culture or learning, but they possessed something more important: Money. Their fortunes were the largest in the world. Reflecting the social atmosphere of the time, artist Charles Dana Gibson published in his 1902 collection of sketches a rather unbecoming symbol of this new breed of American whom he called simply "The Heiress." Next to the drawing he wrote: "She cannot talk, She cannot sing, She looks a Fright; But Folks Aver Ten Millions Have been set apart to talk and sing and look for her."

The late mythologist Joseph Campbell surmised that the tallest buildings in a civilization reflect its cultural emphasis. As the twentieth century approached, places of business grew ever taller in the increasingly urban landscape. With commerce a key cultural feature, the wide-eyed newcomers' social power grew. After a reign of some two hundred years, the Old Guard, whose ancestors dated back to the earliest Colonies, no longer ruled the American upper class. The opportunistic industrialists, riding the crest of the Industrial Revolution, burst onto the New York social scene and claimed the social capital of New York as their own. Their triumph was inevitable because the modern American upper class is a non-aristocratic class, so one's status in it withers without wealth. As a result, America's upper class today includes few descendants of the first stalwarts of Society such as the Van Cortlands and Verplancks. Nor does it include any Jeffersons, Washingtons, Hamiltons, Madisons or Franklins—the descendants of the original political class. Rather, Vanderbilt, Rockefeller, Whitney, and Mellon— wealth once considered shockingly new—are the names known around the world. But those powerful turn-of-the-century industrial families are not alone on the social pinnacle or the tale would end there, in New York, as a minor sideshow in American social history. These families are joined today by New York's Nouvelle Society of Trumps and Steinbergs and Kravises who, along with their wives, further emblazon the flag of high society in the public mind. But the New Yorkers now have some very, very unexpected company.

A Rendezvous with L.A.

A new player has burst onto the scene like an earthquake, creating its own set of rules. The Los Angeles upper crust, propelled by the vast fortunes of the motion picture industry, has met the New Yorkers head on. The Angelenos have become not just a second feature, a nice afterthought in the contest for social distinction—but the main attraction. Once, Selznick and Astaire would work in Hollywood but trek across the country to play in New York. Now, Ovitz, Geffen, Lansing—the new breed of Hollywood moguls—are content with nothing less than changing the rules of upper class lifestyle. They are tearing down the tired remnants of the WASP-only and male-only signs and dispensing with the once obligatory Old World designs in art, architecture, dress and even cuisine.

While sitting in her stunning Pasadena home chatting over afternoon tea, Joan Hotchkis, President of the Blue Ribbon, a top women's group in Los Angeles, explains how this restructuring of L.A. Society has affected the arts community in Los Angeles: "Well, when Michael Ovitz ruled over Hollywood, he collected contemporary art, which gave the impulse to a lot of other people in the Business." The Hollywood trendsetters are creating a social renaissance, reinventing an American upper crust stale with traditionalism. Black and white is out; color is in. The Hollywood style is to be both hip and haute. New is in, old is out. Get the picture? This is not the Los Angeles spotlighted in the *noir* films such as *Chinatown* or *L.A. Confidential*, the caricatured L.A. of the seedy and the ignorant. This is the L.A. of style and glamour that so many seek to emulate. It is the real Hollywood in its actual social setting.

In this modern tale of two cities, in this "yin and yang of America," as essayist Richard Rodriguez calls California and New York, Los Angeles is now a counter-attraction to New York for national upper class leadership and the adulation of all the other classes down the line who, caught in the social whirlpool, compete in the contest for social distinction. Once again the new arrivals have come with a winning hand. This time the card of the joker is not just big money, mere cash, which exists in several states, wherever business ownership is concentrated. L.A.'s trump is named Donald as in Duck, symbolic of that whimsical yet immensely powerful enterprise of image creation called the entertainment industry. Hollywood culture has taken on New York economics and won out in a game of social chess.

In George Orwell's *Animal Farm*, some animals are more equal than others; in industry, some businesses wield greater social clout than others. In the modern mass society based on the revolution in communications, that industry which creates image tends be the most powerful. Great political theorists from Plato to Machiavelli have warned that image creates reality. And when that image has real muscle, economic power, behind it, no other type of social influence can compete. Los Angeles, blessed with the awesome power of Hollywood, witness to the marriage of image creation and economic power that Hollywood embodies, and graced by one of the greatest greenbelts of residential real estate in the world—the Beverly Hills/Holmby Hills/Bel-Air triangle—transmits its unique, trendsetting image throughout the country and then abroad. As New Yorkers clank around in their traditional armor à la ancient Rome, Los Angeles takes center stage as the new home of cultural prophets, explains L.A. author Carolyn See.

Faced with a cultural barrage of films, television shows, mega-stars and finally Presidents, the social nation has succumbed. The children of farmers in Kansas and industrial workers in Kentucky viewed the mythic California lifestyle, now indomitably très L.A., in television shows such as "Melrose Place," "Beverly Hills 90210," and "Baywatch" and were quickly hooked. American youth want a taste of L.A. And the Los Angeles lifestyle is imbued by that phenomenon which so dominates it: Hollywood. When confronted with the rising image of L.A., the New Yorkers fell not at the drop of a hat; they fell at the drop of a cell phone and movie camera. "You wouldn't have had an O.J. trial anywhere else," sums up L.A. Society photographer Alan Berliner. For better or worse, such spectacle can take place only in Los Angeles, where the mix of wealth, media power, intrigue and celebrity forms an irresistible point of attraction. But L.A. is crass, L.A. is crude, object New Yorkers—in fact, per New York physiology, New York is the brain and L.A. is the genitals. "Where would you rather be?" asks Carolyn See.

As observers of L.A. culture have pointed out, the idea that Los Angeles has no brain is as old as the city itself and is a myth adhered to even by many of its residents. As *L.A. Times* book review editor Steve Wasserman explains, there is much more to Los Angeles than "Baywatch," yet even Angelenos have tended to be unaware of their city's complexity. "People write about this place as if it were heaven or hell," affirms Carolyn See as she explains that literature depicts Los Angeles as excess, exploring what happens to you if you get everything you want in this city of hopes and dreams. But even historian Mike Davis, known for his bleak books on L.A., admits that "On the West Side of

12

Los Angeles there is now an intellectual and cultural life that is easily comparable to that of New York or Boston."

But all this supposed complexity is just hoopla. The key ingredient is Hollywood. "L.A. is Hollywood is Southern California," confirms Alan Ladd, Jr., Academy-Award winning producer of *Braveheart* and *Chariots of Fire*, sitting in his office on the historic Paramount lot off Melrose in Hollywood. A soft-spoken child of Hollywood who grew up on this same lot watching his father shoot movies in the 1940s and 1950s, Ladd gets to the heart of the matter. It should not be surprising, then, that the U.S. Postal Service has changed mail sent from Los Angeles post offices from being stamped simply "Los Angeles" to "Los Angeles/Hollywood." The mayor of Hollywood, Johnny Grant, applauds the new designation: "So many tourists who come to visit write to say they're disappointed when they find out that postcards mailed from Hollywood don't say 'Hollywood.' Instead they say 'Los Angeles.'" To add another touch of Hollywood, postage stamps will be cancelled with the words "Home of the Stars."

Hollywood is entertainment is the movies. Ladd, a former studio head at MGM/UA and 20th Century Fox, acknowledges the tremendous global reach of film, attributing this influence more to the American than to the Hollywood mystique: "They buy our films and not so much the other way around. Film is one of our leading exports." In France during the summer of 2000, seven out of the top eight films were American. One August week saw an astounding 91% of movie ticket sales going to American (read Hollywood) films. Imagine what the French Minister of Culture might have said (expletives deleted) upon viewing those figures.

The L.A. influence, not respecting national borders, strikes out around the globe, and point Hollywood/L.A. is where the world turns to watch and wonder and emulate. One Beverly Hills insider confirms, "The film business has had an enormous impact on the world. People view the United States through Hollywood." Much to the chagrin of the French, the Avenue Champs-Elysées in Paris exudes a definitive Hollywood beat that captures not only foreign tourists but French youth as well. Walking down the famous Avenue, you can't help but think of Hollywood. The street has that glitzy, commercial edge to it, as if it were a live, ongoing television ad. You keep looking for the cameras. Noted author Ray Bradbury remarks, "Whenever I go to France, the French people want to know what's happening in Los Angeles. They don't ask about New York. . . . They see Los Angeles as the place that creates the world's culture, and they want to know what's going on here."

And so Charles, Earl of Newmarket, a member of the British House of Lords, visits L.A. to do a bit of old-fashioned but very proper courting, getting a feel for the city and trying to line up literary representation for his proposed writings on L.A. culture for an English audience. Former L.A. Museum of Contemporary Art president Lenore Greenberg, sitting in her artsy Beverly Hills spread near the former homes of Lucille Ball and Jimmy Stewart on a street which has also been called home by Madonna and Peter Falk, states in a modest tone, "I don't feel I have to go to New York all the time for food and culture. We have it all here in L.A. now." Today "Tinseltown" has to be taken seriously. The "outcasts" are now at the top of the heap. Just like in the movies.

Upon viewing this emerging L.A. spectacle, the New York upper class has tried to remain content, still possessing Wall Street, the mighty lever of financial control over corporate America and the supreme creator of great new fortunes. Wall Street has continued renewing the ranks of New York's upper class, long ago expanded beyond the industrial wealth of the robber barons, often challenging its WASP core by producing the new names—Kravis, Steinberg, Perelman—with the dollars: 50 million, 100 million, 5 billion and counting. Yet here too the New York upper class was surprised from outside its ranks. For a time in the 1980s, amidst the glitzy streets of Beverly Hills' commercial district, a new J.P. Morgan, one Michael Milken, humbled mighty Wall Street by changing the face of the American economy with something new: "Junk" bonds. And his address was not Wall Street but Wilshire and Rodeo in Beverly Hills. All of corporate America shuddered. Although the courts later fined and imprisoned Milken for securities violations, New Yorkers are too astute not to have seen some power move west.

As if to add to the growing affront, a very popular ex-President retired in the late 1980s in the Golden Triangle of Los Angeles' wealthy Westside. L.A.'s top social circles claimed the crown jewels of Nancy and Ronald Reagan as their own. Underscoring the unperturbed and almost jaded atmosphere of L.A.'s Westside, a high-end Beverly Hills realtor remarked matter-of-factly, "He's just another President moving into the neighborhood." A Bel-Air resident explained why so few neighbors came to pay homage to the Reagans outside their home upon their return from Washington, D.C.: "In this neighborhood, if you're invited to the White House and have dinner, that's the way you meet the President." Before Hillary Rodham Clinton became New York's junior Senator, husband Bill was reportedly slated to make Dreamworks SKG studio his new office, joining his pals David Geffen and Steven Spielberg in the Business that trumps politics. Clinton and Hollywood? Imagine the possibilities.

Planeloads of Washington officials flying West for late studio mogul Lew Wasserman and his wife Edie's 50th anniversary bash, ex-presidents taking up residence in L.A., and campaign fundraising in the city's most stunning mansions offered unmistakable signs of L.A.'s new political clout, a power derived from the city's already undeniable economic and cultural importance. Washington, D.C., the nation's political capital, has never been able to compete socially with New York. Better to have social clout first, the L.A. way, and then compete. And so L.A. kicked off the new century by hosting the Democratic national convention.

The four days of the August 2000 convention saw Hollywooders feast on an orgy of politics. Hollywood's brightest fluttered and shone at the convention itself. Paramount chief Sherry Lansing; Imagine Entertainment's Ron Howard and Brian Grazer; actors Tommy Lee Jones, Sean Penn, Sarah Jessica Parker, Warren Beatty, Annette Bening and Jimmy Smitts; director Rob Reiner and DreamWorks executives Steven Spielberg, Jeffrey Katzenberg and David Geffen—all were in the thick of the activities. Outside the convention, throughout the city's tony enclaves, Hollywood money and hospitality drew out the eager politicos for a chance to hobnob with celebrities at private parties. At a home in Mandeville Canyon, John Travolta toasted President Clinton: "I wish we could have you for another eight years." Kevin Costner's home was the scene of another party, and at Lawrence Bender's Holmby Hills home, the producer of *Pulp Fiction* and *The Mexican* greeted still more of the Hollywood acting corps including Billy Baldwin, Michael Douglas, Frances Fisher, Robert Forster, Harry Hamlin, Salma Hayek, and Mila Jovovich. The potent mix of celebrity and politics flowed enticingly through L.A.'s top neighborhoods like an elixir. From the youthful Brad Pitt and Jennifer Aniston to the venerable icon Gregory Peck, the stars played out a real-life role perhaps more meaningful than any for which they may receive an Oscar.

Small wonder that the Hollywood political elixir carried Republican movie super-hero Arnold Schwarzenegger to the governorship of California. The L.A. spectacle in August 2000 represents something much more than mere party affiliation or nuts-and-bolts campaigning. Let the tinsel fall where it may, let the party balloons burst, put away the banners, dim the lights, let George W. Bush be President, and something much more telling surfaces. Author Neal Gabler seizes on a deeper and broader meaning of the political convention spectacle: "We are a society driven by entertainment." And the engine, the transmission and the fancy hubcaps all stem from point L.A./Hollywood.

Haim Saban, another entertainment mogul who dabbles in politics, made a record-breaking contribution of 7 million dollars to the Democratic National Committee to build a new headquarters. Saban was quickly followed by film producer Steve Bing with a $5 million donation to the Democratic National Committee. Like so many latter-day movie moguls, Bing's influence extends from film to politics to sociological and environmental concerns. In 2003 Bing, who is also a co-writer of *Why Men Shouldn't Marry* starring Nicolas Cage, sponsored a Rolling Stones concert in L.A. to benefit the National Resources Defense Council. The concert was attended by Leonardo DiCaprio, Cameron Diaz and Pierce Brosnan among others.

Politics is always there to do whenever you want it in a city that has so many, many other avenues of self-definition and gratification. Politics does not dominate Hollywood despite the fact that in 2002, the entertainment industry ranked 4th among industries in federal campaign contributions. And therefore, not surprisingly, in early 2003, the major Democratic hopefuls for President were already poking around Hollywood, where politics usually plays second fiddle to style, to the Business, to culture, to whatever.

Nowhere do business and play, personal life and enterprise mix more than in Hollywood. So, also in 2003, a host of Hollywooders—Brad Pitt, Jennifer Aniston, Mike Myers, Warren Beatty, Courtney Cox, and on and on, attended a charity event, Project A.L.S., to raise money to combat Lou Gehrig's disease. Brad Grey of Brillstein-Grey Entertainment rounded up the gang. Paul Simon did a little singing at the Regency Beverly Wilshire Hotel affaire. It just so happens that Grey has also started a movie production company with Pitt and Aniston that is slated to make ten movies. In Hollywood, networking is everything.

To be sure, the New Yorkers still dominate the major print media that project the opulent display of Park and Fifth Avenue living to the nation in *Vanity Fair*, *Town and Country* and *Vogue*. But the proud and once staid New York-based "news" magazines become glossier and glossier until one writer on celebrity remarks, "Now everything is a celebrity magazine," with the tinseled edge of entertainment about it. "That's show biz" has become "Everything's show biz." *Time* magazine and *People* magazine become the same side of the same coin. New York also dominates television news, but to the chagrin of news purists, most hard news drifts across the once forbidden abyss, becoming soft entertainment news. The line between the network nightly news and entertainment news shows becomes ever so fine. Television news sells stories, which is the business of Hollywood. Popular authors such as Tom Wolfe and Dominick Dunne still wrote bestsellers about the New York haute lifestyle in the 1980s. In the 1990s the New York lifestyle reappeared in television shows. But to what avail? A re-packaged New York is no match for the alluring glamour of the new social frontier that is L.A.

Music is always at the cutting edge of culture. Tom Whalley, president of Westwood-based Interscope Records, which has recorded such 1990s acts as Nine Inch Nails and the Wallflowers, speaks of L.A. as still being far and away the center of rock and roll heaven: "The California dream is real when it comes to musicians around the country, and it draws them here year after year." In L.A., musicians really do "rock-around-the-clock," rehearsing, recording, writing songs and making videos at all hours of the day and night in the many cutting-edge studios dotted across the landscape.

The symbolic expression of the haute lifestyle in the eyes of the American audience begins in L.A., with top drawer cars, Beverly Hills mansions, Rodeo Drive shopping and stars galore. A New Jersey high school girl writes to her aunt living in Pasadena, now her idol for having trekked to Dreamland, U.S.A. from the East Coast: "I want to come and live with you. You are living your dream. The sun . . . the excitement. I want to live in Malibu." The Southern California image is just as alluring to the "Baywatch" generation as it was decades ago during the California boom years of the '50s and '60s. David Brown, former president of one of the world's most prestigious commercial art schools, The Art Center College of Design in Pasadena, reacts to what he sees as vestiges of the caricatured view of L.A. as a bunch of "nuts and fruits": "Los Angeles is one of two driving forces of change in world culture, the other being Silicon Valley. Entertainment and technology are twin engine driving forces, and they are both anchored in California."

So *Ecology of Fear* author Mike Davis misses the point as the dark soothsayer denouncing an L.A. culture and lifestyle run amok with itself and the environment. The L.A. story is not that there are earthquakes, urban sprawl, social isolation and all else that plagues modern societies. The L.A. story is that the city offers something new and therefore brings hope. Cutting-edge culture proves its worth on L.A. streets or fades away. Los Angeles, not New York or Paris, is the contemporary symbol of all that is hip and all that is haute. Down in the streets or tucked away in the gated mansions—all eyes look to L.A. That is the story.

Throughout most of American history, all eyes looked East. Now New York, its compactness revealing starkly contrasting images of wealth and poverty seemingly side by side, is in danger of becoming stodgy and irrelevant, the lavish lifestyle of its upper class appearing inaccessible to the casual observer. In New York, points out Beverly Hills realtor Jeff Hyland, co-ops can keep people out—witness the rejection by a co-op Board of super-singer Mariah Carey's application to buy a residence owned by Barbra Streisand. But in L.A., summarizes Hyland, you can buy anything: "The only color that matters is the color green."

Integral to the L.A. allure are the seemingly endless opportunities to reinvent yourself. "People come west to become what they always wanted," comments L.A. writer Carolyn See. You can dispense with your original identity and change identities even within the city. As See explains, you can reside in Hancock Park and pretend to be old rich, you can live the Valley life of domestic tranquility, or you can do the Westside dance of chic new wealth and physical culture. As the booming plastic surgery industry so aptly indicates, you are always a work in progress in Los Angeles.

The L.A. spread, with its more gradual transitions from neighborhood to neighborhood, beckons middle America. At a glance, the upper middle class appears to be on a more similar footing with the very wealthy, or at least seems to have a shot at their world of haute consumption. L.A. mega-developer Eli Broad elaborates on the L.A. phenomenon: "I love Los Angeles. It is a true meritocracy. You can come here without family background, of any religion, and if you have the right ideas, you can succeed." "Whatever I want to do here, I can find a way to do it," affirms Michele Lamy, one of L.A.'s most successful French restaurateurs. In New York, you try to gain entrée into the top social circles: In L.A., you create them.

Dubbed "the city of the millennium" by publicist Coralie Langston-Jones, Los Angeles is winning the battle of democracy as its alluring image flashes openness and attainability to middle America. New Yorkers, by contrast, appear impenetrable and imposing in their European-style fortresses. Los Angeles is to New York what Princess Diana was to the Royals—Diana always came out on top because she won the public relations battles.

And now that Europe, too, has succumbed to the L.A. charm, the contest is all but over. The Valentinos and the Armanis—the great fashion designers of the world—now must **obligatorily** come to L.A. when they visit New York. Or do they **stop** in New York on their way to L.A.? Donatella Versace went straight to L.A., where she co-hosted one of the city's top events: The Fire and Ice Ball at Universal Studios. For some perspective on one of L.A.'s biggest celebrity evenings, consider that one hundred years ago, when the battle for social dominance between the robber barons and the Knickerbockers was being fought in New York, Los Angeles was but a land of open fields, a tiny western outpost of rugged settlers promoted by the Southern Pacific Co. simply as a sunny place of splendor and affordable real estate.

The 1998 Fire and Ice Ball, an event started by Lilly Tartikoff, widow of NBC studio executive Brandon

Tartikoff, was hosted by Jerry Seinfeld, fresh from his number-one-rated television show. Tickets went for $1,000, tables for up to $50,000, but celebrities entered free of charge. "They're doing me a favor," says Tartikoff. Watching Naomi Campbell and other top models in the Versace fashion show held to raise money for the Revlon/UCLA Women's Cancer Research program were Jack Nicholson, Dustin Hoffman, Lynn Redgrave, and a host of studio executives including Paramount chief Sherry Lansing and Universal's Ron Meyer. But why stop there? Add to the list of celebrities at the Fire and Ice Ball: Madonna, Kurt Russell and Goldie Hawn, Maria Shriver, and the late Carolyn Bessette Kennedy, who brought a final East Coast crowning to the event. Even the bartenders were special—model types and aspiring actresses dressed in Versace. New York Society columnists Liz Smith and Aileen "Suzie" Mehle would be hard pressed to come up with comparable social power to write about on the New York social scene. Star power and studio power are unique and unmatched social power because wealth and celebrity flow from the same elixir. "Publi-ciety," as the late Society observer Cleveland Amory called it, is a thoroughly modern power, and Los Angeles is in the lead.

Fashion, too, has become an L.A. event, and the Oscars are the world's greatest fashion show. In 2000 the haughty, New York-based Council of Fashion Designers of America awarded its own statuette, the Trova, to the Academy of Motion Picture Arts and Sciences for its contribution to fashion through the Oscar show. A billion people worldwide watching designer-clad starlets prance down the red carpet can be a great impetus. And so Eastman Kodak paid $75 million to put its name on the new Hollywood Boulevard Theater, which became the permanent venue for the Oscars in 2002. This was the largest amount ever paid for naming rights of a building outside the sports world.

The 3,300-seat Kodak Theater at Hollywood Blvd. and Highland Ave. is, fittingly, across the street from the

Hollywood Roosevelt Hotel, which hosted the first Oscar ceremony in 1929. That first Oscar event was attended by 270 Academy members and had a family-like atmosphere. Academy President Douglas Fairbanks hosted the event as members dined on broiled chicken on toast—all for a $5 admission. The second Academy event took place at the famous Cocoanut Grove at the Ambassador Hotel and was broadcast on KNX radio. Perhaps the true precursor to the cultural bang that Oscar night now carries was when ABC first telecast the event in 1961.

The Kodak Theater stands where the now demolished Hollywood Hotel, the first Hollywood hotspot that opened in 1903, once stood. Rudolph Valentino honeymooned at the old Hollywood Hotel, and anybody who was anybody frequented the Hotel in Hollywood's earliest days. The Kodak Theater has 28 opera boxes from which the V-VIPs can view the stage and nominees below. The Governor's Ball reception takes place, on that night of nights, in a 25,000 square-foot ballroom above the Theater. The 2002 Oscar ceremony, the first held at the Kodak Theater, lived up to its historic importance as Oscar came back to its original Hollywood setting and African-Americans Halle Berry and Denzel Washington won, in unprecedented fashion, the awards for best actress and best actor. Thirty-second ads for the 2003 Oscars sold for $1.3 million a pop, and justifiably so considering that the Oscars was the second rated show in 2002, exceeded only by the Super Bowl.

The Oscar event has become so hot that Christie's Beverly Hills held an auction of past Oscar gowns to benefit the American Foundation for AIDS Research (AMFAR). Purchasing an outfit worn to the Oscars by a star is purchasing a piece of fashion history, whether it be Sharon Stone's playful outfit mixing Valentino and the Gap, or Cher's Bob Mackie harem dress. It's hard to believe that the first Oscar night in 1929 at the Hollywood Roosevelt Hotel was merely a quiet banquet comprised of a mere thirty-six tables, or that the fabulous Oscar parties only took off into the social stratosphere after 1982 when super agent Swifty

Lazar began throwing his bashes at Spago's restaurant, where Wolfgang Puck does a little cooking. Unglamorous gatherings and ordinary food have given way to the best cuisine in the world and a night when stars and VIPs hop from one haute event to another.

The 1999 Oscar scene saw the Beverly Hills Hotel's Polo Lounge hosting the Miramax party for *Shakespeare in Love* and *Life is Beautiful*, with Robert DeNiro, Nick Nolte, Jay Leno, Disney's Michael Eisner, Uma Thurman, Kevin Costner, and Kim Delaney enlivening the bash. And this was only one of the major parties on Oscar night. Beverly Hills bursts with activity the week before the Oscars as hair stylists, make-up artists, jewelers such as Harry Winston and top designers from Donna Karan to Randolf Duke to Giorgio Armani fall over backwards for a chance to dress the stars. Everyone seeks to capture that invaluable patina of star quality that could rub off on them and their special products and services. Even the great Armani can get a little flustered at all the fashion doings surrounding the Oscars. Attending a performance by guitarist Eric Clapton at Quixote Studios in West Hollywood in 1999, Armani remarked offhand, "It's [Oscar-night fashion] become ridiculous because magazines and newspapers just talk about what a star is wearing and not about the movies. That's the first question they ask."

With Hollywood as a backdrop, fashion can only be spectacle. After all, everyone in L.A. expects to be discovered. Rodeo Drive, the symbol of L.A. haute style, has become such a hot address that some retailers on the street have shops there not because they make money, but as advertising tools. In their ads Beverly Hills gets listed right along with London, Paris and New York—an implied center of everything haute. Rodeo Drive now has its own walk-a-thon, and its first plaque embedded into the sidewalk lies in front of Armani with a fitting quote from the master: "Fashion and cinema. Together for life." A Beverly Hills or Los Angeles address "is almost a built-in marketing opportunity," says New York trend analyst Tom Julian. Rodeo Drive is a major tourist destination for Americans,

Europeans and Asians. Recall that Mrs. Howard Ahmanson, world traveler and great Los Angeles lady, has said in regard to fashion that, "The California image is copied all over the world." In Asia "California" means Hollywood, glamour, sun, gorgeous women and Beverly Hills; the state's name is increasingly used as a marketing tool in the Far East. And that California image is not from Bakersfield, Santa Barbara or even San Francisco, but from the glitzy, sun-drenched city to the south.

So Katherine Bates, editor of *Harper's Bazaar*, the nation's oldest fashion magazine, comes to L.A. in 2000 to capture a piece of the L.A. fashion spectacle for her magazine. Hosting a star-studded party at Mr. Chow's restaurant in Beverly Hills, meeting retailers, and writing stories about the city, Ms. Bates emphasizes that *Harper's* wants to "establish a presence here." Commenting on the opening of her Miu Miu boutique on Melrose, Italian designer Miuccia Prada affirms, "Los Angeles [has] young, hip, more eccentric people there. The film industry seems more and more interested in fashion because fashion and cinema are very connected." Only in L.A. does the hip crowd of Miu Miu and the like complement so well the couture world of top fashion designers, and the two meet in Hollywood.

Nicholas Coleridge's "Shiney Set" described in *The Fashion Conspiracy*— the select group of women catered to by the world's greatest fashion designers who together set the trends in couture for America's upper class—these women who define impeccable taste exist in L.A. as well as in New York. Their presence at a social event or party gives the event an "A" status. The Shiney Set exists in other major cities in the United States as well. But today the upper classes of these cities must pay homage to L.A. style, just as all of the upper class has bowed before the court of New York ever since the robber barons married their "Dollar Princess" daughters to European royalty and draped their Fifth Avenue walls with the world's greatest art.

But chic wasn't always so easy to find in Los Angeles. When former *L.A. Times* Society editor Jody Jacobs came to L.A. for *Women's Wear Daily* in the 1960s, she was hard pressed to find a venue where she could send a photographer to snap shots of the city's best dressed women. She had to rely on the Bullock's Wilshire tearoom to catch upper crust women in daytime clothes. Jacobs could count on a few women such as Mrs. Jules Stein, wife of the Universal Studios head; Denise Minnelli, second wife of Oscar-winning director Vincente Minnelli; actress Rosalind Russell; and Mary Jones of Pasadena to offer distinct looks. One day when Ms. Jacobs asked Mrs. Billy Wilder, wife of the noted director of the classic movie *Sunset Blvd.*, what she was wearing, Mrs. Wilder replied, "My mother made it." Dressing up was clearly not an L.A. priority. Of course, Ms. Jacobs had trouble getting any of her L.A. photos into *Women's Wear Daily* in those days as she was met with snickering from her New York-based editors, who had little respect for L.A. taste.

Yet times do change. *Women's Wear Daily* decided finally—decades later in the year 2000—to expand its L.A. staff and coverage, which will now be second only to New York in scope. *Women's Wear Daily* worldwide president Stephanie George explains the decision to the fashion faithful: "Los Angeles is the second-biggest market domestically and the market with the most potential for the future." The *Women's Wear Daily* president's statement is as telling as it is still understated. Today the fashion industry hovers about the city as so many vultures ready to swoop down on any new L.A. style, be it hip or be it haute.

Buyers for Manhattan-based Henri Bendel show up in Los Angeles to look for L.A. "seasonless" design, or in the words of one executive buyer, "a deconstructive thing— vintage taken apart and reconstructed." The Bendel buyers are not disappointed as they buy T-shirts from a pair of young designers who describe their clothes as "urban white trash chic." Their T-shirts are embroidered with words such as "shalom," "candy," or "pervert." What could be more

L.A.? Independent avant-garde fashion designer Jeremy Scott leaves Paris to set up his Melrose studio. The young designer, who did a collection of clothes paying homage to skyscrapers, quips, "L.A. is an inspiring, inspirational, magical city... It's like dreamland." Scott's 2002 collection, including metallic micro-dresses and revealing suede beachwear never intended to be worn in water, will be shipped to his biggest market: Asia. Scott's business plans are a fitting example of L.A. as a crossroads—as a clearinghouse of the new, the triumphant, the ridiculous, and the extraordinary.

But before exploring further L.A.'s triumphant arrival at what was previously an exclusive New York performance at the center stage of American and world culture, we must find our historical bearings and set our own stage. We must go back in time to witness the creation of the modern American upper class. This fantastic voyage will take us back a century, to a period in the formation of high society not lost but largely forgotten—a time when changes in the upper class rendered its once staid structure dynamic and opened the door for even bigger changes as the approach of the millennium witnessed a once minor city, Los Angeles, challenging New York for America's social crown. The end of the unpredictable ride will find L.A., the most unlikely of cities, standing almost alone at the top of the social heap wearing that trademark Jack Nicholson grin.

PART TWO

TOP OF THE TOP:
THE MAKING OF THE L.A. UPPER CRUST

CHAPTER TWO

Celebrity Goes West: The Early Hollywood

A fool and his money are soon invited everywhere.

—Elsie de Wolfe

The Battle for New York: The Social Onslaught Begins

Wealth imbibed with celebrity is a given in contemporary American society. That this modern mindset linking wealth with celebrity is so ingrained in our psyches is ironic, since from America's Founding Fathers to New York Society at the turn of the 20th century, the American upper class had eschewed publicity and celebrity. The modern attraction of the top social circles to celebrity began as late as the 1920s. Joined by actors, writers and artists, New York's wealthy moved much of the social scene from private residences to very public cafés. Many decades were to pass before celebrity pointed unequivocally toward Hollywood, and Los Angeles of the 1980s emerged as the ultimate venue for the marriage of wealth and celebrity.

Apart from celebrity, even great wealth as it is understood today had not been part of American upper class ambiance for most of its history. It has been fashionable in recent decades to denigrate the Founding Fathers as just another group of rich white men. This revisionist view of history is not entirely accurate. The estate of Thomas Jefferson was bankrupt at his death, forcing his heirs to sell his beloved Monticello to pay creditors. So depleted was James Madison's estate that his widow Dolly sold their grand plantation, Montpelier, and lived largely off the generosity of friends. Franklin and Washington's estates were not especially large, and most of their wealth was held in land. Colonial fortunes were not great by European standards, and most citizens owned at least a small plot of land. Stephen Girard, who in the early 1800s possessed one of America's first large fortunes derived from shipping and banking, lived as a relative miser. Wealth in the Colonies was not fluid—most of it was held in tangibles: Land, livestock, clothing, jewels, carriages, and slaves. Yet it was the closest America would ever get to the European aristocratic tradition.

The top citizens of the newly formed United States would often take days to travel to each other's estates for social gatherings that were strictly private affairs. Men entered political life as a civic duty, not for money. It was important to be well read and well-mannered, and the country gentleman was known for his hospitality even to strangers. Prominent men were leisurely lawyers who practiced only occasionally. They were sculptors or painters. They often traveled to Europe as if fearful of remaining too long in a New World devoid of cultivation. Jefferson and Madison, although often at odds politically with Alexander Hamilton, were no less aristocratic than Hamilton in terms of lifestyle. All three men would have been comfortable dining with the King against whom they made a revolution. In short, the energies of most founding families were focused on what Nelson Aldrich, author of the 1988 look at hereditary wealth, *Old Money*, would characterize as standard old money pursuits: " . . . what can be done with money to transcend money." America's Founding Fathers were quasi-aristocrats culturally, yet they led a political revolution against aristocracy.

This social state of affairs lasted well into the 19th century. In *Democracy in America*, Alexis de Tocqueville accurately assessed the United States of the 1830s as "A nation which contains, so to speak, no rich men." He was struck by the fact that noted citizens would mix on the streets with the common man—what he called a "democratic state of society." America was still made up largely of small farmers, craftsmen, and merchants. At Andrew Jackson's inaugural, Americans of disparate means celebrated together in the streets. Even as late as 1871, 70% of Americans were self-employed, a far cry from the 5% working for themselves a century later. Differences in wealth were obscure, as there were as yet no great extremes of rich and poor. The attire of a gentleman was not particularly distinct, first class travel accommodations were rare, and there were relatively few goods to consume that would mark one as a rich man. The wealthy were generally frugal, and the lack of liquidity of their holdings presented an additional barrier to any thought of lavish consumption.

Wealthy citizens entertained privately and according to de Tocqueville, constituted a private society within the state. Dinner parties and balls in public venues were considered improper. This pre-Civil War upper class formed in New York City and among the Southern plantation wealth. De Tocqueville noted a budding class of manufacturers, but the founders of companies were usually miserly, looked raggedy, and were saving every penny for investment. Ostentatious consumption was not part of their lives or even their mindset. To the extent that a class of manufacturers existed in the 1830s and 1840s, they went largely unnoticed in social life.

Private parties were described as unspectacular as late as the 1870s by prominent members of Society themselves—Ward McAllister, who actually made lists of those who should be accepted into Society along with detailed prerequisites for entry; and Mrs. John King Van Rensselaer, who came from one of the few land-based colonial families whose wealth had not been substantially depleted. Not until the latter part of the century did pockets of isolated local wealth, increasingly accessible because of advances in transportation, coalesce into a cohesive national upper class.

The word *millionaire* was not heard in America before 1843, and even by 1859 there had been only three of them: John Jacob Astor, William Vanderbilt, and August Belmont. There was quite a sensation when press clippings noted that the estate of John Jacob Astor at his death in 1849 was in the twenty to thirty million dollar range. People were aghast at the Astor wealth, yet Astor was not considered a man of Society upon his death. His son William B. Astor married into Society through his union with Caroline Schermerhorn, whose ancestors dated back to 1636 in the Colonies, and the Astors were accepted by notable citizens because of the women in their family.

But as de Tocqueville put the finishing touches on his book, the rumblings of what Mathew Josephson in *The Robber Barons* called the second American Revolution, the Industrial Revolution, were beginning to alter the economic landscape of the United States. The railroad had helped make capital fluid, as the American economy turned from production for personal use to production of commodities for the market. Great fortunes would soon arise like so many weeds after a storm. By the turn of the century, in a span of fifty years, the United States not only boasted the largest fortunes in the world—those of the Rockefellers, the Morgans, the Mellons, the Vanderbilts, the Astors, the Dukes, the Carnegies and on and on—these fortunes were estimated to be twelve times greater than the top British fortunes, the Queen excluded.

These newly wealthy families converged on New York Society to play, to stake out a place at the top of the social heap. Their social aspirations were matched by their bank accounts. With eager eyes they arrived, flushed with money begging, burning, demanding to be spent. Their formidable purchasing power coincided with the rise of the professions and the middle class market. Department stores appeared on the scene, catering to a growing class of women who, fully supported by their husbands, could afford to pass the days in pursuit of the latest trends. The expanding market for goods of all kinds to enhance one's appearance provided more ways for the newly wealthy to spend money—and spend they certainly did. In an instant, the miserly type concerned only with his business who incessantly hoarded money had become a sociological relic.

On the social front, as early as the Civil War era, old-line families lamented the decline of Society, the end of intellect and culture. But they were not the first to foresee the trend. Four decades earlier, Thomas Jefferson understood that his vision of a meritocracy based on moral and intellectual excellence would never be more than a dream. Wealth pure and simple was too powerful, its magic too alluring. Good manners and a thoughtful mind were doomed from the outset to be mere afterthoughts in this country of transplants continually on the move, where to live has always been to do.

That the old Knickerbocker families of Dutch and English descent could hold on to America's social crown for so long, even remaining steadfast in the 1870s in the teeth of this social onslaught by the robber barons, was a tribute to their tenacity. The icy stare of an Old Guard matron froze the social aspirations of many a Society wannabe. Yet in the end the original families are but an amusing footnote in American social history. As their children began to attend the lively balls of the nouveau riche and marry their sons and daughters, the Old Guard lamented that Society was dead. What they did not know was that they had witnessed not a death but a birth: The social foundations of the modern American upper class had been laid in New York.

New Money and the Demise of the Old Knickerbockers

Cornelius Vanderbilt died in 1877, leaving to his heirs America's first great industrial fortune—some 100 million dollars derived from railroads and steamships and uninhibited by any estate taxes. According to New York Society *grande dame* Mrs. John King Van Rensselaer, he "neither sought nor received acceptance from the exclusive society of his time." But this was not true of the Vanderbilt descendants. Son William K. Vanderbilt's $2,000,000 New York mansion built on Fifth Avenue in 1880 rang the bell so loudly that even the once entrenched Knickerbocker families had to respond. The message of the Vanderbilt mansion and others that followed was clear: "We are here to play the game of Society. We want in!" What power could the Knickerbockers muster to compete with a Vanderbilt fortune worth at least $200 million by the 1880s?

In his *History of the Great American Fortunes*, Gustavus Myers responded to the Vanderbilt phenomenon for the too polite Knickerbockers, who disdained confrontation, with a pointed commentary on Cornelius Vanderbilt: "Neither knowledge nor appreciation were required, with the expenditure of a few hundred thousand dollars he instantaneously transformed himself from a heavy-witted, uncultured money hoarder into the character of a surpassing 'judge and patron of art.'" Political economist Thorstein Veblen described this sociological sonic boom unleashed on the New York Old Guard as "conspicuous consumption." The Old Guard, the ancestors of America's first and only aristocracy, clinging to the meager remains of their dwindling landed fortunes, could do little but hold up their good names and disdainfully turn their heads at the impropriety of the great walls of dollars built in the form of brownstone mansions along Fifth Avenue by the arrivistes.

This was not the first social onslaught on the old New Yorkers. Possessors of pre-Civil War wealth, the "silvergilts" and the "goldfish" as they were called, had come to New York to seek social fortune. Those who prospered from the Civil War, the "Shoddyites," came next. But for these groups of newly wealthy, there was a long probationary ordeal, a grueling rite of passage. They had to wait two generations for acceptance by the Old Guard, and this only when their social standing was augmented by a convenient marriage into an old Knickerbocker family. Yet this was easy entrée compared to what social arbiter Ward McAllister, the happy list maker, would allow, insisting that the cultivation of a gentleman took four generations.

The Old Guard, as a great defensive line in football, represented a bulwark of steadfastness to these parvenus. But they were to be no match for "shoddyite" Mrs. William K. Vanderbilt, who truly wasn't very shoddy and who had the whip of one of the first great industrial fortunes in hand.

Before the arrival of Mrs. Vanderbilt, Ward McAllister had deliberately created a closed group of fine gentlemen called the Patriarchs that consisted primarily of those with old New York roots. "Let the heathen come" was the attitude. "We will keep them out by building high walls, a great wall of Society." Parties were held which only a select group of ladies and gentlemen could attend—the Old Guard Knickerbockers. A smattering of new members or notables was allowed in to assuage boredom, but manners and not money would be the prerequisite for participation.

The key to the cohesion of the Knickerbocker families with ties to the original Dutch and English colonial land tracts was the smallness of their group. They often held court in the small Academy of Music that had few really advantageous boxes. Individually decorated by the family, the boxes were passed down from generation to generation. The homes of the Old Guard were not large enough to hold the grand balls of the 1880s and 1890s put together by the nouveau riche, who might invite up to 1,000 people. To enter the realm of the social Mt. Olympus, the nouveau riche were forced to create a counter-attraction to New York Society. Their strategy was of the classic carrot/stick variety. They tried to marry into old New York families whenever convenient to obtain a notable name and family tradition in one fell swoop. This was the carrot strategy. But it was the strategy of the stick—of creating their own haute venues for social life—that felled the Knickerbockers from their 250 years atop the perch of American Society.

Whatever their strategy, the nouveau riche industrial families would return again and again for social battle, from snub after snub, stare after stare from the Old Guard, who nicknamed them the "Bouncers" for precisely their capacity to bounce back in the social arena. This group of troopers, the founders of the modern American upper class, must have invented the saying, "Sticks and stones may break my bones, but names will never hurt me." The names "Shoddyite" and "Bouncer" bounced right off them, and the only really effective stone throwing going on at the time was the construction of brownstone mansions along Fifth Avenue by the upstart class.

You can't get into the Academy of Music for the opera, so what do you do? You build your own opera house, the Metropolitan. The Met opened in the 1880s with boxes that sold for 60,000 real dollars. And who bought these boxes? None other than the Goulds, the Rockefellers, the Drexels, the Vanderbilts, the Whitneys, the Morgans and so on. You can't get invited to the parties of the Old Guard led by McAllister and the incomparable Mrs. William B. Astor, so what do you do? You hold your own parties and make them bigger and better than the others until even the properly raised youth of the Old Guard look eagerly up the street at the goings on.

Mrs. John King Van Rensselaer, responding to this social onslaught in the name of America's founding families, was quick to point out in her 1924 book, *The Social Ladder*, that this so-called American upper class was not a blue-blooded lot but nouveau riche to the barbarian core. Yet even a stalwart such as Mrs. Van Rensselaer could see the inevitable: "They (the social climbers) were outside the pale, but that did not worry them. They aimed for social distinction not by assault upon the established caste, but by counter-attraction. They appreciated the value of publicity and employed it." "Obscure" ancestry? "Different" values? Not to worry—vast wealth was then, as it is now, the great American leveler.

Unfortunately, for the Old Guard as well as for mere commoners, a name cannot be used for collateral at the bank. In the emerging pecuniary society of American capitalism, of what value was it that their families had settled the Colonies? Good manners and proper speech are charming, but in the contest for social distinction based on consumption and display, proper demeanor could only be secondary, a social grace to be cultivated after one had amassed his fortune. You could be rude and crude, but if you had money it didn't really matter. By 1908 one observer remarked, "We have one material which actually constitutes an aristocracy that

35

governs the nation. That material is wealth." When compared with the dollars that were being spent relentlessly by the arrivistes, who now commanded America's great industrial combines, the "good taste" of the Old Guard conveyed as much clout in terms of social distinction as a pistol fired beside a cannon. Decades later *Vogue* editor Diana Vreeland may have put it best: "As soon as you have money, you're old."

This social civil war, this New York battle to secure the social crown of the United States, could not last long, for the Old Guard had not the means to compete. As their blue blood turned red, necks stiff in the air, chins up, they peered out into the social wilderness as they slowly carriaged up Fifth Avenue into their private sunset. But then a social sea change occurred. Mrs. William B. Astor, a key social arbiter of the Old Guard, paid a social visit to Mrs. William K. Vanderbilt, whom she had never previously acknowledged, to seek an invite to Mrs. Vanderbilt's 1883 ball. Most of New York Society followed suit and attended the event. "Let us not quibble over trifles" was the new attitude. After all, Mrs. Vanderbilt was from an old Southern family, was she not?

This historic compromise between the Vanderbilts and the Astors symbolized the social ascendance of the modern American upper class, already dominant economically through their control of key sectors of an industrializing United States: Coal, oil, railroads, steamships, steel and so on. The inevitable social arrival of a small class of people propelled by the economic explosion of the American Industrial Revolution would soon set the pace for the entire emerging world economy. Free of income tax, John D. Rockefeller's fortune from the Standard Oil trust grew from 200 million in 1901 to 900 million by 1913. Incredibly, his fortune had grown bigger than those of the Astors, Vanderbilts, Carnegies, Harrimans and Morgans combined. The sky had truly become the limit, and the American upper class would soon be reaching for the social stars.

Hollywood's Trump Card:
The Marriage of Wealth and Celebrity

The old Knickerbocker society demonstrated its social distinction by virtue of the rituals it so keenly observed, whether something as mundane as a table setting or as erudite as a liberal arts education from a select school. It identified culturally with the European aristocracies however much it differed with nobility politically. Ward McAllister himself promoted French cuisine, the European cuisine of excellence, which had become mandatory at Old Guard affairs by the 1870s.

The Old Guard, disdaining showiness, did not seek or use publicity as a way of disseminating its image to the rest of society. In other words, there were no P.R. people around. On the contrary, as political economist Thorstein Veblen pointed out, self-serving publicity was scarcely possible due to the undeveloped communication channels of the time. The balls of the Old Guard were relatively simple private affairs. Celebrities might attend an affair—after dinner—to entertain. The Knickerbocker families were at the head of society by historical right, as their families had been given the original colonial land grants. They needed no justification of their status. The men participated in public life as an obligation of their position as much as to bolster their own economic interests. By the 1840s, they began leaving political life to intermediaries.

For the families of the robber barons, the situation was quite different. They could claim no right to America's social crown and were as unprepared to receive it as the next citizen on the street. What they did have was more money than they knew what to do with, and they began spending it and publicizing this consumption as a way of legitimizing their presence at the top of society. They too turned to Europe, mimicking its architecture, fashion, food, and buying its most cherished art.

There is a sense of charade in this first wave of the modern American upper class living in all its splendor. Their fortunes were based on industrial capitalism in a country that made a revolution against aristocracy, but their style of consumption mimicked all the trappings of aristocracy. The mania for antiques was a symbolic compensation for the newness of their wealth. Their ancestors had not made a democratic revolution as had those of the Knickerbockers, so how could they justify their standing as a special class in a political democracy?

The forerunners of the modern American upper class, despite their tens of millions, were a rather insecure group. That is one reason Goulds and Vanderbilts so quickly married into European royalty. If the American upper class was a shaky lot, they could hire the decorators, the art experts, the couturiers, the cooks and so on to help present themselves to the world. They could buy taste. A need developed for a new class of entrepreneur, a need that still exists today: One who serves as a social arbiter and sells haute products to the upper class. Fifth Avenue in New York was an outgrowth of the need of the robber barons' families to cultivate themselves by spending their money in a socially impacting way. The development of a class based on great industrial wealth had created a market for haute products and in its wake the beginning of mass-produced versions of exclusive goods. With the spread of mass communication, the upper class lifestyle eventually became the mark of success throughout the country in spite of a growing middle class presence.

With the collapse of the Old Guard, the new upper class began to tire of its own parties. Having wrested the social spotlight away from the Knickerbockers, they found fewer reasons for social display. The battle of New York had been won. Entertaining was still done in private homes or in select hotel ballrooms, but the younger generation grew restless. The novelty of conspicuous consumption had worn off, and the children of the new Society often found themselves in dance halls dancing the latest dance and eating outside in public. Even before World War Two, the younger set began foregoing Fifth Avenue mansions for apartments where they could live less formally. The new old wealth of the Vanderbilts and Whitneys could not differ much in social articulation from that of the Knickerbocker group it had replaced. The victors mimicked the vanquished. In other words, the New York social scene remained dull.

The emergence of Broadway changed the social dynamic of New York, creating a new social marketplace. By the mid-'20s the theatre crowd, including writers and artists, would gather at the Algonquin Hotel. This group had no particular social distinction, but prefigured a long wave of celebrity that would transform American society. A mass culture was flowering, and the moneyed were soon at the Algonquin's tables taking it in. When the Old Guard attended the opera at the Academy of Music, they had refrained from associating with the performers, who were not of Society. The arrivistes were not hampered by such considerations. The new game of Society was to appropriate all excellent things.

The families of the robber barons, now far removed from the industrial enterprises that created their family wealth, went out socially with clean hands to New York cafés to hobnob with the notable people: The writers, artists and musicians. They were there in the spotlight for all to see. After all, the heads of their families had founded the great enterprises that moved the nation. As they sat with drink in hand at choice tables, looking about the room, they were experiencing a new form of success: High public honor. "How gauche!" the Old Guard might have clamored, but to no avail. From this point forward the American upper class eschewed any pretext of establishing distinct manners and morals which would delineate its social status. With these distinguishing features gone, the top social circles could only waffle back and forth between haute consumption and celebrity as the prime indicator of class.

Prohibition gave rise to the high grade speakeasy and brought the emerging artistic elements of American mass culture and the New York upper class together in an environment where class barriers were further blurred.

Everyone was tossed together in one illegal mix of dance and drink. The modern New York upper class had never really developed a unique character, first mimicking Europe and then embracing celebrity. The upper class love affair with celebrity so visible today has its roots in the top social circles of the 1920s and '30s which wined, dined, danced, chatted and gossiped out in the open, *en evidence*, at New York cafés. The heirs of what were now "older" fortunes joined the newly rich to mingle with actors, writers, top dancers, Hollywood beauties, producers and eventually celebrities of all kinds in a social stew that journalist Maury Paul called Café Society.

And now the media was there to write about this new Café Society based in New York. And write about them they did, as the main show in the country. But as Cleveland Amory noted in his book *Who Killed Society?*, the world of celebrity would prove as hard to control as a mix of volatile substances in a chemical reaction. Celebrity tended to overwhelm the Café Society crowd of the upper class through publicity. And that publicity could only lead west to the sweet land of sunshine. Celebrity was something the upper class could not control. Celebrity unashamedly ended up adorning that "non-city," that most unexpected rival thousands of miles away: Los Angeles.

The Broadway crowd spawned and was then overrun and surpassed by the Hollywood crowd, as movies were to have a far greater impact on American culture than theatre. Celebrity by its very nature needs to be photographed, and the newspapers were eager to oblige. By the 1930s this social cocktail of wealth and celebrity could be found in a few New York cafés or at one of the famous parties of Elsa Maxwell, who acted as both social arbiter and catalyst for New York Society. At her parties the new old wealth of the Vanderbilts, Whitneys, and Astors mixed with such Hollywooders as the Selznicks and Astaires, creating a social novelty.

The purpose of this entertaining was to gain publicity. Back before television, an avid reading public still provided a reliable audience for columns on high society doings. Newspapers had real power. Magazines such as *Vanity Fair* and *The New Yorker* were captivated by the new social scene and filled their pages with its doings, proving the truth of Elsa Maxwell's claim that, "Society is not made by society, it is made by its reporters." In 1937 *Fortune* magazine published a list of the players and those on the sidelines in this game of social musical chairs. The list was based on how often certain people appeared with key players and were photographed for or mentioned in Society columns. The spotlight of the camera could now amplify the drama of social distinction and transmit these images for all to see.

Today, press coverage still distinguishes New York's Nouvelle Society, as pointed out by John Fairchild of *Women's Wear Daily* in his book *Chic Savages*. It also sets apart the top players in Los Angeles. Yet the irony of the emergence of the L.A. upper crust in the 1980s and '90s is that press coverage of Society functions in L.A. waned just as the city's top circles attained global recognition. As newspaper circulations decline along with their coverage of high society events, the visibility and influence of the top social grouping become shaky. As L.A. art collector and socialite Joan Quinn explains, "The death of the news media is the death of Society." But the basic dynamic remains: If you are photographed at the major charity functions with the key players, you have arrived. Of course you need major money to be in such a position.

The contemporary cultural scene, imbibed with celebrities galore, has its roots in the new social mix of the '20s and '30s. Increasingly, the hot new happenings could be broadcast to the wider public in magazines, newspapers, and even movies as the audience for mass media began to develop. Telephone, radio, and highways were also making the American cultural landscape less vast, with radio in particular exerting a unifying effect unlike any until T.V. In 1927 sound became a fixture in the movie industry, and increasingly the power of advertising was making itself felt.

The development of a mass market of consumers and the mass production of commodities—goods patterned after each other with slight variations in form and based on advertising and a differential pricing scale—is a 20th century happening. In the initial decades of the new century, personal care products in particular became popular. Elizabeth Arden cosmetics was founded in 1910, and the early 1920s saw the first Society woman, Mrs. O.H.P. Belmont, endorse a product: Pond's face cream. More and more products were being created and then advertised, planting the initial seeds of the contemporary upscale marketing scene epitomized by the designer boutiques of Rodeo Drive.

New York's Café Society was eventually overrun by artistic types and hangers-on without social distinction, leading to a more Bohemian scene. But another far more exciting and formidable development was challenging the hierarchy of Café Society and about to create a new stage in American social history. The New Yorkers could not control one peculiar, unique outcome—in which locale wealth and celebrity would become interchangeable. And that is precisely L.A.'s claim to social distinction: The very public marriage of wealth and celebrity. The celebrity of Hollywood in the New York cafés glistened with such social power that its presence made even the nonchalant upper class blink. The Hollywooders were the first bi-coastals—now in Los Angeles, back to New York to play and back again to Los Angeles. The Hollywood actors, producers and studio heads had money, even big money. And more great wealth was going west under the names of Hearst and Getty. This combination of money, power and celebrity social clout was a new creation, a child of the mass society. The New York upper class had to be eclipsed by this marriage of power to power, of money to social distinction that Hollywood embodies. When the bulk of motion picture and television production shifted to Los Angeles in the 1960s, L.A. inevitably would become the first real counter-attraction to New York Society.

Finally in the 1980s a relatively tranquil street in Los Angeles, Rodeo Drive, began to awaken as the great European designers who create and cater to upper class tastes arrived there to see the marvelous new happenings. A new section of the American upper class was strutting its stuff, displaying newly accumulated fortunes in the entertainment and communications industries. The newspapers, books and magazines of New York that had conveyed the upper class lifestyle to the nation were to be no match for the direct hit of films and television shows of this now developed L.A. upper crust. The alluring image and the special power of its Industry created a kind of biting awe. Who or what could compete with Oscar parties where even the stars get star-struck? What were the New Yorkers, the new old wealth, to do? After 300 years the American upper class would have a new geographic focal point, and the contest for social distinction would reignite.

Glamorous Hollywood, Provincial Beverly Hills: Truth and Consequences

How was it that L.A., rather than San Francisco or some other major American city, produced an upper crust that could rival New York for social dominance? There was nothing particularly notable in L.A.'s early history that would have foretold such a fabulous outcome. For a city founded as far back as 1781 by the Viceroy of New Spain (Mexico), Los Angeles showed no signs of distinction in its first hundred years. The culture of the native Gabrielino Indians quickly gave way to Spanish mission and ranchero life.

The Southern Pacific railroad connected with Los Angeles in 1872. By the 1880s, Southern California was being sold to Easterners as a dreamland with sweet sunshine and ample opportunity. All classes of people bought into the mythic image, beginning a 100-year-long trek to California, and in particular to the L.A. basin. By the early 1900s, the wealthy had built a string of Victorian-style homes in downtown L.A. on Bunker Hill, and Pasadena had become known as a winter vacation spot symbolized by a string of mansions along Orange Grove Avenue called "millionaires' row."

The old Spanish land grant families in California had congealed around the same time as the Southern plantation Society, and many of them identified strongly with where they were, points out UCLA architect and history buff Tim Vreeland, son of the late *Vogue* editor Diana Vreeland. Los Angeles' first families date back to founders such as Antonio Pico, one of the forty-six signers of the 1849 California Constitution. Pico and other "Californios" spoke Spanish and English. Many of the Spanish names prominent about the L.A. basin as either names of streets or cities—such as Pico and Del Amo—are among the First Families. Some Hispanic groups consider their roots "old" if an ancestor was in California before 1848, near the time of statehood. Others consider "old" only the eleven commonly recognized founding families of Los Angeles, among them the Verdugo, Bandini, Sepulveda and Dominguez clans.

Anglo first families are even less "old." Alyce Williamson, past President of the First Families, explains that the Anglo members of her group date their ancestors' arrival in Los Angeles back to the 1860s. Mrs. Williamson's husband, Warren B. Williamson, comes from the Chandler family, which helped to found the *Los Angeles Times*. Harry Chandler arrived in Los Angeles in 1882 and at the time, the newspaper he ultimately controlled printed a paltry 400 copies a day. Mrs. Williamson's great-grandfather, Germaine Pellissier, was known for raising prize sheep and had a ranch in the 1880s and '90s on Wilshire Blvd. near the old Ambassador Hotel. The Los Angeles city limits did not even reach that far west, and the Southern California economy was still mainly agricultural. Alyce Williamson, brought up in the wealthy enclave of Hancock Park and a graduate of Marlborough School, recalls how Los Angeles, even in the 1940s, had a small town atmosphere. "I knew everyone in Hancock Park," Mrs. Williamson remarks wistfully. "It was the time of great private parties and dinner dances in homes, and women would wear hats and gloves." The Hancock Park home she grew up in now houses another member of the Chandler publishing family. Alyce's father, Henry de Roulet, developed part of what is now the mid-Wilshire district and built the Wiltern Theater.

But in spite of such efforts by its top citizens, the development of Los Angeles into a world-class city was anything but pre-ordained. L.A. had the weather, but that wasn't enough. Because of the gold rush, San Francisco was originally the largest city in California. The 49ers, 100,000 strong, paraded out to California in 1849, most making their way to the northern half of the state where gold was discovered. So it was not even clear that Los Angeles was destined to be the most significant city in California, much less one of global import.

By the turn of the century, the families of the original Spanish land grants had already begun to divide and sell off land, and as is the case in New York, these original land-based families do not make up the modern Los Angeles upper crust. The Del Valle family, which was granted a whopping 46,000 acres in 1839 near the Valencia area and what is now Magic Mountain, sold off what remained of their rancho in 1924 for $300,000. L.A.'s current top social circles are not comprised of Spanish surnames any more than the New York upper class is comprised of families exclusively of Dutch or English descent dating back to the Colonies. There is not a Dominguez, Verdugo or Sepulveda on the L.A. charity circuit.

Before the motion picture industry set up production in Southern California in the first quarter of the 20th century, L.A. was still little more than a sleepy outpost. Its open land spread out into two great valleys jettisoned by mountains on one side and the Pacific Ocean on the other. That Hollywood became the entertainment capital of the world was little more than an accident. Legendary director Cecil B. DeMille ended up among the orange groves of a then rural Hollywood when he found the Arizona of 1913 uninviting for his western shoot. DeMille wound up filming *The Squaw Man* in a barn at Selma and Vine, that is, Vine as in Hollywood and Vine.

By 1920, much film production had shifted to Hollywood. After their much-fêted marriage, silent film stars Mary Pickford and Douglas Fairbanks joined Charlie Chaplin and D.W. Griffith in 1919 to form United Artists, one of the first major studios.

The early Hollywooders found in L.A. a wonderful open playground but little else, at least in terms of high culture. A few oil fortunes—those of the Greens, the Dohenys and the Bells (Alfonso Bell founded Bel-Air with his fortune in 1926)—dotted the landscape. Surprisingly, the motion picture industry folk were not particularly welcome. Actors, seen as seedy, were often shunned as renters in Hollywood, and Alfonso Bell initially refused to sell to "movie people" in Bel-Air. Only during the Depression did the first Hollywooders enter the Bel-Air enclave. Symbolically, as Tyrone Power, Alfred Hitchcock and Cary Grant bought homes in Bel-Air, guards were removed from the two famous Bel-Air gates still standing today.

Back in the '20s and '30s, the Hollywooders had their own little playground all to themselves. But they lived in social isolation. With no social peers and no standard local Society to conquer, they spent their time making movies and traveling to New York for an occasional social splash. Irene Selznick recounts in *A Private View* how she used to travel with David O. Selznick, producer of *Gone with the Wind*, to the big city, New York, for social happenings. When Elsa Maxwell, the great social arbiter of New York Café Society, visited Hollywood in the 1930s she wrote, "I had gone there expecting to see parties that reflected the stock-in-trade of the movies—glamour." But Maxwell found the Saturday-night-only parties "methodical." One reason for the lack of socializing was that the production of movies took long hours, often including Saturdays, and people were simply exhausted, with little inclination for a party circuit. Maxwell concluded that Hollywood was a "cultural vacuum" in the 1930s.

When the Hollywood crowd did socialize, television did not yet exist to transmit the vibrant images of directors and stars in this emerging western playground to a mass audience. Beverly Hills and the entire Westside was largely open space when the distinctive Beverly Hills Hotel opened in 1912. A magnificent rural retreat was really what Douglas Fairbanks built for his wife, Mary Pickford, in 1919 near the Beverly Hills Hotel. The house, named Pickfair, was used as a hunting lodge and dubbed the "White House of Hollywood."

The early Hollywood bashes were more reminiscent of the gatherings of the old Knickerbocker aristocracy than of the splashy affairs of the New York upper class and its Café Society. Producers, directors, writers and stars would often visit each other's estates to spend a few days with their families, to horseback ride or just relax. The setting was as much rural as urban. Or they would trek to the beach at the Santa Monica Gold Coast, where the Hollywood top brass such as Louis B. Mayer, Darryl F. Zanuck, and Irving Thalberg mixed with the latest stars. There were no paparazzi swarming about, and the scene was not brought to the nation on "Entertainment Tonight."

But with due respect to Ms. Maxwell, Old Hollywood did have some noteworthy nightlife which began to heat up in the 1930s. Stars did not necessarily let an early morning shoot prevent them from partaking of the emerging social scene. Billy Wilkerson, founder of the *Hollywood Reporter*, opened Café Trocadero on the Sunset Strip between Los Angeles and Beverly Hills in 1934. Sunset Strip had been an old cow path surrounded by poinsettia fields and avocado groves until the 1920s, but by the 1930s a series of small boutiques and restaurants had opened. Wilkerson was tired of running all over town to meet with agents and stars for his paper, and his solution was to build his own restaurant. He patterned Café Trocadero after Parisian outdoor cafés and New York speakeasies. Agents soon moved their offices to the Sunset Strip, which quickly became known as the place where the stars dined.

At Café Trocadero a Saturday night poker game in the back room included regulars Irving Thalberg, Darryl

Zanuck, Carl Laemmle, Jr. and Samuel Goldwyn. The Sunday night amateur hour, where aspiring talent could audition for producers such as Selznick and Zanuck, featured Judy Garland, Phil Silvers and Jackie Gleason. The ambiance was formal, with French decor and tuxedo-clad waiters. When Hollywood dined out, the men sported black tie attire while the women donned evening gowns. Café Trocadero boasted enough star power to catch anyone's attention. Robert Taylor, Tyrone Power, Betty Grable, Fred Astaire, Jean Harlowe, Clark Gable, Barbara Stanwyck, Jimmy Stewart, Olivia de Havilland, Vivien Leigh, Lawrence Olivier and Bing Crosby often filled the dining hall. Nat King Cole was a regularly featured singer. Guests dined on beef forestière, not free-range chicken. History does not reveal the name of the chef, but he was definitely not Wolfgang Puck.

Old Hollywood was focused on creating and defining an industry. They adopted the upper class opulence imported from Europe and duplicated in New York as it existed without further ado. Old Hollywood was definitely not minimalist in either art or décor. During Café Trocadero's heyday, Hollywood hip was still a long way away. L.A.'s triumphant rendezvous with modernity had to wait. It would be several more decades before Hollywood players truly opened their eyes, surveyed the L.A. geography and embraced California Cuisine and modern art, creating a new avenue of haute taste.

By the late 1920s, L.A. high culture smacked of bits and pieces of aristocratic European taste amidst a sea of Midwestern-style towns dotting the L.A. basin. The Hotel Chateau Marmont, patterned after a French chateau in the Loire Valley, opened in Hollywood. Since the hotel was considered more private than the Beverly Hills Hotel, Harry Cohn told his stars William Holden and Glen Ford, "If you must get into trouble, do it at the Chateau Marmont." The Garden of Allah, another hotel, had opened on Sunset in 1927 and served the artistic crowd and Hollywood stars. It was leveled in 1959, prompting Joni Mitchell to sing her famous lament, "They paved paradise and put up a parking lot." Meanwhile developer Charles Toberman was transforming the city of Hollywood, building landmark theatres such as the Egyptian, the Chinese, and the El Capitan, which opened to live theatre with such performers as Clark Gable, Buster Keaton, Rita Hayworth and Douglas Fairbanks, Jr.

Wilkerson, not content with the magic he had created at Café Trocadero, opened Ciro's in 1940. On opening night Tony Martin and Judy Garland spontaneously sang for the throng, and the nightclub remained a Hollywood hotspot into the 1950s. The walls at Ciro's could undoubtedly tell some compelling stories. Touching scenes. Funny scenes. Party scenes. Ciro's saw the likes of Sammy Davis, Jr. moping around one night, despondent after being told by Harry Cohn that he had to break up with Kim Novak. Another night Frank Sinatra was spotted dejected and drinking after his break-up with Ava Gardner.

But Ciro's was a happy place too. Howard Hughes enjoyed himself in Ciro's parking lot in the back seat of a Chevy with a starlet as his guests partied inside. Rock Hudson, Tony Curtis, Peter Lawford, and Robert Wagner could be found backstage. On many a night, Marilyn Monroe and Walter Winchell sat at a little table surveying the crowd. On the dance floor could be any Hollywood notable, maybe Barbara Stanwyck dancing with Joel McCrea. One night Mickey Rooney stepped in to do duty as a waiter. Desi Arnaz entertained for Lucille Ball, Joan Crawford, and Cary Grant. Ciro's booked Dean Martin and Jerry Lewis as rising stars in 1950, and Sammy Davis, Jr. made his comeback appearance there after a car accident took one of his eyes. He was introduced that night by Frank Sinatra.

Hollywood columnists Louella Parsons and Hedda Hopper made Ciro's their home away from home. Studios sent young actors and actresses to roam about so they could be photographed. Fondly remembering the glory days of Hollywood night life, publicist Dale Olson recounts that the studios demanded that the stars be socially driven: "The social element was terribly important." When they were not working on a shoot, the stars were working on their image. During the 1950s special ringside tables were always kept in reserve for a Lana Turner, for Sinatra, for Monroe, for Jack Lemmon or for Zanuck.

Other dining hot spots of the era included La Rue, also run by Wilkerson, and Romanoff's. Romanoff's opened in 1939 on a then tranquil street, North Rodeo Drive, with the backing of many studio heads as well as East Coast upper class marquee names: Jock Whitney, Laurence Rockefeller, and Alfred Vanderbilt. On any given night the "A" tables at Romanoff's might seat John Wayne, Lucille Ball, Greer Garson, Frank Sinatra, or Ronald Reagan. But the restaurant also brought in top L.A. Society names such as the Chandlers (newspaper publishing) and the Dohenys (oil). Owner Michael Romanoff called himself a prince, claiming he was descended from Russian royalty. Many Hollywooders happily went along with the story. After all, it was Hollywood.

This Hollywood version of Café Society already had too much star power for New York to outpace. But Los Angeles was still several decades away from being able to challenge the Big Apple for top social distinction. Fortunes were on their way west, homegrown wealth was at an incipient stage, L.A. hip had not yet arrived and perhaps most important of all, media coverage of Hollywood was still in its infancy. And it is this media projection of Hollywood—not just as stardom, but as culture, as style, as Society—that has finally challenged the heretofore indefatigable New York upper class as the head of the social nation.

Las Vegas would soon hire away Hollywood nightlife talent. As 1960 approached, L.A. seemed to be fading, if only for a moment, reclaiming its role as the "double Dubuque," an apt phrase coined by H.L. Mencken. While the stars would never shine as brightly as they did in the glory days of Hollywood, they would soon shine louder at the Oscar parties of the 1980s and '90s to which, as the story will be told, there has never been a parallel world around. But if you stop and look, you can still see a glistening from the past, when Hollywood looked more like Society.

The yearning for a Hollywood gone by, of simpler times, lingers in a 1999 tribute to Tony Duquette, set decorator and interior designer extraordinaire, thrown by the Decorative Arts Council of the Los Angeles County Museum of Art. Duquette once numbered J. Paul Getty, David O. Selznick, Mary Pickford, and Elizabeth Arden among his clients and designed a set for Vincente Minnelli's *Ziegfeld Follies*. The created setting for the evening: Mocambo—a smaller nightclub of Hollywood's golden era, once across the street from Ciro's and decorated by Duquette himself.

Old Hollywood was not just a free-for-all at the nightclubs nor merely a rural retreat without a social structure. Unlike today, stars lived almost exclusively in Beverly Hills, which had its own special aura. Shops catered to the locals, and few tourists were about. Helen Chaplin, who has worked for both the Beverly Hills Hotel and the Beverly Wilshire Hotel, recalls that when she went into a restaurant, "I would know everyone there." People met at each other's homes, only a stone's throw away, and mingled at functions on studio lots. Parties were often grand, and there was a clear social hierarchy.

Hollywood publicist Dale Olson, whose clients have included Gene Kelly and Lawrence Olivier, explains that Hollywood's social circles were ruled by a dozen or so women, including Ann Warner, Micki Ziffren, Fran Stark, Edie Goetz, Edie Wasserman, and Ruth Berle. "They dictated who was in and who was out," says Olson. The group's head was Doris Stein, whose husband Jules Stein started the studio that became Universal. Edie Wasserman's husband, Lew Wasserman, was Stein's right-hand man. To be invited to an Edie Wasserman luncheon was a badge of honor. It meant that you had made it. Irene Mayer Selznick, daughter of MGM founder Louis B. Mayer and wife of David O. Selznick, was part of this party-giving crowd and competed socially with her sister Edie Goetz. But for all this studio power, for all the star power and newspaper gossip columnists, the traditional Hollywood did not have the social impact of Hollywood today. And Los Angeles at that time was scarcely mentioned as a city in any regard.

As late as the 1970s, despite the building of the Music Center and other cultural markers, L.A. remained largely nondescript, indistinguishable from many other American cities. Los Angeles, similar to other major cities, had developed certain economic power groupings composed of the top families in newspaper publishing (the Chandlers, owners of the *L.A. Times*); banking (the Tapers and the Ahmansons); various industrial concerns and later, especially after World War Two, aviation and real estate development. Important aerospace firms had emerged in Southern California: Lockheed, McDonald Douglas Corp., Northrop Corp., and Hughes Aircraft. These groups worked with government officials to promote economic development as in any other large American city.

Yet these traditional movers and shakers in L.A. had little social impact prior to 1960. They existed largely in the shadow of the movie set, whose private parties on the estates of Beverly Hills and Bel-Air combined wealth and leisure with stardom and celebrity. The traditional upper crust spawned by banking and the like did not really mix with the Hollywood set. Whatever culture Los Angeles had was imported from the East and Midwest. Los Angeles before the 1960s showed few signs that it was a mere snapshot away from social stardom. There was no L.A. haute scene, no L.A. look, no L.A. attitude. Beverly Hills itself had been called by actor Jack Lemmon "one of the most beautiful small towns that I have ever been in in my life," referring to life there in the 1960s. But changes were forthcoming that would remove the adjective "small" from any description of the L.A. social scene.

So it's worth reposing the question: How did Los Angeles, a standard American city, take off into the social stratosphere? How did the L.A. upper crust come to rendezvous with the New Yorkers to become an haute couple? Amid today's smog and earthquakes, the unique allure of L.A.'s geography tends to recede in the image of the city. Los Angeles' fortune was its warm weather amidst a terrain that included both mountains and the ocean. It sat farthest to the west in the United States, beckoning the individualistic social pioneers of the movie industry to come out, visit and then stay. They could whet their artistic appetite all year around, uninhibited by social traditions or the weather. Just as historically the Germans have had a strong attraction to the light and warmth of Italy, so L.A. represented a perpetual working holiday for these creators of fantasy and interpreters of social reality.

Not just the artistic crowd but all types of people, drawn to the West Coast by its seemingly eternal sunshine, trekked out to California throughout the 20th century with Los Angeles garnering the lion's share of this movement. The California economy grew at a stunning rate, and one Industry in particular took on a special meaning—the Industry of image creation, of cultural amalgamation, of great fortunes and of mass society par excellence: The motion picture industry. It grew at the heart of the entertainment industry as the importance of leisure in American culture became firmly rooted by the 1960s.

Hollywood's images were soon to be beamed directly to the mass audience by film's sweet sister, television, spawning a powerful dual force of image creation. By the 1960s television production had largely gone Hollywood. The rock and rollers of the record industry were hobnobbing at the local hangouts on the Sunset Strip and partying in the hills above Hollywood. The development of television and the continual growth of entertainment media via VCRs and cable propelled the L.A. scene into the national spotlight with an éclat never before experienced in American culture. In the 1970s, the Silicon Valley-spawned, California-based computer industry emerged as an adjunct to this new technological surge of records, films, modems and faxes.

The East Coast-dominated print media, however

important, fell into the background in this revolution in communications. The images of mass culture transmitted daily to Americans came from Hollywood in television shows, movies, theme parks and records. L.A. was at the heart of the emerging entertainment industry that in turn fed on the revolution in communications and the shift in the economic power structure to high-tech industries. New York was still the head of finance, but capital now flowed worldwide. By the 1970s Los Angeles was becoming home to foreign investors staking serious claims in private and commercial real estate. Hollywood movie and television production alone added 16 billion dollars to the California economy in 1992, $27 billion in 1997. Hollywood produces wages 70% higher than average. Yet if Hollywood were only an industry like the others, L.A. haute culture today would be on a train with Chicago and San Francisco with New York as its engine.

But Hollywood is a special Industry that transmits image. With the wealth of New Hollywood injected into the broadening, vibrant L.A. upper crust developing after 1960, Los Angeles has created a social outcome unique in American history. An unlikely player, L.A. now sits at the head of the poker table looking across at its counterpart, New York, and winking with a sly, Warren Beatty-style grin. And the cards at L.A.'s disposal—the many facets of the now global entertainment industry—can hardly be considered a bluff. Every social power must be backed up by an economic power, and in the Los Angeles of the 1960s that economic basis was largely in place. All that was lacking was for L.A. to have its coming out party. The guest list would be truly spectacular.

CHAPTER THREE

Making it Big: The Social Invasion of Los Angeles

"The one who dies with the most toys wins."

—1980s bumper sticker

Wealth Moves West

Just as Mrs. Astor did for the Knickerbockers when she embraced the upstart Mrs. Vanderbilt a century earlier, so too has the modern New York upper class finally thrown its own pretension to the wind and grudgingly acknowledged its crude partner, L.A. Threatened with irrelevance by the challenge of Los Angeles and not wanting to lose the social limelight, the New Yorkers have blown kisses to the L.A. crowd and embraced the new princesses from the West as their social equals. The top circles of New York and L.A. preside jointly over American high culture and the social nation. Emblematic of this alliance of heavyweights and super-heavyweights, of the sharing of the social crown, is the fact that many members of these two groups are now bi-coastal, buying homes and spending time in both cities.

Rupert Murdoch, Steven Spielberg, and Ronald Perelman represent a growing contingent of bi-coastals. Spielberg has long owned a home in Pacific Palisades, and he and his actress wife, Kate Capshaw, also have a home in the Hamptons in New York. They purchased a 2.8-acre horse ranch in Brentwood for 5.75 million dollars complete with horse trail access to the Santa Monica Mountains. Murdoch, who owned the Los Angeles Dodgers for several years and is the head of News Corp., which runs the Fox TV network and the 20th Century Fox film studio, has been spending more time in New York since his divorce proceedings from his long-time wife, Anna Murdoch, and remarriage to Wendy Deng, one of his T.V. executives. New York investment banker Perelman has held major positions in the Hollywood companies Technicolor, New World Communications Group and Marvel Entertainment and now holds a large stake in Panavision, Hollywood's top camera supplier. It is business interests, especially in the entertainment industry, that so intertwine L.A. with New York, driving the bi-coastal dance of jet planes, multiple residences and top social affairs.

Fashion, too, does a New York-Los Angeles two-step. Fashion designer Richard Tyler, the darling of Hollywood, whose creations grace the likes of Julia Roberts, Sigourney Weaver, Angelica Huston and Ashley Judd, owns a home in South Pasadena. Tyler already maintains a 37-room home in New York. Many high-end retailers who sell haute products to the upper class are following this bi-coastal trend. The venerable department store Barneys New York is now Barneys New York/Beverly Hills. A symbol. An event. The opening of Barneys New York in Beverly Hills featured New Yorker Ronald Perelman, head of Revlon, making a 1.2 million dollar donation to the UCLA Women's Cancer Program. The Fire and Ice Ball highlighted the store's opening. With seventeen chandeliers hovering overhead, women in designer gowns floated up the spiral staircase to the festivities. A happening. An L.A. statement. Hollywood flashes. In the crowd mingled actors Dustin Hoffman and Jack Nicholson; actresses Melanie Griffith, Sharon Stone and Helen Hunt; writer Jackie Collins; singer Olivia Newton-John; and the usual smatterings of the super wealthy flung together in an awesome display of social power. Wolfgang Puck prepared the almond-crusted salmon.

Like stress on an earthquake fault, L.A. social power was cumulative until it burst forth like an explosion in the 1980s and '90s. Since the 1920s, possessors of large fortunes generated in other states had been moving to Los Angeles to reward themselves in this new playground, to stake their claim to social distinction and play among the Hollywood stars. By the 1980s, such a move was not merely fanciful but almost mandatory as a way of achieving distinction on the American social panorama. When one speaks of Society with a capital S in America, one has always spoken of New York—until the arrival of Los Angeles.

There's good reason why budding entrepreneurs sell maps just below the hills of Bel-Air on Sunset Blvd. guiding tourists to the homes of the rich and famous, or why visitors to L.A. must obligatorily take their rental car and poke around in the hills above Rodeo Drive. It's astonishing to discover the host of families who reside or have resided on L.A.'s Westside. What began as a trickling of wealthy families has become an outright social invasion.

Early arrivals included members of the Guggenheim family and the Hormel meatpacking clan. George A. Hormel, company founder, built a home in Bel-Air in 1927. One of his descendants, San Franciscan James Hormel, became Ambassador to Luxembourg in 1999 despite conservatives' objections to his openly gay lifestyle. The Guggenheim family built their Beverly Hills mansion in 1929. Burton Green, a Massachusetts transplant, established the Beverly Hills Hotel in 1912 amidst little more than open fields. For many years the hotel was an upscale rest area on the trip from L.A.'s downtown to the sea.

Chicago-based Philip Knight Wrigley, Jr., who founded the chewing gum company in 1892, vacationed in Southern California. In 1914 he built his Pasadena mansion, which later became headquarters for the Tournament of Roses. He purchased most of Catalina Island, just off the Southern California coast, a few years later. The Island's Victorian-style Wrigley mansion is now a tony bed & breakfast where for the right price you can sleep in the Wrigley bedroom.

With his father's Dallas oil fortune in hand, Howard Hughes entered the Hollywood scene in the 1920s, becoming a producer and eventually buying the controlling interest in RKO Studios in 1948. He founded Hughes Aircraft, for which he is perhaps best known, in 1932. Besides dabbling in film production, Hughes married into Hollywood and was at one point a permanent resident in one of the Beverly Hills Hotel's famous bungalows. He purchased the now renovated

Pantages Theatre in 1949; since the theatre's recent facelift, some claim to have seen the ghost of Howard Hughes haunting the corridors. Old Hollywood, it seems, does not let go easily.

J. Paul Getty, another Texas transplant, moved to Los Angeles and lived there for many years in relative obscurity vis-à-vis the general public. Only after a 1957 article in *Fortune* magazine designating him the richest American did Getty garner public notice. He later became even better known when he founded the Getty Museum in Malibu. The lavishly funded foundation he created eventually established the Getty Center, an art Mecca perched high on the hills above L.A.'s posh Westside.

Armand Hammer of Occidental Petroleum, who founded the Hammer Museum in Westwood, lived and worked in L.A. in his later years. Hammer's fortune began through the buying and selling of Soviet art. Acquainted with the Soviet Union's revolutionary leader Lenin and all Soviet heads of state thereafter, Hammer made the bulk of his fortune when he took over Occidental.

Norton Simon, another art patron, came to Los Angeles from Oregon, built a fortune buying and selling companies on the stock market and bought a scintillating array of the world's greatest art, much of which is housed at the Norton Simon Museum in Pasadena. He connected with Hollywood through his marriage to actress Jennifer Jones.

Doris Duke, heiress to the Duke tobacco fortune, spent much of her time in Beverly Hills until her death in 1993. Like many in the upper class, Duke had several residences. She could well afford her stays in Beverly Hills, as it was reported that her income in 1984 alone was 35 million dollars, 14 million of which arrived in her bank accounts tax-free from municipal bonds.

Armand Deutsch, a grandson of Sears, Roebuck and Co. founder Julius Rosenwald, came west with his wife Harriet to be a Hollywood producer. He was later part of Ronald Reagan's Kitchen Cabinet, a group of wealthy businessmen instrumental in Reagan's election as Governor and then President.

Another insider in the Reagan circle is Betsy Bloomingdale, a native Angeleno who resides on the Westside and is a major player on the Los Angeles social scene. She married Alfred Bloomingdale of Diner's Club and department store fame. Mr. Bloomingdale was another bitten by the Hollywood bug and lured west to make movies. Betsy Bloomingdale is a close friend of Nancy Reagan and was dubbed the First Friend during the Reagan presidency. Partly because of her European connections forged during her husband's Diner's Club days and also because of her longtime friendship with then First Lady Nancy Reagan, Betsy Bloomingdale received an invite to Princess Diana's wedding. Her social radar seems to find all the top events from coast to coast and across the Atlantic as well.

The late Walter Annenberg, whose family owned Triangle Publications Inc., publisher of magazines such as *TV Guide* and the *Daily Racing Form*, entertained President Reagan and many of the Hollywood crowd on his winter estate, Sunnylands, filled with the world's most expensive art and located in Palm Springs, a moneyed enclave two hours from Los Angeles. During the summer Annenberg often occupied Bungalow 5 at the Beverly Hills Hotel, where he entertained guests and enjoyed the private pool built specially for him by the hotel. For a time he was also one of the top shareholders of General Motors Corp., owning some two million shares. Annenberg, a Philadelphia transplant, paid 40.7 million dollars in 1989 for Pablo Picasso's "Au Lapin Agile," which then found its way to a new home in his desert oasis. His daughter, Wallis Annenberg, resides in Beverly Hills, where she is active in top L.A. social circles and charitable endeavors. She organized the 1998 Music Center tribute to L.A.'s *grande dame*, the incomparable Caroline Ahmanson. Wallis Annenberg pledged 10 million dollars for the Los Angeles County Museum of Art in 2002 through the Annenberg Foundation to fund art acquisitions and to support educational programs and exhibitions.

This relentless march of transplanted wealth seemed

to momentarily peak in the 1980s, sending home-pricing tremors throughout L.A.'s Westside. But how high is too high in a place where everyone dreams to be? In the 1980s Ted Field, heir to the Chicago-based Marshall Field department stores, bought silent film star Harold Lloyd's house in Beverly Hills for 6.5 million dollars and began producing movies. He sold it in 1993 for 15 million dollars, but not before he had hosted on his estate President Clinton's biggest Hollywood fundraiser prior to the 1992 presidential election. Field then moved to a smaller house in the area that he only rented for $40,000 a month.

Bi-coastal Rupert Murdoch, based in New York, moved to an L.A. home for a time to look after his media interests, including 20th Century Fox Studios and the Fox Broadcasting Co. The Fox Studios Richard Zanuck ran in the 1960s has been likened to a boutique compared to the giant corporation Murdoch owns today. In 1986 Murdoch purchased a 7 million dollar Beverly Hills estate once owned by MCA founder Jules Stein and built in 1927 for Fred Niblo, who directed stars such as Douglas Fairbanks, Sr. and Rudolph Valentino. Finding the ubiquitous Murdoch in Los Angeles is like finding a fish in water. Apparently feeling at home in L.A., Murdoch ponied up one million dollars for the 1996 California Republican Party campaign. He then purchased the Los Angeles Dodgers baseball team from the O'Malley family. But Murdoch's family life took a nasty turn as estranged wife Anna filed for divorce after a thirty-one year marriage, and the couple put their estate on the market for $19.5 million. Mrs. Murdoch sought division of all the couple's property plus alimony, and hired lawyers whose sole job was to determine Murdoch's net worth, which Forbes magazine estimated at 5.6 billion dollars in 1998.

Steve Tisch, producer of *The Truman Show* and the Oscar-winning movie *Forrest Gump*, is the son of Preston R. Tisch of the New York-based Tisch brothers. Family holdings wrapped up in the Tisch Corp. are worth close to two billion dollars. Tisch spent 8.5 million dollars in 1997 buying the home of agent Bernie Brillstein, whose clientele has included Brad Pitt and Nicolas Cage. Tisch has also caught that L.A. art bug, joining the ever-increasing stream of new collectors of contemporary art. Larry, the other Tisch brother, bought a controlling interest in CBS in 1986, becoming its president and chief executive officer. The Tisch family now has solid L.A. roots.

The Mansionization of Los Angeles

The fountain of Westside wealth flows constantly as new players continually appear on the scene. The list of names could go on to the point of sounding trivial, yet this largely transplanted economic force is anything but trivial. In the virgin soil of Los Angeles, it was a key catalyst in the birth of an identifiable L.A. upper crust. Real economic power means real social power, and economic power is spread over the hills of West Los Angeles like so many transplanted trees that provide the instant old foliage to the mansions of the area. People, trees, and houses, whether new or old to L.A., blend together in a colorful hue as if there since the tectonic plate on which Los Angeles teeters first rose out of the ocean.

When you walk into the office of Mr. Westside Real Estate himself, Jeff Hyland, you really understand the milieu of high-end real estate on the Westside. Hyland's partner is Rick Hilton of Hilton Hotels fame. Down the street is Spago Beverly Hills where Wolfgang Puck is at work. As you walk into Hyland's penthouse suite you are struck by enlarged, decades-old pictures of the Westside, when barren spaces rather than lush foliage, streets, and mansions dominated the terrain. Hyland's office is appropriately spacious for someone who handles multimillion-dollar properties daily. The staff is as courteous as you would expect considering the next referral may be a billionaire looking for a 20 million dollar property. The office handles Christie's high-end real estate, which has included the former Valentino home owned by the late billionaire Doris Duke. The firm's selected client list includes Barbra Streisand, Merv Griffin, Lionel Ritchie,

Rupert Murdoch and George Hamilton.

Hyland appears sans tie and understandably so considering over half his clientele comes from the entertainment industry where beyond cool is the proper demeanor. Hyland knows the history of most any Westside property off the top of his head. But he rarely gets to show the office to his clients. They meet him either at the prospective property or for lunch. As for the movie stars, the only time he sees them is when he shows them a property. If the house is right and the sale is pending, Hyland works with their business managers and attorneys to close the deal.

Fred Sands, another successful Westside realtor, explains that, "People on the Westside want to know the pedigree of the person they are working with." If an agent works the high-end market, "they'd better know the names of the celebrities and others living in the neighborhood." And you don't hand out cute little notepads or pens as realtors do in middle class areas, at least not if you want to be taken seriously by the L.A. super rich. One high-end Beverly Hills realtor remarked that were he to advertise in this way, he would lose all of his clients. Word of mouth is the main advertising tool in Westside real estate heaven. Almost all clients are repeats or referrals, and trust is the main draw. The Jon Douglas Co., another top Westside realty, has put out a glossy magazine portfolio of distinctive estate properties marketed worldwide. The wealthy may pick their multimillion-dollar L.A. home out of a catalogue and purchase it with a simple phone call if they are too busy to look.

The Westside real estate frenzy knows no bounds. Money is but a minor detail in a lifestyle contest that pits the most unlikely people against one another. One such battle erupted over a proposed 56-foot-high home in Bel-Air in a serene neighborhood that Elizabeth Taylor, Rosemary Stack, and Joanna Carson, Johnny's ex-wife, call home. Do these gargantuan dream homes of couples wanting to make their presence felt on the Westside get built? Usually. Neither trees nor environmental impact reports, not even a feature article in the *L.A. Times* by Patti Davis, whose parents Ronnie and Nancy Reagan live close by, can stop this real life game of monopoly: You build and I'll build better.

On one street alone, South Mapleton Drive in Holmby Hills, this social drama of wealth and power played out in posh Westside neighborhoods has unwound with particular éclat. In the 1980s television producer Aaron Spelling purchased a 15,000 square-foot home from Patrick (Papermate pens and Schick razors) Frawley for 10 million dollars. Across the street Frawley owned yet another house where he never lived (he lived in a third house next door), which he sold for 11 million dollars. Part of the social cachet of the Spelling home was that it was formerly owned by Bing Crosby. Down the street, having relocated from Chicago, lived none other than *Playboy* magazine's Hugh Hefner in the Playboy mansion of Playboy parties, centerfolds and adult fantasy.

For his part Spelling began immediately to demolish his new home. The destruction of the Crosby home raised a few eyebrows and brought protest for the ensuing disturbance from another neighbor, J.P. Guerin, former chairman of PSA Inc. The new Spelling home covers 56,000 square feet and sits on six acres of prime real estate. The home's features include a bowling alley and an ice skating rink. Mrs. Spelling's closet alone takes up some 7,000 square feet. The Spelling estate has become somewhat of a symbol for excess around Los Angeles, yet everyone secretly wants to get a look inside. But the Spellings have been very guarded about sharing their palace's interior. The deceased Crosby would perhaps have given his usual wry grin at the irony when Spelling, who spent a purported 48 million dollars on his new mansion, took a contractor to court for a leaky roof.

Leaks aside, the Spelling home risked being second best even as the decorators put the finishing touches in place. Merv Griffin, of game shows "Wheel of Fortune" and "Jeopardy," bought a mountaintop of eleven level acres and over two hundred acres total in the Beverly Hills area with plans to raze it and build a 58,000 square-foot mansion. Apparently Griffin reconsidered his plans, though, and later sold the land to Mark Hughes, founder of Herbalife. Hughes was building an Italian Mediterranean-style home with a million-gallon lake on the former Griffin property overlooking Beverly Hills before his untimely death. Of course Griffin can always live in the Beverly Hilton Hotel, which he has owned since 1987. He also owns a 157-acre site that he purchased from Princess Shams Pahlavi, the late Shah of Iran's sister, another royal transplant and nouveau Hollywood celebrity who called Los Angeles home from the 1930s until her death in 1996.

On the compacted Westside, what the wealthy want above all, it seems, is an estate, meaning a large home on several acres of land. One lot is apparently no longer enough. Gary Winnick, founder of Global Crossing communications company, bought the prized estate of Henri Salvatori in 1998 for 16 million dollars before his company ran into financial difficulties and filed for bankruptcy just four years later. Salvatori had been a member of Ronald Reagan's Kitchen Cabinet. After purchasing the Salvatori mansion, Winnick then bought the home next door, once owned by Merle Oberon, for $10 million with plans to tear down both homes and combine the lots. The Salvatori home was designed by renowned architect Paul Williams. No matter.

Not to be contained, Winnick later bought the estate of David H. Murdock, chief executive of Castle & Cook, for $11.5 million. The house boasts 64 rooms, including a dozen bedrooms and a dozen bathrooms. Named Casa Encantada, the mansion symbolizes upward mobility. It was originally built in 1934 for a New York nurse who married her wealthy patient and decided to come west in style. Winnick's own father was a Long Island businessman who went bankrupt. Winnick worked under Michael Milken in his junk bond department on Wilshire and Rodeo in the 1980s. His fortune came as he raised 20 billion dollars in 1996 to start Global Crossing with the goal of wiring the world with fiber optic cable. Winnick was forced to resign as Chairman in 2002 as the company filed for bankruptcy, wiping out $54 billion in investors' equity. But before Global Crossing shares began to tumble, Winnick sold off some $600 million worth. He can presumably still afford his home purchases. If not, ten people are in line to take his place.

The house wars that sprang up in the 1980s in the Golden Triangle—Beverly Hills, Holmby Hills, and Bel-Air—were not confined to wealthy Americans outdoing wealthy Americans. Foreign nationals also got into the act. The Sultan of Brunei bought the Beverly Hills Hotel from Marvin Davis. Davis himself was another transplant, and transplant himself he did, in style, moving from Colorado to a 21 million dollar mansion in Beverly Hills and using his oil fortune to buy not only the Beverly Hills Hotel, but a major studio, 20th Century Fox, which he later sold. Davis purchased the hotel from Dallas-based Caroline Hunt, heir to the Hunt oil fortune, whose private investment concern, Rosewood Financial Partners, manages her one billion dollar fortune. Davis and his wife Barbara quickly became major players on the L.A. social scene by hosting grand parties and through work on the charity circuit.

From Europe came former waiter Giancarlo Paretti, who along with his partner had allegedly bribed the French bank Crédit Lyonnais to extract a credit line of two billion dollars. In 1989 Paretti bought out MGM/United Artists with the money. He also bought Tramp, then a hot nightclub in the Beverly Center catering to L.A.'s rich and famous and an offshoot of the Original Tramp in London. Paretti luxuriated in an 11,000 square-foot Beverly Hills home complete with tennis court, guesthouse, and gym. He purchased the house, once owned by Vidal Sassoon, for 8.9 million dollars, one of the largest Westside real estate transactions that year. After playing in L.A. in a big way, Paretti later fled the United States, returning to Italy to avoid being brought to justice for a perjury conviction. Paretti's partner, Florio Fiorini, was convicted and sentenced to 41 months in prison. Paretti's stint in the Southern California sunshine shows how easily a relative nobody with big bucks can break into the L.A. scene, yet how ephemeral one's place may be.

Even the Russians have made their mark on Los Angeles. Leon Rudyad, a Russian industrialist who owns a chain of video stores there, and his wife Mila bought a 14,000 square-foot Mediterranean-style home for 6.5 million dollars in Bel-Air. Asians are increasingly players in the haute Los Angeles real estate game. Martial arts star Jackie Chan purchased a $3 million Beverly Hills house in 1998. The 7,000 square-foot home features four fireplaces, a pool, a five-car garage and a motor court securely ensconced behind gates.

Homes made famous as sets in blockbuster films are also put up for sale, sometimes in rather unconventional ways. The Beverly Hills mansion used in the 1987 movie *Beverly Hills Cop II* went to auction and could have been had at a bargain basement price of about one million dollars. The house boasts padded silk wall coverings, a gourmet kitchen with a built-in wok and a temperature-regulated toilet. The U.S. Customs Service forced the sale of the home after Japanese owner Ken Mizuno was convicted of tax evasion and fraud in Japan.

Another famous property came onto the market in the late 1990s: Falcon Lair, once the home of screen legend Rudolph Valentino. The home got its name because Valentino himself had etched "Falcon Lair" on the front gate. Built in 1924, the 4,700 square-foot Benedict Canyon estate rests on more than four acres only five minutes from the fabled Beverly Hills Hotel. Features include a library/music room, a kitchen with four ovens, a motor court, staff quarters and a guest apartment. Tobacco heiress Doris Duke died there in 1993 after owning the property for thirty years.

You knew the "techies" were going to show up in West L.A. since everyone does sooner or later. Billionaire Paul Allen, co-founder of Microsoft, purchased a 120-acre estate in Benedict Canyon overlooking Beverly Hills for a little under 20 million dollars in 1997. Noted architect Wallace Neff had designed the 10,000 square-foot home known as Enchanted Hill. Allen is a major investor in the new Hollywood studio DreamWorks SKG, co-founded by Steven Spielberg, ex-Disney executive Jeffrey Katzenberg and David Geffen. Allen lost no time making a splash in Hollywood as a DreamWorks partner. He hosted one of the most exclusive parties at the 1996 Cannes Film Festival in France, flying in by charter jet a select group of 200 stars and executives from Los Angeles, New York, and Microsoft. The purported one million dollars Allen spent on the party buttresses his 500 million dollar investment in DreamWorks. True to L.A. haute style, guests received gold-engraved invitations sent inside treasure chests and were lodged at hotel rooms running $500 per night. Allen seems determined to put to rest the "nerd" label for computer whizzes once and for all.

The Internet, too, has arrived on L.A.'s Westside to join the party as Geocities founder David Bohnett has parlayed a few web pages into his new $5.95 million Holmby Hills home once owned by actor Gary Cooper. Bohnett sold a stake in Geocities to Yahoo, the Internet search firm, and still holds company stock valued at upwards of 100 million dollars.

Then there's the music industry, which has moved to Los Angeles in a big way. From the Hollywood Hills to Malibu, music money permeates the uppermost levels of L.A. wealth. Take the listing of Freddie DeMann's 20,000 square-foot Bel-Air home for 23 million dollars. DeMann is Madonna's former manager and co-founded Maverick Records with her. Perched on a promontory, the home features city-to-ocean panoramic views, maids' quarters, a guesthouse, a state-of-the-art projection room, climate-controlled wine cellar, hair salon, gym, sauna, spa, pool and tennis court—all on about three acres. Not bad for the former manager of the material girl.

Tired of staying in hotels when he visits the city, the most famous living Beatle, Paul McCartney, decided he needed a home in L.A. too. So when McCartney gets the L.A. urge, as all the music types and movie types do when they want to close business deals and massage relationships, he can comfortably reside in his Hollywood Hills home bought from singer-actress Courtney Love. Staking her claim on the Westside, pop singer Christina Aguilera bought a Mediterranean-style home in Beverly Hills. Aguilera then acquired a Hollywood Hills home in 2003 for $5 million with a waterfall and city views. And what about "shock rocker" Rob Zombie, with his custom made contact lenses that turn his pupils into black pinholes, moving into a home in the venerable, wealthy enclave of Hancock Park in 1999? Zombie brought his heavy metal to test the walls of a home built in 1924. Among other feats, Zombie designed the Horror Night maze for Universal Studios Hollywood that featured creepy creatures and a 30-foot replica of Zombie's head. Music industry people are no longer content to roam only in the Hollywood Hills hinterland, buying also in Brentwood, Beverly Hills and Malibu and becoming another element in the mix of financial power and cultural clout that distinguishes Los Angeles from any other city in the world.

R&B and pop music producer Kenneth "Babyface" Edmunds has moved up by selling his Holmby Hills home for $6.3 million and buying another for $13 million just a stone's throw away from Hugh Hefner's Playboy mansion. The Grammy-winning Edmunds has written songs for Whitney Houston, Michael Jackson, and Madonna. He also produced the 1997 movie *Soul Food*. The new Edmunds dining room can seat forty people—not surprising considering that the 20,000 square-foot home boasts five kitchens.

Motown on the Westside? Barry Gordy, who founded the label in Detroit in 1959, established himself in Los Angeles by the 1980s. The Motown label, whose stable of stars included the Supremes, the Temptations, and Stevie Wonder, was sold in 1988 for 60 million dollars. In the 1990s Gordy sold some of the rights to the songs for 132 million dollars. Not bad for a kid from Detroit.

Another Detroit boy making his presence felt in Los Angeles is Eli Broad, Chairman of SunAmerica. Broad was bitten by the L.A. contemporary art bug, serving as founding chairman of the Museum of Contemporary Art. Broad owns his own museum-quality collection of contemporary art, and his Frank Gehry-designed home in Brentwood was visited by President Clinton for a fundraiser. Broad's Malibu home was designed by Richard Meier, architect of the Getty Center. Broad was instrumental in raising money for L.A.'s latest modernistic showcase: The Disney Concert Hall, new home of the L.A. Philharmonic. And just a few miles away, in his 12,000 square-foot Bel-Air home is another man who made a name in Detroit, Lee Iacocca, who is known far and wide for his leadership in saving Chrysler Corp.

Often L.A.'s elite seem to come and go on a whim. Rocker David Bowie and his wife, model-actress Iman, have gone since selling their Beverly Hills condo to rap star Heavy D for $850,000. Sylvester Stallone was temporarily out of the picture, having moved to Miami, but the Hollywood draw proved too powerful. He returned in grand style with a 10 million dollar custom home in Beverly Hills that includes a huge library; a gym; a theater; a 900 square-foot bathroom with copper sinks, a copper tub and two chandeliers; and his and her home offices overlooking a newly planted forest of some 300 trees. Stallone also bought the house next door for relatives for $16 million. Stallone later sold his Beverly Hills property in 2002 for $15 million.

Billionaire five times over Kirk Kerkorian is also back bigger and better. Kerkorian, who regained ownership of MGM Studios for the third time in the late 1990s, sojourns in L.A. when not in his Las Vegas outpost, where he is chairman of the MGM Grand Hotel and Casino. So he took Stallone's old house off his hands. The home is one of several on Kerkorian's 31-acre Beverly Hills estate overlooking Benedict Canyon that includes the former tracts of Sonny Bono and Yvette Mimieux. But in this case, forget the house. What could be more fun than the buying and selling of movie studios for which Kerkorian is so well known? For sheer headiness, it sure beats acting. But someone has sour grapes about the Kerkorian spread. The property apparently has water run-off problems, and Kerkorian is being sued for 3 million dollars. Kerkorian's driveway, which has been compared to a freeway, is also a contentious point in the lawsuit.

And then there is the just plain ridiculous. One Beverly Hills property on Sunset Blvd. two blocks east of the Beverly Hills Hotel at Alpine Drive became a haven for lookey-loos in the late 1970s when it was purchased by Saudi Sheik Mohammed al-Fassi, who painted the house lime green. But what caused the real uproar was the Sheik's taste in art: He installed white plaster nude statues on the front veranda painted in natural hues and complete with pubic hair. The sheik was shocked at the commotion. After all, it would have worked in ancient Greece.

Not everyone in Beverly Hills is a homeowner. The city does have its renters, too. Producer Matthew Mellon of the Pittsburgh banking Mellons and grandson of Gulf Oil's founder along with his cousin Ginger Grace, descendant of the founder of W.R. Grace & Co., leased a two million dollar estate in Beverly Hills for $8,000 per month. The country French estate boasts five bedrooms and a guesthouse in 7,000 square feet. Meanwhile, pop diva Mariah Carey came out to L.A. for a T.V. special and rather than stay at a luxury hotel, leased a three-acre English estate for $25,000 a week.

Dodi Al-Fayed, who died in the tragic car crash with Princess Diana and was heir to a billion dollar oil fortune, often rented homes in Beverly Hills with monthly prices ranging from $20,000 to $35,000. Apparently Beverly Hills does not believe in rent control. Al-Fayed came to Hollywood for what else: To produce movies. He helped finance Academy Award-winning *Chariots of Fire*, among other films. Al-Fayed was known for his lavish parties which included many celebrities and beautiful women. He was also known for not paying his rent from time to time and was often sued for skipping town or bouncing checks. Al-Fayed must have felt that the landlords didn't really need the money.

When heading Universal, Seagram chief Edgar

Bronfman, Jr., dispensed with renting. Bronfman, who years earlier came out to the Hollywood playground to produce a movie, became an L.A. homeowner when he bought comedian Bob Newhart's Malibu home for 6.5 million dollars in 1997. The house boasts eighty feet of beach frontage and was once owned by Robert Redford. Every home has a story in the fabled environs of L.A.'s Westside. Yet the unpredictable Bronfman never actually lived in his Malibu home, and sold it in 2000 for 10 million dollars.

The mansionization of Beverly Hills was the logical outcome of the massive movement of wealth to L.A.'s Westside that by the 1980s had impacted the area like an economic sonic boom. By 1995 the Beverly Hills city council had moved to put a limit on the size of hillside expansions of homes. This ruling was precipitated by the proposal to build an 18-bedroom, 21-bathroom, 46,000 square-foot mansion by London financier Robert Manoukian. The house was to be larger than a football field. This proposal naturally raised the ire of surrounding homeowners including the late Jack Lemmon, then MCA President Sidney Sheinberg, and Ticketmaster baron Fred Rosen. Manoukian intended to live in the house one or two months a year with his seventeen-member extended family.

Is there no escape from mansionization, from homes where the house staff outnumbers family members? Arnold Schwarzenegger and Maria Shriver bought into Pacific Palisades in 1986. Now with four children, they have patiently bought out neighboring homes, making three purchases over fifteen years, one of them the home of actor John Forsythe. The couple's compound now totals some 5.5 acres. The three Palisades homes include a stream, three swimming pools and three tennis courts. The couple bought into a gated community in Brentwood for $11.9 million in 2002 and listed their Palisades compound for sale in 2003 at $18 million. Such changes are not uncommon in Westside real estate, where busy schedules and changing needs often mitigate grandiose plans.

Los Angeles vs. New York:
The Cost of Playing in the Upper Crust

O.K., you made it. You are in Los Angeles staying at one of the famous bungalows at the Beverly Hills Hotel. Now, how do you become an L.A. player? Today, the upper classes of L.A. and New York are as open as a dollar bill. As one Beverly Hills insider put it, "You buy your way in everywhere." The late Nancy Vreeland and her husband Tim, son of the late *Vogue* editor Diana Vreeland, affirmed that L.A. is "one of the cities in which you can establish yourself quite quickly because almost everyone else is new also," and the emphasis is on accomplishment. But New York? Contrary to the old misleading conceptions about heritage, demeanor and the like for entry into the upper class, one only needs dollars to play whether in New York or L.A.—many, many dollars. A net worth of 20 million dollars minimum with considerable liquidity might get you close. As the character Goddard Bolt states in Mel Brooks' 1991 film *Life Stinks*, "Five million dollars is nothing." The difference between New York and Los Angeles is that L.A. admits its addiction to the mighty dollar. Money talks. In Los Angeles, money is the ultimate calling card.

Still, mere inheritance of money does not always guarantee easy entrée into the top social circles. In fact, nothing could be more bizarre than the events surrounding the inheritance of Doris Duke's estate. The heiress to her father's tobacco fortune died in 1993 at her home above Beverly Hills, Falcon Lair, the former home of film legend Rudolf Valentino. She left a 1.2 billion dollar estate to be administered by her pony-tailed butler. Duke had no natural heirs and had made as many as five wills late in life. One will left the execution of her estate to Chandi Heffner, a Hare Krishna she met at a dance class and adopted as her daughter. Heffner was one of several who contested the will. She eventually settled for 65 million dollars.

The designation of Duke's butler Bernard Lafferty— onetime butler of Peggy Lee and described as "the perfect girlfriend" by wealthy women for whom he had worked and fussed over—as executor of the Duke estate left the usual contingent of lawyers and bank officers hovering around the fortune in a tizzy. It was simply a question of a billion dollars plus, growing daily, that had everyone up in arms. Duke even had a will designating her one time New York doctor as executor. He too joined in the legal banquet of sorting out who got what. Duke, distrustful of lawyers, had asked (who else?) her plastic surgeon, Dr. Harry Glassman, husband of actress Victoria Principal, to suggest a legal counsel. It seems Glassman received a $500,000 gift a few weeks before Duke's death. Duke's last will assigned the bulk of her estate to a Doris Duke Charitable Foundation to benefit art and wildlife, while giving Lafferty $500,000 a year plus 5 million dollars in executor fees.

Predictably, Lafferty's credibility was immediately challenged from all sides. Lafferty had continued to live in Duke's estate and reportedly had personal servants and a chauffeur. "I don't drive because I have always had a chauffeur," Lafferty stated in a police report. He had run up a huge credit card bill on Rodeo Drive at Georgio Armani and Cartier, where he bought a gold and diamond watch for $35,000. Lafferty eventually settled for a 4.5 million dollar payment and $500,000 a year to relinquish his role with the estate, but he did not leave without some parting shots: "I have a ponytail. I have an earring. I look maybe eccentric to them. I don't fit into the mold they've got ... It doesn't belong to lawyers and bankers. The Doris Duke estate is not a pie, and it's not going to be cut up... It belongs to the poor, the sick...the elderly, for AIDS."

Lafferty, no longer a butler, purchased a seven bedroom, 11,000 square-foot, 2.5 million dollar home in Beverly Hills with his inheritance from the Duke estate. How's that for upward mobility? Walking distance from Falcon Lair, the home includes a bedroom with a twenty-foot ceiling and a headboard that was part of a door from a Vanderbilt mansion in Newport, Rhode Island. And former butler Lafferty hired his own butler. Unfortunately, Lafferty did not live long to enjoy his new social status: He died of heart failure in 1997 at the age of 51 just after purchasing his trophy home.

If inheritance hasn't unlocked the top social doors for you, another way to earn a little recognition and hobnob with the upper crust is to do some gift giving. Again, the New York social scene is not radically different from that of Los Angeles even though the New York upper class has a much longer history, noted old-line families and fixed social institutions. Author Tom Wolfe, known for hobnobbing in New York's top circles, offers his take on the New York social scene: " . . . today if you have money, you can become a socialite in two years no matter how crude you are. The magic ticket to making it socially in New York is to support the Metropolitan Museum of Art or the Museum of Modern Art. And the reason is that if you give a lot of money to a museum, they want to get more, assuming you have more, so they will put you on the party circuit." Should you be hesitant to give to cultural institutions in Los Angeles, remember that Caroline Ahmanson, herself at the pinnacle of the L.A. upper crust, says, "There are no walls." Status in L.A. depends on whether or not the individual is participatory. To be accepted you must be generous with your time and money. So get out your checkbook, and be prepared to keep it out for a while.

In New York, investors Saul Steinberg and Henry Kravis gave heavily as they became generous benefactors of the Metropolitan Museum. Henry Kravis made a 10 million dollar tax-deductible contribution that founded his own wing. Both men used their wives to great advantage. Kravis married and later bankrolled Carolyn Roehm as a couturier, and Steinberg's third wife, Gayfryd, quickly became one of the queens of New York as a hostess of lavish parties. In 1989 she spent one million dollars for Saul's 50th birthday party in the Hamptons. Donald Trump also used his then wife Ivana to great advantage, as her sense of style gave him legitimacy. Trump, consciously creating his own persona, bought the fabulous estate Mar-a-Lago in Palm Beach. He would fly down key socialites in his private jet for his own stellar parties.

Eli Broad, a huge player on the contemporary art scene in L.A. has remarked, "I'd say 90% of donors want recognition of some sort." You could have a gallery or a corner in a museum, or you could simply have your picture in a prominent place. Art museums have followed a trend set by universities to name whole buildings after donors. The L.A. County Museum of Art (LACMA) has Ahmanson, Hammer, Anderson, and Bing wings.

Museums are the hottest game in town. The Museum of Contemporary Art in Los Angeles renamed its Temporary Contemporary facility the Geffen Contemporary in 1996 after receiving a 5 million dollar gift from David Geffen. The late Armand Hammer wanted the Los Angeles County Museum of Art to name an entire floor after him in exchange for his considerable collection. When the Museum balked, Hammer established the Armand Hammer Museum in Westwood near UCLA. Broad himself gave a stunning 60 million dollars to the Los Angeles County Museum of Art in 2003 for a new building that is tentatively called the Broad Contemporary Art Museum at LACMA. The museum will house post-1945 art and will probably also be the destination for much of Broad's world-class collection of contemporary art.

Modern day social climbers always have several irons in the fire. Former corporate raider Ronald Perelman, who took control of Revlon, hired Nancy Gardiner, *Town and Country* editor, as his social secretary and married Patricia Duff Medavoy, ex-wife of Orion Pictures' head Mike Medavoy. Presumably to do his civic duty, Perelman became an honorary chairman of the New York Public Library. To hedge his bet, he put California-based Ann Getty and Nancy Reagan on the board, and soon created a foothold in L.A., where he is often seen at Hollywood bashes. With the Perelmans and the Trumps and others, New York high society, built on great new fortunes quickly christened "old" money, is merely getting its comeuppance.

As in New York, marriage has often been the elevator ride into the L.A. upper crust. Socialite Joan Quinn recalls that as Jews tried to gain a foothold in an L.A. social scene dominated by WASPs, some Jewish studio heads married out of their faith to enter the fold. Women who marry into great wealth often come from humble backgrounds—manicurist, secretary, even high class hooker—and then marry their way up the social ladder. Today, with Viagra, quips one insider, women have to work for their money and social standing, as they cannot assume that their often much older husbands will not stay sexually active.

Marrying up is the stuff movies are made of, and quite literally so in the case of Darva Conger. Conger beat out a bevy of beauties to win the "Who Wants to Marry a Millionaire" show on Fox only to find that her husband was not compatible (surprise), nor was he necessarily a millionaire. Conger undoubtedly found out the hard way that it is a better bet to hang around the hot and tony Westside hotels such as the Mondrian, the Peninsula or the classic Beverly Hills Hotel to meet your true millionaire or billionaire. Or perhaps, as in Conger's case, posing for *Playboy* and hanging out at the Hefner mansion might be the thing to do.

The aforementioned Patricia Duff Medavoy Perelman met studio head Mike Medavoy while working on the Gary Hart campaign. After divorcing Medavoy, she married the immensely wealthy Ron Perelman. The Perelmans have since gone their separate ways. They were locked in a child custody battle, and Patricia Duff spent over 2 million of the 30 million dollars awarded to her for her three-year marriage to Perelman fighting for custody of their child. She demanded even more money so that the daughter could live a comparable lifestyle to that of her billionaire father. Duff was eventually awarded some $13,000 per month in child support.

Still, marriages, messy or not, are a way to catapult into social stardom. If your husband has big bucks but is short on taste and social graces, you can take him "from K-Mart to Tiffany's," as the character Caroline Sexton claims to have done for husband Brad in the 1997 film *For Richer or Poorer*. Take the example of former Oregon chicken farmer Darcy LaPier Robertson Rice Van Damme Hughes. Darcy catapulted onto the Malibu shores as the late Herbalife founder Mark Hughes' wife after three previous marriages. Native American Darcy became Oregon's Miss Hawaiian Tropic in 1986 and later married Hawaiian Tropic's founder, Ron Rice—or so it seemed. It turns out Darcy had never divorced her first husband. Rice later commented on his unexpected bachelor status: "We had a $2 million party that I thought was a wedding."

The determined Darcy then turned an affair with actor Jean-Claude Van Damme into yet another marriage. After a rocky marriage with Van Damme, Darcy met Mark Hughes on a blind date and once again wedding bells were a ringing. The two married in 1999, and Hughes promised Darcy $1 million a year for their first five anniversaries—a nice incentive for Darcy to stay married. Hughes and Darcy lived in both Beverly Hills and Malibu, spending over $1 million decorating the two homes.

Mark Hughes died unexpectedly less than two years later. Darcy, after trying to lay claim to the couple's Malibu beach home, decided to return to Oregon with a $34 million package, giving up—at least for now—her Beverly Hills residence as well. Predictably, Suzan Hughes, a former Hughes wife, has filed suit on behalf of her son Alex, Hughes' sole heir, calling the LaPier settlement a giveaway. One old-line Angeleno comments on this familiar tale of money and marriage: "Blood and money—that's the bottom line. You marry to make up for your deficiency." It's been the same story since the first great American fortunes thundered at the gates of Old New York.

Whether or not a strategic marriage is part of your ladder to social stardom, you'll need to donate some money. The key institutions involving charitable giving in L.A. are the Music Center, the Museum of Contemporary Art, the Los

Angeles County Museum of Art, Cedars Sinai Medical Center, USC, UCLA, and various children's charities. If Los Angeles has a social core, the Music Center is it. "The Music Center still has that certain cachet if you want to feel that you are society," explains Marcia Newberger, a former Center executive. "Your best way into certain circles is to buy your way into the Music Center."

Supporting the Music Center garners more social cachet than contributing to hospitals such as Cedars Sinai or St. Johns because it is more glamorous. High culture has always been seen as a hallmark of the upper class, and the established wealth patina of the Music Center can rub off on those who support it. To be a benefactor of the Music Center costs $150,000, a grand patron one million dollars. Your wife can become a part of the prestigious Blue Ribbon of the Music Center for a paltry $2,000 if she can secure an invite. But the clothes she would need to wear to its yearly events might cost $50,000 or more, not to mention the ongoing contributions to the charities the Blue Ribbon supports. Chalk up another $50,000 to $100,000 a year for that. And don't forget—your wife needs big jewelry to come out and play.

Ron Burkle, head of Ralph's Grocery Co. and Food 4 Less, hardly symbols of social distinction, pledged 15 million dollars into the kitty for the construction of the stunningly modern Disney Hall. He bought Greenacres, the old Harold Lloyd estate sold by Ted Field, and is on the Music Center Board of Governors. Move over, Marvin Davis? No—there is plenty of space to make a statement in L.A. high society. Michael Ovitz, the super agent turned super manager, left a short stint at Disney with a much talked-about 90 million dollar severance package and gave 25 million dollars to help rebuild the UCLA Medical Center in 1997. A 1968 graduate of UCLA, Ovitz has gone from super agent to super alum.

As a board member, Ovitz was instrumental in bringing in A. Jerrold Perenchio, a billionaire Hollywood producer, to help the Medical Center with another extraordinary gift of 150 million dollars in the name of President Ronald Reagan. Perenchio, a long-time Republican and neighbor of the Reagans in nearby Bel-Air, is also head of the Spanish language television company Univision. The UCLA Medical Center will be named after President Reagan at the end of the fundraising campaign. DreamWorks' David Geffen added $200 million to the UCLA Medical Center fund in 2002—the largest single gift to a medical center in the United States. What would a mere million dollar donation get you these days in L.A.? A cool million will see your name on the meditation room/chapel of the UCLA Medical Center. Hey, you only live (and die) once. It could be a bargain.

Although medical centers and the like are almost universally regarded as worthy causes, many Hollywood types prefer political activity—moguls such as Geffen, Spielberg, Katzenberg, Warner Bros. head Alan Horn (who became politically involved through the influence of producer Norman Lear), Barbra Streisand, actors Tom Hanks and Warren Beatty, director Rob Reiner, Fox Family Channel Chairman Haim Saban—all regularly contribute to Democratic causes. Arnold Schwarzenegger, of course, gives to the Republicans. Mrs. Vincente Minnelli describes some of this new group of Hollywooders as "movie-movie—not very 'social.'" Whether social or political, the new Hollywood movie moguls are determined to leave their mark on the city in their own way, and they have not only the mindset but the cash to do so.

Of course you can take a circuitous route and contribute to a number of charities. No bargain here. The donations add up quickly. Charity events have replaced the private Hollywood dinner parties of a quieter though no less glamorous time. John Loring, senior vice-president of Tiffany & Co., states, "You absolutely simply cannot have a simple charity ball . . . The costume party is obviously a thing of the past. Now it's the rooms themselves that are costumed," reflecting the theme of the evening. Beverly Hills' *Inside Events* magazine's focus is the way major venues such as museums and studio lots are dressed up for charity events. Talk about a specialized magazine. The première/party format is no longer as popular with some, so Cedars Sinai Medical Center has switched to an antique show for its fundraising event. Tickets to charity events start at as little as $250, but you are expected to augment this bargain basement admission price with a generous donation.

You do get some good news. A portion of your contributions to charity is tax deductible. You get to attend lavish parties, do a good deed and get a tax break from Uncle Sam. Some of the costs of your parties will be underwritten by major corporations so that expenses won't eat up all the charity dollars. Who underwrites the underwriters? You are not a politician. Let them worry about it. At least you will get some tangible benefits from this Society thing, and sometimes you get little presents when you attend, too— maybe a silver card tray from Cartier. Everyone likes something for free, even the L.A. upper crust.

The 20 Million Dollar Man and His Wife

But first things first. What about your home? You must live on the Westside to gain any credibility. Preferably you should buy in Beverly Hills, Bel-Air or Malibu. Hollywood Hills is for, well, actors, or those directors or producers who aren't yet part of the cosmopolitan elite set. You are talking 2.5 to 5 million dollars just to get in the neighborhood, 10 to 15 million dollars to make a splash. After all, if you succeed in getting the big L.A. players to attend your party, you need to have something to show off: High ceilings; spiral staircases; designer chandeliers; private guest suites; separate master suites; separate maids' quarters; long driveways embraced by lush landscape; private parking for guests; plenty of trees to ensure the visual privacy of your abode; a pool, tennis court and fitness room; possibly a projection room; and the best sound system available. Universal Studios spent in the range of 2 million dollars to build a screening room at the home of its then chief executive, Frank Biondi, who was to have the option to buy the screening room when he left the company. It was not clear how the studio would get the screening room back if Biondi chose to pass on the option. But unless you are top dog at a major studio, you will have to pay for your screening room yourself. To achieve the right effect in your home you will need to hire architects, draftsmen, designers, decorators, builders, carpenters, drapers, heating engineers, lighting engineers and maybe even a curator. Your furniture must be custom made.

To avoid all the headaches, you could just hire Santa Monica-based Kathryn Ireland to decorate your home. She'll decorate a six-bedroom house for $500,000 to $1 million, not including artwork or her fee. And you could say that the interior designer of Steve Martin and Caroline Kennedy Schlossberg decorated your home.

The labor in your home must be specialized. Someone who can do a little of everything well, filling the roles of maid, housekeeper and cook, is not quite good enough. You hire a chef to prepare your food. Nothing less would be accepted by your palate. You may pay $3,000 to $5,000 a month in food bills, but the good news is that it's cheaper than eating out. Once you make a name for yourself you may want to follow the Davises' lead and seldom eat in because you are out every night at top social events, parties or restaurants. It seems the Davises have a huge staff, including a chef, at their Bel-Air residence. All that staff and you may hardly ever eat at home.

But you are not ready to luxuriate just yet. You need to plop art on your walls, not just any art, but the world's greatest art, the kind you purchase at Sotheby's. Although paintings and sculpture by recognized artists can be had for as little as $30,000 to $40,000, the top flight art needed to make a big splash is often in the millions. Your art collection, including your sculpture, should be worth nearly as much as your house, say 10 million dollars minimum. Ten plus ten—that's 20 million dollars. Get out your calculator.

You need an army of maids and gardeners. You need

a trainer so you and your wife can stay in shape. You need to hire a chef or go to a culinary service for your party. If you're worried about the cost, remember that closing Spago for the evening would do even greater damage to your checkbook. Fresh flowers should appear everywhere. Only the finest flatware may enter your custom doors. You must pay attention to every detail. Even your dog must match your decor or vice versa. Since occasionally a goat or some other unusual animal has been spotted walking down Rodeo Drive on a leash, you may not be satisfied with the minimal attention an ordinary dog would attract. But if the traditional canine is your preference, remember that dogs also go in and out of style—Golden Retrievers were hot for a while, but soon the Dalmation took over the top "spot." You'll need to keep abreast of the changing fashion in canines.

You need a special designer invitation made. You need a social secretary and even a publicist to make a big splash. You may want to hire Warren Cowan & Associates or maybe Lee Solters or Dale Olson. You can count on the publicist to invite prominent clients to your party so you can begin to network. Insiders say that while living in Denver, the Davises met stars through Harry Finley, social arbiter and owner of Flower Fashions, and flew them up for the Carousel of Hope Ball for diabetes.

Unless you're gay, you need a wife. And even if you are gay, a wife can still come in handy. Society sparkles through the make-up, couture clothing and jewels of its women. If you need some introductions, it's easy to get started. And don't worry if you fall into the senior citizen category. As Henry Kissinger purportedly once said, "Power is the greatest aphrodisiac." You can go through a publicist, as many of them make their entire livelihood out of making such introductions, says publicist Dale Olson. Or you can get leads through friends. Denise Hale, second wife of Vincente Minnelli and later the wife of Broadway department store magnate Prentice Cobb Hale, arranged a meeting between Sharon Stone and the Executive Editor of the San Francisco Examiner, Phil Bronstein. They were married for 5 years.

Once the vows are pronounced, you need to dress your wife. Gowns cost three to five thousand a pop. If she's a member of the Blue Ribbon, which she should be, Armani and Chanel are the preferred designers. She needs to spend big bucks at a Rodeo retailer to convince the retailer that she is an important customer worthy of introductions to his other clients. She needs to be dressed for each season, year after year. She needs shoes and accessories. She needs jewels.

With her jewelry, you had better sell a portion of your company stock to get some liquidity. Pieces start at $50,000 to $100,000, and you need a blockbuster million-dollar necklace for the Davises' Carousel of Hope ball for diabetes charities. After all, no less a Hollywooder than Lee Minnelli has called it the "Oscars of charity balls" and the most glamorous ball in America. Mrs. Minnelli adds, though, that a lot of charity balls are attended by "people who want to get somewhere," and she personally doesn't go over and over to the same charity balls—eating rubber chicken, waiting two hours for your car to be brought by the valet, and possibly being seated with someone you don't like gets old. Still, few could afford to turn down such an invite, so should you choose to go, you may find yourself at a table near Whitney Houston, Kurt Russell, Goldie Hawn or Dustin Hoffman. You might sit next to Quincy Jones or Warren Beatty. Across the room you may see Hillary Rodham Clinton, Barbra Streisand, Steven Spielberg, Plácido Domingo and Tom Hanks. You may wish to wave to Sherry Belafonte or Rod Stewart or Jane Seymour. You may want to pay your respects to L.A. royalty Marion Jorgenson or tell Joan Collins how good she looks.

For her ball, Mrs. Davis uses highly paid publicists and has a reputation for knowing how to bring out the big stars whose presence ensures national press coverage. "The Davises court Hollywood," confirmed the late Nancy Vreeland. And remember that you are in the presence of a master: "No one in the world can put together a ball like Barbara Davis," affirms Joan Hotchkis, one of Pasadena's top citizens. Society photographer Alan Berliner points out that big formal events such as balls are waning in an era in which even the President won't put on a tux except for a state visit—Society is less formal, more fun. Given this trend, Mrs. Davis' talent for pulling off such a grand affair seems all the more remarkable. You may personally want to thank Marvin and Barbara Davis for coming out to Los Angeles from Colorado to help organize L.A. Society and Hollywood. All the world may be a stage, as Shakespeare observed, but at the Davises' ball and other key events, you had better put on your best performance, as you wouldn't want your name "overlooked" next time around.

You need your own photographer. The photographer of choice in L.A.'s top circles is Alan Berliner, a native Angeleno and UCLA alumnus whose career took off after he did freelance shoots for the *L.A. Times* Society section in the 1970s, working closely with then Society editor Jody Jacobs. Sitting in his two acre Malibu spread down the street from Nick Nolte and across from a property owned by Luane Wells, widow of late Disney president Frank Wells, Berliner relates his now pedigreed history. "Once I did the Chandler wedding of Otis and Bettina Chandler, I guess I became known." Chandler's family controls the *L.A. Times*, from which he retired in 1986 after having served as publisher. Berliner soon received a call from publicist Lee Salter who offered two of his clients: Frank Sinatra and Marvin and Barbara Davis. "I wish I had a buck for every time I've held Barbara Davis' diet coke," says Berliner, who is now sometimes offered diet coke when he enters an event since people assume that's what he drinks. Berliner has gone on to shoot Tom Hanks and Rita Wilson's tenth wedding anniversary, along with private photos for Dustin Hoffman, Michael Douglas, Tom Cruise, Nicole Kidman, and Sharon Stone.

In L.A.'s top circles, you especially need to watch over whom you let into your home. When featured in an issue of German *Vogue*, L.A. super socialite Betsy Bloomingdale paid Alan Berliner to do the shoot instead of using the photographer assigned to her by the magazine. She told Berliner she didn't feel comfortable having a stranger in her Holmby Hills home. And you don't want to step out for any old thing. New L.A. power broker Ron Burkle, who has contributed to the Disney Concert Hall, had Berliner come to his home to do a passport photo. The upper crust does not pop in at the one-hour photomat for a passport photo, and ironically, the movers and shakers of Hollywood scarcely have time to have a picture taken even in private. Berliner had a tough time getting the top executives at Creative Artists Agency to sit still even for a company-mandated photo shoot.

You need to get on the waiting list for the Bel-Air Country Club, which requires an initial fee of $75,000. You had better not get a divorce or you will have to ante up big time and you will then still need a new wife. And she will need jewels and clothes and . . . No, you can't ask your former wife to give back some of her jewelry.

When Johnny Carson settled with his wife Joanna in 1985, Joanna asked for $220,000 a month to maintain her lifestyle. She had to make do with $35,000 a month for six years. She did get the Rolls, a Mercedes and an economy car. Even the upper crust drives economy cars or 4-wheel drives for errands, especially in L.A. The couple split stocks and bank accounts and sold the Bel-Air Country Club membership. Joanna got the Picasso painting, Johnny the Lipschitz sculptures. She got the Bel-Air house and the three New York City apartments while Johnny got the Malibu house, the condo in New York and eight properties in Las Vegas, Arizona and California.

Still not convinced of the financial perils of divorce? Then look at the example of the late Howard B. Keck and his wife, Elizabeth Avery Keck. Remember their horse, Ferdinand, won the 1986 Kentucky Derby. The Keck family inherited an oil fortune worth several hundred million dollars, and the couple lived in their Bel-Air mansion known for world-class French art. Well, they got a divorce. Keck's wife had her own bank account worth 11 million dollars. Her settlement gave her a monthly allowance of $5,000 for groceries, $3,300 for dinners, $1,200 for lunches, $10,000 for dinner parties and $25,000 for clothes—for a total of $44,500 per month. So take the advice of your team of financial advisors and stay married.

And let's not forget those custody battles over children you have fathered and maybe one or two you have not fathered. Take the example of billionaire MGM mogul Kirk Kerkorian. Kerkorian was married to former tennis pro Lisa Bonder for one month. Kerkorian agreed to marry Bonder to legitimize a child he supposedly had fathered, but only if Bonder agreed to a divorce immediately thereafter. Bad decision. Bonder says that she was left "heartbroken" and when their relationship began to chill, Kerkorian withdrew use of his private plane from Bonder and tightened the purse strings. Kerkorian was paying upward of $20,000 to $30,000 cash a month to Bonder and the child while they lived in an 8 million dollar home in Beverly Hills not far from Kerkorian's own estate. Of course, Bonder sued Kerkorian in 2002—for her child—for monthly living expenses including $144,000 for travel, $14,000 for parties, $7,000 for charity, and so on. In total, she asked the court for $320,000 a month in child support even after the 84-year-old Kerkorian gave DNA proof that he was **not** the father of the child. Kerkorian asked the court to award *only* $50,000 a month in child support. A judge ruled in September 2002 that Kirkorian indeed "only" had to pay about $50,000 a month to support Bonder's 4-year-old daughter. Bonder, having admitted she had faked the DNA paternity test by getting saliva from Kerkorian's adult daughter, plans on appealing the decision. As part of the $50,000 a month, the 4-year-old daughter is still to receive $2,400 a month for equestrian activities, $1,400 a month for French and ballet lessons and $8,500 for travel expenses.

Kerkorian actually hired a private investigator to take dental floss out of the trashcan of multimillionaire producer Steve Bing in an attempt to prove that Bing was the father of the child. Bing, whose grandfather built New York luxury apartments before the family moved to L.A., naturally counter-sued Kerkorian for invasion of privacy. Bing also had problems of his own, as he sued actress Elizabeth Hurley to force a DNA test after she claimed that he was the father of her child. Later he agreed to pay $158,000 per year to be held in trust until the child turns eighteen. Despite his legal woes, like any good Angeleno, Bing went on to have a very busy 2002, buying some half-dozen properties in Bel-Air.

Divorce battles even heat up in the upper crust confines of the L.A. Opera. Not even Mozart or Beethoven could allay the battle of corporate takeover artist and L.A. Opera Chief Executive Leonard I. Green and his wife, Jude. Jude, originally a physical therapist from Michigan, chaired galas for the opening night of the opera and one for Plácido Domingo. When the marriage failed, the couple predictably fought over use of the Gulfstream jet and a vacation home in Aspen. Jude asked for $500,000 a month for spousal support including an $83,000 allowance for furs and jewelry. It is uncertain whether or not Leonard has become an animal rights activist since the divorce proceedings. What we do know is that Johnny Carson seems to have cut a good deal with Joanna back in 1985, even taking inflation into account.

Did we say a minimum of $20 million net worth for entry into the L.A. upper crust? Better make that $20 million plus with real liquidity, and then you are on the bottom rung unless you are a celebrity or a social arbiter selling to the upper crust on Rodeo Drive. Even if you are a movie star, you had better be a big star and be independently wealthy, or you had better marry wealth to keep your place in the L.A. solar system. Falling stars are only pretty in outer space.

PART THREE

HOW L.A. BECAME THE CULTURAL
ASPIRATION OF THE WORLD

CHAPTER FOUR
Building L.A. High Society

To be in society is simply a bore,
but to be out of it is simply a tragedy.

—Oscar Wilde

Who Rules Los Angeles: Some Notes on L.A. Power

Billionaire studio mogul David Geffen hosts a dinner for a small group of business and entertainment industry leaders including then Universal head Edgar Bronfman, Jr., film producer Steve Tisch and recording industry executive Jerry Moss, formerly with A&M Records. The occasion features a special guest. These Los Angeles movers and shakers welcome to this intimate fundraiser then President of the United States, Bill Clinton. Clinton knows that the Southern California-based entertainment industry contributes heavily to political campaigns, having given some 23 million dollars to parties, PACs, and candidates from 1991 to 1996. If you are a major player in the L.A. upper crust and politically inclined, meeting the President face to face in your own home is only fitting.

Special events such as the Geffen fundraiser often mark important historical changes, in this case the emergence of an L.A. upper crust with major social clout. The growth of L.A. social power is part of a repositioning of power in the American economy symbolized by yet another event, a 1994 Sun Valley, Idaho gathering. The Sun Valley conference featured an array of leaders of the new power structure in the American economy representing new centers of capital accumulation and large fortunes. This group that *Vanity Fair* called "The New Establishment" plays far above the confining structure in which government and corporate bureaucrats, the real "Establishment," function. They symbolize the emergence of a dynamic entrepreneurial faction based on today's booming industries—entertainment and communications—that for the most part are L.A., not New York, based. Most who own and control these enterprises either live in Los Angeles or spend time and do business in Los Angeles.

The conference participants included powerful L.A. players such as David Geffen, now with DreamWorks Studios; Michael Ovitz; Steven Spielberg; Disney's Michael Eisner; current Universal chief Barry Diller; and Barbra Streisand. New York and Hollywood financier Ron Perelman; Edgar Bronfman, Jr.; Microsoft Chairman Bill Gates, the world's richest man; cable mogul John Malone of Tele-Communications Inc.; and Ted Turner of Turner Broadcasting Systems Inc. also attended. Such a gathering of business entrepreneurs represents a new group of movers and shakers who have a major impact on the American and world economy and culture. Their grand Power should not be confused with the petite power of the bureaucratic "Establishment" sitting in cubicles initialing documents.

Herbert Allen, an investment banker with extensive financial interests in Hollywood studios, hosts the Sun Valley conferences. At the 1995 conference, Michael Eisner ran into Warren Buffett, then ranked by *Forbes* magazine as the second wealthiest American and the largest individual shareholder of New York-based Cap Cities/ABC Inc. Eisner proposed the merger of Walt Disney Co. with Cap Cities to Buffett, who immediately brought up the deal with Cap Cities chairman Thomas Murphy, who just happened to be down the road at a picnic, a long way from New York headquarters. If there are power lunches—and there are, daily, on L.A.'s Westside among the L.A./Hollywood crowd discussing movie deals, tuning in on the latest gossip and so on—then the Disney/Cap Cities deal could be seen as a power picnic held, in of all places, Sun Valley, Idaho.

A symbol is worth a thousand words. With the Disney/Cap Cities/ABC merger, a Hollywood studio would now own a major television network. Once largely based in New York, television, which as a medium once threatened the film industry's hegemony, is now mainly an L.A. production. Cap Cites/ABC is a subsidiary of Southern California-based Disney. When Eisner so graciously appeared in New York for a press conference with the retiring Murphy a short time later, Eisner was clearly at center stage.

With the economic base of the powerful entertainment industry coupled with the flood of wealth from the outside tearing down multimillion-dollar houses in Beverly Hills, the recognition of L.A. as a major social power seemed inevitable. As outside wealth put up "I'm Here to Stake My Claim" signs, ready to play in the top L.A. social circles, they realized that, if anything, L.A. was late in arriving. The "outsiders," transplanted wealthy from around the world that came to L.A.'s Westside, at first must have been disappointed at what they found. L.A. was there for the taking, but there was little, in terms of social distinction, to take. As late as 1960, a rather provincial Los Angeles had little to suggest that it would be a leader in American and world culture. L.A. had no cultural center. Rodeo Drive was far from being a world-renowned hotbed of haute style, and even the Hollywood entertainment industry shared considerable power with New York at the time. L.A. hip, if it existed at all, had not yet found its own unique expression.

This L.A. open playground contrasts with the firmly established New York of the 1880s, scene of the original social battle of New York between the Knickerbockers and the invading captains of industry, the robber barons. The New York social war endured for decades as new wealth repeatedly attempted to stake a claim to social stardom. Cornelius Vanderbilt, Jr. wrote in his 1935 book, *Farewell to Fifth Avenue*, about one such social battle: "Even today, thirty years after the first million dollars was made in the automobile industry, they [the New York upper class] continue to keep the 'Detroit Crowd' [the automobile fortunes] out of their two sanctuaries [the Union Club and

New York Yacht Club]." But today even the New York upper class succumbs to a single trump: Big money.

In Los Angeles, in spite of existing traditional enclaves of established wealth from banking or real estate development, symbols of the building of a distinct upper crust came slowly. The most watched late night talk show, "The Johnny Carson Show," which was taped in New York, moved to Los Angeles in the 1960s. Television, which had become universal in American households, was by the 1960s a predominantly Hollywood-based production. Around the same time the recording industry was relocating to L.A., and clubs such as Gazarri's and Whiskey-A-GO-GO came alive with rock music on the Sunset Strip. The Academy Awards saluting the year's best motion pictures soon became an exclusively L.A. affair, as the principal movie stars now all lived in L.A. There was no need for a New York half of the broadcast.

Los Angeles wealth built the city's first great cultural center in 1964 when the Music Center opened for theatre and symphony and later the opera. The Music Center was the brainchild of Dorothy Chandler, whose family controlled the *Los Angeles Times*. Earlier, Chandler had worked to save the Hollywood Bowl from bankruptcy. It is hard to imagine that the Bowl—a venue so in tune with L.A. outdoor living, where the Beatles shone in 1965 and where today all social circles of Angelenos flock to concerts under the stars, listening to Beethoven and eating brie—could have once been on the verge of going under. After saving the Bowl, Mrs. Chandler had little trouble raising the money from L.A.'s already large group of enormously wealthy for the proposed Music Center. One gala, referred to as "the Eldorado Party" because a Cadillac was auctioned off, alone raised $400,000 in 1955. The event took place at the old Ambassador Hotel with performances by Jack Benny, Dinah Shore and Danny Kaye. Christian Dior put on a fashion show. The gala prompted composer John Green to call Chandler the greatest fundraiser since Al Capone.

Contemporary L.A. art collector and longtime Blue Ribbon member Joan Quinn recalls that Mrs. Chandler was resented by many of the old-line factions of Hancock Park and San Marino, who had social standing but not necessarily enormous wealth, for bringing Westside Jews, who had money but no social standing, into the Music Center fold in exchange for their substantial contributions. Alyce Williamson recalls the lingering prejudice toward Jews and the Industry in general: "Neither found much mention in the paper. But that changed after Dorothy Chandler's efforts." Mrs. Williamson, who says her mother was Dorothy Chandler's best friend, does not hesitate to describe Mrs. Chandler as "ruthless" with regard to raising money for the Music Center. L.A.'s old-line wealthy took the lead in raising money for the Music Center as the Hollywood movie studios, not known even today for funding the arts, remained largely in the background.

A group of about thirty businessmen ran Los Angeles at the time. They included Ed Carter, who controlled the Broadway department stores; Harry Volk, president of Union Bank; Asa Call, head of Pacific Mutual Insurance; Ed Pauley of oil money and Frank King of First Interstate Bank. This group frequented the California Club downtown and golfed together at the Los Angeles Country Club. Carter and banking magnate Howard Ahmanson of Home Savings and Loan worked with financier/art collector Norton Simon to provide Los Angeles with a freestanding first class museum. Camilla Chandler Frost, sister of *L.A. Times* publisher Otis Chandler, and Sidney Brody, a well-known art collector, were involved in the planning of the museum. Of course, egos clashed and Norton Simon left the project, eventually founding the Norton Simon Museum in Pasadena.

The Los Angeles County Museum of Art opened in 1965 as part of an emerging foundation of high culture in the city. This downtown business elite provided quick support for the Music Center, with Ed Carter becoming a founding member. And this pioneer power grouping was tenacious. Some forty years later, Hannah Carter donated her rich cache of Dutch paintings to the Los Angeles County Museum of Art. Such cohesion of power had its advantages, but it wouldn't remain self-contained. The tight-knit flavor of the downtown business group would have become increasingly incongruous in the entertainment industry-dominated Los Angeles of today. The growing Jewish wealth on the Westside and the economic boom of Hollywood after 1970 would have eclipsed any exclusively downtown-based, WASP grouping of money power.

The Los Angeles Country Club was not only WASP—it would not admit entertainment people either. The Club even turned down Bing Crosby. Actor Victor Mature, who did over seventy films in the 1940s and 1950s including *Samson and Delilah* in 1949 under Cecil B. DeMille, and who was under contract at 20th Century Fox in the 1950s for a then hefty $5,000 a week, when turned down for the L.A. Country Club on the grounds that he was an actor quipped, "Not true. I've never been an actor—and I've got seventy movies to prove it." Hollywooder Randolph Scott alone gained entry only because his then wife, Mariam Du Pont, was "Society." This fission in the L.A. upper crust still exists to some extent today, with traditional old-line groupings and Hollywood for the most part taking separate paths. The Jewish upper crust continues to flock to the Hillcrest Country Club, established in 1921, when the Los Angeles Country Club did not admit Jews. The movie group often sends their kids to Westlake School in Holmby Hills instead of to Marlborough School, mostly attended by students from old-line families.

More important, though, is that the social game has changed. Country clubs have given way to charity events as the key venues, and the social marketplace of charity functions allows women major involvement. Big business is now transacted all over the L.A. basin—on the Westside, in Orange County and in Burbank—by the movers and shakers, most of whom are entertainment moguls. The *L.A. Times* ran an article on the "inner circle" of L.A. business which all but bypassed the Hollywood moguls: When something is right in front of your nose, you often miss it. Hollywooders Ovitz, Geffen, and Eisner have been key figures about town, making deals, creating studios and donating to charities. In the meantime the city has lost much of its banking power with the disappearance of First Interstate, Security Pacific and others, and aerospace has declined substantially.

Hollywood Enters the Social Mix

While the days of a traditional L.A. business elite are gone, there has been a renaissance of sorts in terms of a power elite that formed around former mayor Richard Riordan during his term. Developer and former SunAmerica chief Eli Broad, supermarket magnate Ron Burkle, developer Ed Roski and Hollywooder Michael Ovitz were thrust together with the mission of bringing a football team to the city. Football team or not, an attitude is developing among the L.A. moneyed class that it is about time the city struts its stuff and takes on the role of a world class city. Riordan himself intervened in the election process for the school board of the Los Angeles Unified School District, supporting candidates who promised reform instead of the usual apologies for the district's low test scores. Broad has established a foundation with a 100 million dollar gift designed to find ways to improve the public schools. "If we want to be a competitive society, if we want to save our middle class, K-12 is the nation's salvation," explains Broad.

Broad's modernist stamp on L.A. cultural life traverses the city: The Broad Center for the Biological Sciences at Cal-Tech in Pasadena, the Edythe and Eli Broad Art Center at UCLA, and the selection of Dutch architect Rem Koolhaas to virtually demolish and reconstruct the L.A. County Museum of Art (Broad, a trustee, was on the selection committee)—are all examples of Broad's stunning influence. When the Koolhaas plan stalled for lack of funding in 2003, Broad pledged 60 million dollars for a new building at the Los Angeles County Museum of Art, and he chose Italian architect Renzo Piano to design the proposed building which will house, what else, but contemporary art. Broad jump-started the Disney Hall project when it stalled after the original 50 million dollars in seed money from Lillian Disney. Anticipating the opening of Disney Hall and acknowledging the increasing prestige of the L.A. Opera, the heretofore unthinkable has been oh-so-subtly suggested in recent opera publications: Increasingly, Los Angeles is becoming a center of American opera. The Disney Concert Hall is the crowning symbol of the new L.A. pride and is certain to be another must-see venue in the city.

Broad, Riordan and DreamWorks billionaire David Geffen were also part of a team that was instrumental in bringing the 2000 Democratic national convention to Los Angeles. When the financial underpinnings of the convention project were in doubt, then Mayor Riordan, a Republican, organized a fundraiser at his Brentwood home featuring Democrat President Clinton. The event quickly raised 7 million dollars, with Ed Roski and Riordan himself ponying up $1 million each.

Even in the 1950s and '60s, Mrs. Chandler had already sensed that for Los Angeles to blossom, Hollywood needed to be brought into the social mix, however imperfectly. One pundit observed that the movie people didn't even know where downtown was until they had to go there for a divorce. But Chandler was able to enlist the support of Lew Wasserman, head of MCA Universal Studios, who became instrumental in bringing entertainment money into the Music Center project. Wasserman was also the bridge Chandler needed to secure the support of Westside Jews. Actress Rosalind Russell was another early fundraiser, along with actor Jack Lemmon. Bob Hope hosted a site dedication for the Music Center in 1964. Walt Disney himself helped design "buck bags" to collect money, as fundraisers for the Music Center took their quest out to people in the valleys. Rock Hudson attended the first concert in 1964. Another concert at the Dorothy Chandler Pavilion in 1964 saw Frank Sinatra fill in for an ailing Nat King Cole. Gregory Peck and Greer Garson were there to salute the audience at the 1967 opening of the Ahmanson Theatre that featured a performance of *Man of La Mancha*. As one Hollywood insider put it, Mrs. Chandler "brought Beverly Hills into downtown."

Besides the Dorothy Chandler Pavilion, which has hosted the Oscars, the other key Music Center buildings—the Ahmanson Theatre and the Mark Taper Forum—were named after families of banking wealth. The Ahmanson family has been particularly notable in supporting the Music Center since its inception. In 1979, at the request of Dorothy Chandler, Caroline Ahmanson formed the Music Center's Education Division, which does outreach through performances and workshops to students and teachers, touching almost one million people each year. The Division even brings in senior citizens free of charge to enjoy performances. In January 1998 Mrs. Ahmanson was honored for her work in the Education Division in a Music Center tribute organized by Wallis Annenberg with the help of Marcia Wilson Hobbs, then Blue Ribbon President Joni Smith, and Music Center Chairman Andrea Van de Kamp. Although Mrs. Ahmanson was initially reluctant to be the focus of such attention, she acquiesced upon learning that the event would raise a half million dollars for the Music Center.

Dorothy Chandler also created the Blue Ribbon, a social springboard for prominent L.A. women, which would promote fundraising for the Music Center. Curiously, Chandler tried to enlist 400 women in her initial endeavor to build the Music Center. 400? The number hearkens back to Ward McAllister's list of acceptable Society members in Old New York before the invasion of the robber barons. Gregory Peck helped kick off the first Blue Ribbon meeting in 1968 at the Beverly Hills home of Virginia Ramo. Mrs. Chandler had sent out invitations she signed along with Mrs. Kirk Douglas and Mrs. Henry Salvatori. A picture kept in the Blue Ribbon office shows Gregory Peck addressing the some twenty-seven women in attendance. Helen Wolford, the first Blue Ribbon President, recalls that besides Peck, Franklin Murphy, former Chancellor of UCLA and head of the *L. A.*

Times, also spoke at the meeting. Wolford's husband was a prominent lawyer whose clients included J. Paul Getty. She worked hand in hand with "Mrs. C." in the "exciting times" when the city's top cultural institutions were being built. Mrs. Wolford also remembers the early work of Harriet Deutsch and Jean French Smith, women later prominent in the Reagan group. Before the formation of the Blue Ribbon, Mrs. Chandler had relied on Ann Douglas and Veronique Peck to lead women's support groups for the Music Center. With the birth of the Blue Ribbon, another piece of the social puzzle had been put in place as prominent women were given a social lever to control. The group was to become a key ingredient in the emergence of a more cohesive L.A. upper crust.

To the dismay of some older WASP socialites, Mrs. Chandler welcomed wealthy Jewish women into the Blue Ribbon, which today is at least 50% Jewish. But according to recent President Joni Smith, Hollywood does not have a strong presence in the Blue Ribbon. And Smith laments that minority membership is still less than 10%. Mrs. Smith emphasizes that potential members should have time and expertise to contribute, and that a position on the 65-person Board is granted largely on merit, since there's really no "Society" anymore. Joni Smith herself comes from a "social" family, is a graduate of Marlborough and USC, and had begun volunteering by the early '70s. We met Joni Smith while she was still President of the Blue Ribbon in her office at the Music Center. Smith, attired in a brightly patterned black Chanel suit with her shoulder-length blond hair defying the traditional poufed look, jokes that her father was probably the only Democrat in the L.A. Country Club. Mrs. Smith has the reputation of working tirelessly to promote the Blue Ribbon and the Music Center.

Today the Blue Ribbon has over 600 members, but the actual membership list is not available, not even to members themselves. The $2,000 annual membership fee is token. The group raised 2.5 million dollars in 1997, and often provides up to one-third of all the money distributed to

Music Center resident companies. For their $2,000, members receive invitations to events ranging from fashion shows such as an Alber Elbaz Spring Collection preview at Neiman Marcus Beverly Hills to a Body, Mind and Soul Series with Dr. Andrew Weil.

The men's counterpart to the Blue Ribbon is the Fraternity of Friends. The group invites a dozen or so top high school musicians, singers and dancers to the Music Center each year to perform in front of their fellow students in a rousing event with the energy of the young crowd rattling the sparkling haute facade of the Dorothy Chandler Pavilion. The Spotlight Program, as it is called, was created in 1988 by Walter Grauman, producer of "Murder, She Wrote," in an attempt to get Southern California youth involved at the Center and counter the view of the Music Center held by some as an "elite" institution. Bob Bookman, former President of the Fraternity of Friends and one of Steven Spielberg's agents at Creative Artists Agency, relates how he got involved with the Music Center: "I was an executive at ABC (the head of the Theatrical and Motion Picture Division) when someone at the Music Center approached me to get Roone Arledge, the President of ABC, to speak. Well, I couldn't get Roone Arledge, but I wound up working for the Music Center anyway and headed Fraternity of Friends when I was just in my '30s."

Cultural institutions such as the Music Center are not alone in providing a backdrop for the social interactions and charity work of L.A.'s top circles. Private clubs have always been venues for upper class play, and David Murdock created one such club in 1981 with the opening of the Regency Club. Murdock, another notable transplantee, came from the Midwest to seek his fortune. After becoming a major real estate developer in Phoenix, he sought bigger challenges, coming to L.A. in the 1970s. Murdock began acquiring companies, even making a run on Armand Hammer's Occidental Petroleum. He was paid some 60 million dollars to give up his position in Occidental and abort the takeover attempt. He purchased a 64-room mansion in Bel-Air built by Conrad Hilton of the Hilton hotels. The estate consists of 9 acres adjacent to the Bel-Air Country Club. The outsider-now-insider Murdock quickly sensed a void at the top of L.A.'s social scene. His Regency Club displaced in one fell swoop the old Jonathan Club in downtown L.A.

After World War Two, wealth had continually shifted to the west side of Los Angeles, away from downtown; in Hollywood, if you were anybody, you located on the Westside or in Malibu. Both the Jonathan Club and the L.A. Country Club had the reputation of excluding Jews and minorities, and the Jonathan Club had not admitted women, who are critical to the display of high society; the Club was composed more of the political set and white collar business functionaries. Murdock understood where the real power of L.A. lay. Hollywood, led by its ever-expanding stable of Baby Moguls, was the Westside. What was once only a peculiar enclave of Jewish wealth had become the distinguished venue of an L.A. haute culture. Whether Jew or WASP, second generation Hollywood or transplanted wealth, Valley-raised or blueblood, American or foreign—all came to L.A.'s Westside by the 1980s for one big social happening. Los Angeles was to the wealthy what Haight-Ashbury had been to the hippies in the 1960s. One just had to show up.

So Murdock opened his club in Westwood near the UCLA campus, leading one reporter to observe that only in L.A. could "a fellow who once slung hash at a greasy spoon near Detroit" found an exclusive club and tell people what to wear in it. The Regency Club allows corporate heads of L.A.-based industries to meet and is also a venue for top women's groups such as the Blue Ribbon or the Costume Council of the L.A. County Museum of Art to organize charity events. The Regency highlights the changes which have overtaken exclusive clubs: Originally designed as places for inheritors of great wealth to "take refuge from the world of doing and simply be," as *Old Money* author Nelson Aldrich explains, they now function largely as settings for high stakes business dealings and large scale philanthropic planning.

Especially in Los Angeles, one must be "doing things," or one's star fades quickly. Taking their cue from Hollywood, wealthy Angelenos as a whole value exciting, creative pursuits. Those who shine in the top L.A. circles are either actively working in business or entertainment and/or participate in several charitable causes, from the Music Center to the Museum of Contemporary Art to AIDS. In order to shine at the Regency Club, prospective members need to have five people attest to their good character. They are admitted based on wealth and reputation. Of course there is a long waiting list to get in. Ironically, Murdock himself went to great lengths to convey a traditional aristocratic ambiance both at the Regency and at his Westside mansion (since sold to supermarket magnate Ron Burkle, a rising power broker on the L.A. scene), where he dined at home in suit and tie. Suits and ties, after all, belong at the Jonathan Club.

CHAPTER FIVE

Oscar Parties, Super Chefs and World Class Art:
L.A. Culture Makes Its Mark

Oscar Takes Center Stage

In the 1980s, super agent Irving "Swifty" Lazar began to throw his A-list Oscar party at Spago in West Hollywood, the new restaurant of the entertainment set and home of super chef Wolfgang Puck. From year to year Spago was the place to be, an event, a happening for all to envy. An invitation became the ultimate "A" ticket, and in terms of social prominence the Spago party quickly displaced the Governor's Ball held downtown for Oscar winners. Many winners would make an appearance at the Governor's Ball and then quickly limo to the Spago party. If you were unfortunate enough not to be invited, you made arrangements to be out of town to save face. Of course everyone wanted and deserved the choicest seating, but social arbiter Lazar had his own seating chart that was observed diligently. After all, a faux pas this year might get you excluded next year.

A typical year, 1990, had a guest list that included stars such as Jack Nicholson, Michael Caine, Joan Collins, Tom Selleck, Warren Beatty, Anjelica Huston, Gene Kelly, and Jimmy Stewart. Also present were singer Diana Ross, studio head Barry Diller, corporate head Ron Perelman of Revlon and L.A. locals Betsy Bloomingdale and Marvin and Barbara Davis. In from the East Coast came Georgette Mosbacher, wife of the elder George Bush's Secretary of Commerce, Robert Mosbacher. Hollywood's ability to get the big stars out, actresses in their designer gowns, and mix with the politicos, corporate heads and wealth in L.A. with the press and the paparazzi swarming about is a social coup unparalleled in American society. This concentration of celebrities is what's different about L.A. Rumor has it that there are people who go to as many as ten parties on Oscar night.

Before Lazar, Oscar parties had not been organized. Stars, producers, directors and company executives would scatter after the ceremony. Many would wind up at Dani Janssen's condominium in Century City, mingling and relaxing in remarkable privacy. Janssen, widow of actor David Janssen of "The Fugitive" television series fame, recalls that the first year she hosted the party there were seven Oscars sitting on the table. Although Janssen resumed the parties after Lazar's death, Oscar night has become too important for the Industry not to get involved directly in the celebrations. Academy member Dale Olson works with the public relations coordinating committee and with top marketing people from the studios for weeks before the event. It is, after all, Hollywood's night out, and on Oscar night L.A. is as happening as any city could possibly be.

1998 was vintage Oscar. *Vanity Fair* held its Oscar party at Morton's restaurant. Who was there? Try Madonna, Barry Diller, Brad Pitt, Warren Beatty, Oliver Stone, Barbara Davis, and Jerry Seinfeld. The Columbia Tri-Star party at Chasen's included Jack Nicholson and Helen Hunt. Spago was back in the Oscar game sans Lazar but with Elton John, as Canon Drive in Beverly Hills was the place to be. John hosted a bash for his AIDS Foundation as Jay Leno, Sharon Stone, Michael Douglas, Arnold Schwarzenegger and Maria Shriver mingled at the tables in the restaurant's open-air design.

But the *Titanic* crew had to be different. After putting up an Oscar night tent on Canon Drive, the *Titanic* entourage also partied into the morning at the famous Polo Lounge and adjacent patio at one of L.A.'s jewels, the Beverly Hills Hotel. A more fitting spot for celebrating Hollywood's big night could not be found—the Beverly Hills Hotel has Hollywood history written all over it. How many years before had Sir Richard Attenborough entered the Polo Lounge after winning an Oscar for *Gandhi*? Longtime maitre d' Nino Osti had held up the Oscar to the spontaneous applause of the crowd. Earlier still, Sidney Poitier danced barefoot in the lobby after winning an Oscar for *Lilies of the Field*. If you're not sure you're in Southern California, you need to visit this hotel—even better, check in. You pass the rows of palm trees, fixate on the unusual green and salmon colors of the buildings, read the street sign, "Sunset Blvd.," and feel the relaxed but haute spread. You will understand why so many people have moved west.

The *Titanic* crew showed up after midnight, walking the hotel's red carpet with the press flashing on either side. Robin Williams, Matt Damon, Helen Hunt, and about 400 others closed the unofficial Oscar ceremonies of parties and hoopla. New York is abuzz and the Society columns are smoking when a few Hollywooders show up at an event. But the winners of the Café Society that began in 1920s New York now hold court on Canon Drive or at the Beverly Hills Hotel on Oscar night. Social distinction 21st century-style begins on the West Coast.

Haute Cuisine L.A.-Style

You are what you eat. Growing culinary sophistication in Los Angeles restaurants is another symbol of a culturally maturing city. Historically, upper classes, irrespective of their economic basis, have eaten better than everyone else. Images of a gluttonous Henry VIII devouring beef legs and Marie Antoinette's legendary "Let them eat cake" come to mind. Food and culture have always had a symbiotic relationship. Ruth Reichl, then the Los Angeles Times food critic, summed up the culinary experiences of Angelenos at the end of the 1970s: "The year 1978 was not a good one for restaurants in Los Angeles. The same cannot be said for any year since." She continued in reference to a kind of pre-history of fine dining that existed before 1978: "I seem to have existed on a constant diet of paté, duck à l'orange and coquilles St. Jacques. For dessert there was chocolate mousse and crème caramel." What came every year after 1978 was nouvelle cuisine, California Cuisine, and almost any other kind of cuisine known or unknown as the L.A. of the 1990s blossomed into a major food capital. The fare's creative. It's innovative. And it happens first in L.A.

Los Angeles has become such a food happening that a 1998 gala dinner for public television and in honor of California winemaker Robert Mondavi gathered together a host of international chefs who altogether have been awarded some ninety Michelin stars for excellence. Noted French chef Roger Vergé was pleased: "I remember the first time I came to the U.S. The only salad green we could find was iceberg lettuce." Michel Fuérard, leader of France's nouvelle cuisine revolution, nodded in agreement: "The 20-year evolution in America is unbelievable." L.A. food is now delectable, creative fun. Put away those Dodger dogs.

The California School of Culinary Arts, which opened in 1994 with a mere twenty students, has expanded into a new Pasadena location with 50,000 square feet and the potential to house some 1,500 students, becoming the largest culinary school in the West. Students rush to get in, forking over $32,000 for a fifteen-month course and the chance to be one of the new wave of chefs, the new cultural icons, who will spread the food revolution in L.A. and throughout the country. Locals cram the school's restaurant to get a taste of the new creations from the next superstar chef.

A quarter of the nation's 300 chef schools have come into being since the late 1980s as Americans try to reclaim a food culture taken over by the mass market of McDonald's mania. L.A. has been a catalyst in the development of nouvelle cuisine. In Los Angeles an invasion of chefs and fresh produce has swept away the old, staid restaurants that mimicked the traditional New York ambiance. Waiters are no longer in tuxedos; menus include mouth-watering descriptions of the meticulously selected, always fresh ingredients and the resulting unique, usually eclectic, dishes. Modern art graces restaurant walls, and the lighting is turned up. Now diners can see each other as so many performers in a real-life novel while they eat their scrumptiously presented meals which themselves are works of art.

Dining out has become a major social event. Much of the credit goes to Wolfgang Puck of Spago and Oscar parties—the first celebrity chef. He has attracted other chefs to the L.A. scene and has raised the level of the culinary playing field. Joan Hotchkis, prominent Pasadena resident, affirms that, "We have top restaurants and top chefs in this town." Hollywood created the power lunch, and like their New York counterparts, L.A. upper crust women "do lunch." The L.A. crowd now eats with the best.

Los Angeles has always had a smattering of famous restaurants usually made popular by the Hollywood crowd frequenting them. Alfred Hitchcock, Clark Gable, Alan Ladd, Barbara Stanwyck and Jimmy Stewart were among a host of Industry types who dined regularly at the old Chasen's. The Brown Derby, Romanoff's, and Scandia were all well-known celebrity restaurants. But both the cuisine and the ambiance were traditional if not staid. The Brown Derby on Hollywood and Vine opened in 1926 as an all-night eatery. The Derby's famous Cobb salad featured bacon and chicken mixed with lots of lettuce. Chasens' specialty was chili—comedian David Chasen had opened the restaurant in 1936 as a barbeque stand in a cornfield at Beverly Blvd. and Doheny Drive. Chasen's was also known for its seafood on ice, creamed spinach, and hobo steak—a slice of New York steak cooked in butter and served on toast with souffléd potatoes. L.A. food was either mundane or classic haute French, and it masqueraded under the label of continental cuisine. Continental cuisine was a poor imitation, even a bastardization of traditional French fare.

The Society restaurant was Perino's on Wilshire Blvd. according to socialite Alyce Williamson, raised in Hancock Park and past president of the Hollywood Bowl Patroness Committee. Betsy Bloomingdale wistfully recalls her first plate of spaghetti bolognese at Perino's. But Perino's classic Italian fare seems light years away from the wave of Northern Italian cooking that first hit L.A. in the

1980s and has since swept throughout the country. The comfy, rich Italian cooking of Perino's would be blasé next to the light, tangy, experimental cuisine of the Italian bistros. First led by Chianti on Melrose and its add-on, Chianti Cucina, Italian bistros are threatening the French stranglehold on haute cuisine.

Earlier, the "new wave" restaurants of the 1970s did not break this haute cuisine, can-you-make-it-richer (creamier) monotony nor the traditional dark, I-have-just-been-to-a-funeral ambiance. Kurt Niklas opened the Bistro in Beverly Hills with the backing of director Billy Wilder, the Bloomingdales and many other celebrity supporters. Niklas had originally been a waiter at Romanoff's. Former *L.A. Times* Society columnist Jody Jacobs recalls milling about the Bistro as a reporter for *Women's Wear Daily* while prominent women, dressed to the teeth, did lunch. But the Bistro and other "breakthrough" restaurants which caught fire in the 1970s—Le St. Germain and Au Petit Café—were anything but innovative. Le Dôme on Sunset was yet another French clone. Nor was Murphy's—opened by Jimmy Murphy, another Romanoff's waiter—out of the ordinary mold.

But then things got interesting. Ma Maison came along. And although Ma Maison came and went like a streak of fireworks in a July sky in the 1970s, it opened the door for an L.A. cuisine from which there is no turning back. Ma Maison did still offer traditional French haute cuisine. The restaurant's name was obviously French. But the place dared to have an unlisted phone number. This created quite a stir among an emerging group of foodies in L.A., a group which increasingly crossed class lines. People were thrilled to tell friends they had the number. They savored recounting how they were greeted by host Patrick Terrail in his Scandinavian clogs as they dined at the restaurant. For the Hollywood crowd it was the place to be for a while. Terrail had an excellent pedigree as nephew of Claude Terrail, the owner of Paris's famous La Tour d'Argent. But Ma Maison was all L.A., the new-look L.A. Orson Welles always had an inside table, while most of the diners sat on the outside terrace. The pretense of the restaurant was in the people. Dining had become spectacle in the city of spectacle.

But that was not all. Ma Maison's break from tradition came from the restaurant's layout or lack of a layout. It was put together on a shoestring budget. It had ghastly Astroturf on the floor. Many diners felt they were eating on a parking lot as they dined on the patio. The kitchen was closed off and on the side. The restaurant was small. But there was light. In the city of sunshine, in the city that produces stars who shine brighter than any in the night, finally there was light. Perhaps just by accident, but there was light. Stars and would-be stars could now be seen.

The unknown chef at Ma Maison with the disheveled hair and the German accent, the shy, short, stocky man to whom you would just as soon say "Let's go have a beer" if you saw him on the street, was the soon-to-be-famous Wolfgang Puck, the future super chef. In those days Puck used to open a window from the kitchen to peek at the heady clientele outside. While visiting our table at Spago Beverly Hills, Puck recalls giving a cooking class at Ma Maison attended by Suzanne Pleshette and Gladice Begelman, wife of then Columbia Pictures President David Begelman. Puck says that in those days he was so shy that he couldn't stand in front of the women: "I stayed in the back of the kitchen most of the time."

The yoke of traditional haute cuisine was broken when Puck opened his own restaurant, Spago, in West Hollywood. Spago quickly became Hollywood's restaurant, but its real significance was that Puck began experimenting with the cuisine. A simple pizza now featured goat cheese and artichokes. Hollywooders and Hollywood wannabes dined in a relaxed atmosphere in a nondescript former private home above Sunset Blvd. The chefs were visible as they prepared fresh and innovative pizzas and pastas. The best tables were at the windows overlooking the city below. The stars—from George Burns to Sean Penn—were there every night, and a private VIP line was kept busy for table requests. But the mix of excellent food in an informal setting gave that special and peculiar L.A. stamp to the proceedings. Los Angeles dining was haute and unpretentious at the same time.

Joan Hotchkis, who commissioned Puck personally to cook for her husband John Hotchkis' sixty-fifth birthday party, with stoves on the tennis courts of their historic Bixby Ranch in Los Alamitos, recalls that Puck's celebrity status brought new chefs to L.A. from around the world. Around the same time Michael McCarty opened Michael's in Santa Monica, cooking with nothing but fresh California ingredients and proudly using the label California Cuisine. McCarty later opened a restaurant in New York. As in France, the L.A. chefs became stars in their own right. Then came the wave of Italian and other types of nouvelle restaurants from cultures around the globe. Everything was experimental.

The roof had been blown off. Food was fun. Haute cuisine took on new meaning in Los Angeles. Dating back to the kings' courts in France, haute cuisine had developed as rich food with heavy sauces. While most people ate a poor diet consisting of a few innocuous items, the nobility could distinguish itself by eating rich foods that the general population could not afford. Only recently has this knee-jerk, cream-based, meat-centered cuisine been challenged. Although Alice Waters of Berkeley's Chez Panisse holds title as the mother of California Cuisine and nearby San Francisco boasts gourmet meatless restaurants such as Roxanne's, Greens and Millennium, it is from L.A. that the lighter fare emphasizing freshness and organic produce has taken off into national culinary stardom.

By the end of the 1990s, Puck was offering California Cuisine at the new Spago Beverly Hills created by a chef clearly in his prime. The restaurant on Canon Drive has that L.A. open-air effect with smatterings of contemporary art on the walls. The food is pure pleasure. White sea bass topped with fresh vegetables in a tangy sauce is an experience you think about for days. During Spago's first few months alone, its private dining room hosted groups from *The New Yorker* magazine; "The Tonight Show"; the Colleagues, L.A.'s most exclusive women's charity group; and Saks Fifth Avenue. The opening featured a kick-off for Race to Erase MS, the charity headed by Tommy Hilfiger and Nancy Davis, daughter of Marvin and Barbara Davis. Other notables at the Spago opening dining on lobster salad and artichoke tortellini included Seth Baker, publisher of *Beverly Hills 213* and his wife, Dee May, whose late husband was heir to the May Co. fortune; Colleagues President Anne Johnson; Joan and John Hotchkis; and Quincy Jones.

Puck now spends his time at Spago Beverly Hills rather than Spago West Hollywood, which he closed in 2001 after commenting that the original Spago "feels like a divorced wife." Puck's casual, off-handed remark came well before divorce proceedings began between him and his wife, Barbara Lazaroff, in 2002 and thus should not be construed to have any bearing on his later marital situation. Puck sees Spago Beverly Hills as the first restaurant that truly bears his own unique mark. Puck's new abode stands on the site of the old Bistro Garden operated by former Romanoff's maitre d' Kurt Niklas. Spago Beverly Hills brings in all of L.A.'s traditional upper crust along with tourists and of course Hollywood. The Hollywood list of regulars is long: Joan Collins, Ed McMahon, Ron Howard, Steven Bochco, Robert De Niro, Shirlee Fonda, Candice Bergen, Steve Martin, Lili Zanuck, Shirley MacLaine, Jeffrey Katzenberg, Sidney Poitier, Denzel Washington, Sherry Lansing, Sylvester Stallone, Glen Close, Aaron Spelling and others. It's a place where you expect to see someone famous at any time. Lee Minnelli, last wife of director Vincente Minnelli and stepmother of Liza, regularly held her annual Christmas lunch at Spago Beverly Hills at two tables of ten people each. Mrs. Minnelli recalls that guests have included Barbara Sinatra, Dominick Dunne, Robert and Rosemary Stack, Frances Bergen, Liza Minnelli, Gregory and Veronique Peck, Henry and Jayne Berger, and Charlton Heston. And she always orders the duck, which she says only Wolfgang Puck, or "Wolfy," as some insiders call him, can make so exquisitely.

Spago has had staying power in a city where restaurants spring forth from nowhere to become stars and then are gone in the wink of an eye. In a city where old is automatically suspect and old restaurants whisper suspiciously of the tired, the outdated and the New Yorkish, Puck's Spago has stayed fresh and dynamic. But new star restaurants surface continually in L.A. and often in the most unexpected places. Just when it looked as if the Italians had won the battle of L.A. cuisine fomenting since 1980, just when the L.A. palate seemed to be permanently draped in olive oil, French cuisine has made a comeback. One darling of the Hollywooders, Les Deux Cafés, where Madonna and Tom Ford dine regularly, has come out of nowhere to save the game for le Tri-color. Leading the charge is a rather unlikely Joan of Arc, Michele Lamy, a former criminal lawyer in France, who, when she came to Los Angeles to be a designer, knew all of one person: "I didn't have his phone number when I arrived."

Lamy is a classic L.A. success story, an unknown transplant who has become what the *New York Times* has called the "Gertrude Stein of L.A." But Lamy's tale is hardly your usual rags to riches variety. Lamy's grandfather, who owned restaurants and hotels in France, was a chef: "I never cooked; we were always around chefs," Lamy reveals. Lamy, having already traveled the world, found her way to L.A. and opened a storefront in West Hollywood in the early 1980s to showcase her work as a designer of accessories. Her family in France includes artisans and artists who design fashion accessories, so the work was familiar. Lamy noticed that the L.A. crowd was either "badly dressed or over-dressed," and so she also designed clothes in a casual chic mode or what she calls a "rough Sonja Rykiel look." But the gregarious Lamy was not content with the designing business and soon agreed to help a friend with her restaurant in Hollywood. The restaurant, Café des Artistes, quickly became part of the new must-see, must-do L.A. restaurant scene.

After five years, Lamy left Café des Artistes to found Les Deux Cafés. "Les Deux" cannot be found from its street address and there is no sign. The authors had to be pointed to the side, away from the street and right off the public parking lot, where a lush vine drapes the discreet entrance. Perhaps this is why Les Deux Cafés is so readily embraced by a Hollywood that likes to be seen in the movies or at movie premières but not in daily life. Though only shouting distance from Hollywood Blvd. in Hollywood, the façade of the building in front of "Les Deux" seems lonely and adrift from the hubbub of L.A. street life. Next to an abandoned theater and still rather run down, the neighboring building was a jazz club in the 1920s and then the first gay club in L.A. when Las Palmas was a Hollywood street with a strong gay presence.

Behind the front building, Lamy renovated a former crack house to serve as an inner dining sanctuary. Though richly adorned in dark polished wood, the interior is not the restaurant's distinctive feature, although it does offer many secluded corners for its famous guests. Only in the Hollywood dream world could a former crack house become a place where the A-crowd hangs out. Outside, in the back, on what was once a parking lot (shades of Ma Maison), Lamy put together a lush, fragrant garden ensconced behind a high, vine-covered wall with a long center fountain reminiscent of those in Avignon, France. "It's all about memories," explains Lamy, describing her restaurant as not a business, but "building a home." Fittingly, her guests dine outside in the balmy Southern California climate, but the scene evokes the warmth and loveliness of France's Provence region. This out-of-doors yet private dining experience—a virtual Provence in the center of Hollywood—is what gives Les Deux Cafés its distinctive quality.

We wait for Ms. Lamy in a small section of the restaurant that rests between the outer garden and the inner house-now-restaurant on an uncharacteristically mild summer day in August. The slim Lamy, in a mauve-toned pants suit with a touch of sheen to belie its understated tone, pulls up a patio chair and sits alongside us, with long auburn hair sleekly brushed back off of her forehead and flowing comfortably down her back. Her skin is tanned, as if she has just come from a day by the pool. Two conspicuous rings and accompanying tattoos on her fingers give her a decidedly Southern California touch. "This is my house," explains Lamy. "I want to offer the best of everything. That includes the food. But a restaurant, ultimately, needs a personality to succeed over time." When asked what it takes to maintain quality, Lamy remarks, "I am here every day. But I have traveled earlier in my life. I am content to come here every day." Shying away from mentioning names of celebrities who frequent the restaurant, Lamy emphasizes, "I like it when all types of artistic people come."

Yet she was struck by one incident at the restaurant involving a few of her more famous guests. Liza Minnelli was at the restaurant, on crutches after a recent operation. As she struggled to the restroom, she caught the attention of Madonna, sitting in the corner. Madonna got up to leave but first went toward the restroom. She yelled greetings to Liza Minnelli through the door, only to get a terse response from Minnelli, who was unaware of the identity of her attentive inquirer. When Minnelli came out of the restroom, Lamy told her it was Madonna who had wanted to talk to her. Minnelli, having unwittingly rebuffed Madonna and feeling bad about the incident, on crutches and with some help scampered out to the parking lot to catch up with a departing Madonna. Coming in at that moment was yet another singer, Joni Mitchell. The frantic Ms. Minnelli passed by the bewildered Ms. Mitchell, panting that she wanted to talk to her also but was in pursuit of Madonna. Apparently, she didn't catch up with her.

Les Deux Cafés is a restaurant that really comes into its own at night, and the garden is the place to be. When the tree-lined and vine-covered walls give way to dark patches of shrubbery and the not very plentiful lighting takes on whatever force it can possibly muster, when the tables are full of happy groupings of diners—this is when the restaurant smiles. It would be wrong to characterize Les Deux Cafés as only a celebrity restaurant. Far from it. The night we were there, not a celebrity was in sight, but everyone else in the eclectic L.A. crowd was there to hang out, Southern California style, partaking and looking around, amidst the patina of Hollywood which is never completely absent from one's mind.

When guests arrive, they mill about near the bar—as if they were in someone's home—before meandering to their seats. Hours are European: Guests rarely take their seats before 8 p.m. Tables are not turned over—diners are there for the night. The food is best characterized as Franco-Californian Cuisine with a penchant for fresh, organic ingredients, though Lamy would point out that she is merely serving food the way her grandfather would when he prepared fresh vegetables from his farms for his restaurants in France. Salt and pepper are rarely seen on the tables, the assumption being that the food is just right: "It is the way it is," says Lamy. And indeed, the seared sea scallops salad is first rate, as is the couscous surrounded by those fresh organic vegetables. We leave the restaurant with that contented feeling that you try to get often after a fine dining experience, but which comes along only rarely, and therefore seems all the sweeter. Add to Les Deux Cafés the equally trendy and no less Hollywood Café des Artistes, and French cuisine, which had been left for dead, has signaled to the faithful that the Italians have not yet won the culinary battle of Los Angeles.

Authors' Note: Les Deux Cafés closed at the end of 2003. Owner Michele Lamy had left the business to her ex-husband, Richard Newton, to manage as she left for Paris with her fashion designer boyfriend, Rick Owens. Owens had been hired by Revillon, necessitating a move to Paris. Sad story? Not at all. Girl comes to L.A. Girl makes it big and then moves on with her lover to Paris, leaving the L.A. hip crowd free to wander off and find some other hot venue. Sounds like a good movie script.

In the new millennium, food and culture prove their worth in L.A. first and are then imported by other cities. Las Vegas, a city ever alert to social trends, is quickly becoming a leader in marketing haute culture to a mass audience. The ultra-deluxe Bellagio Hotel with its Gallery of Fine Art for a time housed Steven Winn's collection including works by Picasso, Van Gogh, Degas, Brancusi, Pollock and other top drawer artists. The Venetian has followed suit by housing a branch of the Guggenheim with an entrance just off the hotel's lobby. Las Vegas has also been infused with a flood of celebrity chefs. Once an undistinguished desert outpost, Las Vegas is now a city with the right recipe for an upscale playground. The giant buffets that brought in droves of the middle class in the 1970s have given way to luxurious hotels such as Mandalay Bay and The Venetian, which are enlisting the world's top chefs. Wolfgang Puck has opened, among other restaurants, a Spago and a Chinois at Caesars Palace; while Sirio Maccioni has opened a version of Le Cirque, the restaurant darling of New York's Society set, at Bellagio. Mary Sue Milliken and Sue Feniger are taking their Border's Grill California Cuisine to Las Vegas' Mandalay Bay Resort, and Nobu Matsuhisa is featuring his fusion of Asian and Latin American cuisine at the Hard Rock Hotel. Matsuhisa has successful restaurants in Beverly Hills, New York, Aspen and London already. But the commercialization of haute culture, like all commercialization, often loses something from the original in the translation.

The opening of an aspiring top-notch restaurant is potentially history in the making, and serious business for Angelenos. A successful Cleveland shopping mall developer invites super chef Puck to Cleveland to coax him into overseeing the opening of a restaurant there. The businessman states, "Most people want what I have—30 acres, two lakes, tennis courts, a health club and steam room on my property." Puck's then wife and premier business manager, Barbara Lazaroff, seems unimpressed. She throws a series of questions at the businessman. She finally asks, "Do people spend their money here?"

Our Hollywood duo were too polite to point out that what the businessman boasted about having was not enough to make a splash in L.A. and that Cleveland, well, is Cleveland and L.A. is L.A. and that the great gulf in between is spelled SOCIAL DISTINCTION. Or as L.A. author Carolyn See puts it, "Cleveland makes cardboard boxes—L.A. doesn't. We're not interested in cardboard boxes. Something else is going on out here." The real interviewer in this exchange was our L.A. power couple and not the outsider. Puck and Lazaroff did open another restaurant—in Malibu. Lazaroff, thinking about the Hollywood enclave in the Malibu Colony, lamented, "All those people with nowhere to eat."

Often whole sections or even an entire restaurant is reserved for a top social event. During its celebrated reign, the Bistro was the scene for many an haute function, but none more tongue-in-cheek than the "coronation" of "Contessa" Alice Cohen. Former *L.A. Times* Society editor Jody Jacobs describes how the entire upstairs was closed off as Contessa Cohen, who wrote a Society column for *Beverly Hills 213* magazine, sat in a high-backed chair and was crowned. Why go to all the bother of marrying into European royalty as the Old New York upper class had done? The coronation apparently stemmed from her children having said that she was like the Barefoot Contessa, referring to Ava Gardner's movie role. Reportedly she took the title seriously enough to require that the help at her home address her as Contessa from then on. Not bad for a girl from Arkansas who apparently met her husband years before while she was an elevator operator at May Co. and he worked in the store's men's department. The coronation may have been taking the Society thing a bit too far, but no more so than some socialites who reportedly pay for their publicity.

Perhaps only in L.A. does the **closing** of a restaurant become a major event. L.A. restaurants go out like a burst of fireworks, with the end more spectacular than the beginning. Someone may even make a movie about the closing, such as the documentary *Off the Menu* about the closing of the original Chasen's. Later, Chasen's memorabilia was auctioned off: A picture of Frank Sinatra with friends, a telegram from Howard Hughes and even the booth regularly occupied by Alfred Hitchcock. Everyone tried to get in to have one last meal at Madame Wu's before its closing in 1998. The first to serve haute Chinese food on the Westside, Madame Wu catered to a clientele that included Hollywood legends Cary Grant, Frank Sinatra and Mae West.

The 1996 finale of the famous Bistro Garden, where Beverly Hills ladies did lunch regularly, was a black-tie and big jewels affair and brought out billionaire Marvin Davis, members of the Keck and Doheny oil families, and The Irvine Company's Donald Bren, who seems to own half of Orange County. Bren's father Milton Bren was a Hollywood agent who developed part of Sunset Boulevard and was later married to Oscar-winning actress Claire Trevor; his mother is Marion Jorgensen, important in the Nancy Reagan group and wife of the late Earle Jorgensen, Reagan Kitchen Cabinet member and steel magnate. Also crowding into the Bistro Garden farewell were other Reagan friends and the usual entertainment industry types—just the ordinary L.A. crowd.

If the Bistro Garden goes down as a legend in the annals of the L.A. social scene, not so the once très chic but now infamous Mezzaluna restaurant in Brentwood where Nicole Brown Simpson ate her last meal. The restaurant finally closed in 1997 as people crowded in to bid on anything and everything. Even a single menu was up for grabs as the throng tried to capture through one mighty purchase a fleeting notoriety that will end up as only a dark footnote to L.A. social history. An attorney for Mezzaluna's owner offered what could be read as a sad epitaph for the restaurant. "Take a look around you," he said, pointing to the

L.A.-style spacious picture windows that give way to patio tables right off the boulevard for those "laying out." "Do you think you'd want to eat outside this restaurant when you had 5,000 tour buses coming by each day, people craning their necks and leering out the window to see what you're eating?" The lawyer has a point.

But in L.A., everyone always looks at what you're eating, because eating is spectacle. Hollywood production teams feast in downtown L.A. on location, eating grilled salmon and a tossed pasta salad prepared by special caterers while the filming of a movie takes place. Streets are blocked off. Everyone looks on. The production crew did not stop at the nearby McDonald's to eat.

L.A. Plays the Art Scene

L.A. and art have found each other. In 1995 the renowned art auction house Sotheby's, operating in Beverly Hills since 1971, expanded West Coast operations by moving into a 13,000 square-foot building on Wilshire Blvd. in Beverly Hills. Not to be outdone, arch-rival Christie's, a player in L.A. since the early 1980s, fêted its new, expanded showroom on Camden Drive in Beverly Hills with an auction of what else but Hollywood memorabilia. For a semblance of continuity, Christie's flew out the doorman from its New York premises. Apparently good doormen are hard to find these days. The auction included Claudette Colbert's Oscar for Best Actress in the 1934 film *It Happened One Night*, and Marilyn Monroe's silver gown from *How to Marry a Millionaire*. Clark Gable's Oscar for Best Actor, also for *It Happened One Night*, had sold at Sotheby's in 1996 for $600,000.

"There's no end to the potential here. It's unfathomable," explains Marcia Wilson Hobbs, chairman of Christie's Beverly Hills. Terry Stanfill, International Representative for Christie's Beverly Hills, notes that there is a lot of Pacific Rim business in the L.A. office, and that Christie's sees the L.A. market as "phenomenal." Christie's

Beverly Hills has sold collections owned by director Billy Wilder, Kirk Douglas, Barbra Streisand, the Dohenys and the Chandlers, and also handled David Geffen's Tiffany lamp collection. Christie's Beverly Hills facility may be upgraded to a West Coast auction center to reflect the trend. Lord Hindlip, chairman of the international division of Christie's, responding to a question about whether the Hollywood crowd were good buyers and sellers, quipped in a manner befitting L.A. smug style, "Very."

Key New York art galleries such as PaceWildenstein and Gagosian also established Beverly Hills addresses in the 1990s, signaling the development of an independent art market on the West Coast based in Los Angeles. Such expansions are further affirmations of the emergence of a broad, dynamic L.A. haute culture. Terry Stanfill emphasizes the dominance of contemporary art in the L.A. market: "Except for Norton Simon, people have never collected the Old Masters out here." Her good friend Joan Hotchkis, once a representative for Sotheby's, adds: "Contemporary art is fashionable—many Hollywood producers have been into modern art and that has made it fashionable." Historically, collecting the Old Masters signified wealth, but "contemporary art now equates with great wealth as well," explains Gagosian Gallery's Robert Shapazian. Andrea Van de Kamp, chairman of Sotheby's on the West Coast and wife of a former California Attorney General from a socially prominent Pasadena family, affirms that contemporary art "is the big area for collecting" in L.A. "We are relaxed, colorful, open. We respond to the life we lead here, and contemporary art is very representative of that life."

The opening of the Museum of Contemporary Art downtown represented a beacon in the trend toward modern and contemporary art and a marriage of a hip city with the hip art emerging in L.A. today. The decor in the grand Old Hollywood homes had been traditional, modeled on New York or European art and furnishings. True, most Old Hollywood homes were less grandiloquent, more in tune with L.A. geography, often with a sprawling design featuring

Spanish overtones. The decor was simple, often Industry-oriented with photos and placards, and Old Hollywooders as a rule were not great collectors of art.

The L.A. upper crust still does not collect art on the scale of the New York collectors, although the gap is narrowing. And the decor of a surprising number of high-end homes is still traditional, without the modern flavor of the city. In New York, because living occurs in confined spaces, art collecting becomes a major avenue of social expression; in L.A., the sprawling home design is often statement enough. But as with changes in cuisine, so too come changes in L.A. attitudes toward art. Robert Shapazian, head of the Gagosian Gallery in Beverly Hills, explains that in L.A., "The idea that art is natural and required to live a certain kind of life is growing."

In fact, the L.A. art scene has exploded. The all-in-white Gagosian Gallery in Beverly Hills has returned to its roots. Larry Gagosian first opened a gallery in Westwood near UCLA in the 1970s and began trading in prints and small works of contemporary art. Gagosian became friends with the budding group of L.A.-based artists in the Venice school and met major pioneer collectors of contemporary art such as Marcia Weisman. Gagosian then moved to New York, becoming the preeminent contemporary art dealer handling trophy art, pieces from artists of some repute. 1993 saw the return of Gagosian to L.A., no longer selling prints, but top-notch contemporary art on Camden Drive in Beverly Hills.

What had happened on the L.A. contemporary art scene during Gagosian's brief absence? Robert Shapazian, seated in the offices of the Beverly Hills Gagosian Gallery, explains that many artists in the new pop art scene of the 1950s and '60s—Wallace Berman, Ed Roche and John Baltazar, for example—chose to remain in L.A. instead of trekking off to New York. Yet this development would have been merely happenstance without the social and cultural boom of the city itself. The growth of the L.A. art scene springs from the growing importance of the city—its wealth, style, culture and films—and the explosion in an art market hungry for merchandise. Hollywood—the Industry that thrives on personality, on promotion, on exhibition, on projection—is the motor for this growth. L.A. is the city that best understands and represents the commodification of art as art becomes an entertainment product. Shapazian points to Andy Warhol as the artist who perhaps best understood the conflation of art, product and entertainment: "The soup can painting said that the painting is product." Art is beauty, but it is now also a commodity and as such has its own social space. Art has become a social force, and contemporary art is at the forefront of this thrust, with L.A. a logical world player.

Major L.A. art schools—UCLA, USC, the Otis Art Center, the Art Center College of Design, and CalArts—have provided a continual flow of young artists. CalArts was founded by Walt Disney and is now lodged in the new Disney Concert Hall thanks to a 5 million dollar gift from Patty and Roy E. Disney, Walt Disney's nephew. The CalArts space is called the Roy and Edna Disney/CalArts Theater. Back at the Gagosian Gallery, Robert Shapazian, a Harvard educated Ph.D. in Fine Arts and Literature, states matter-of-factly that until the early 1990s, an L.A. collector would still go to New York for big-ticket items. Now collectors from all over make major purchases in L.A. David Geffen, according to a former president of MOCA, Lenore Greenberg, is a "major, major collector." Hollywood producer Doug Cramer has been a collector for some time and quickly got involved at MOCA when he lived in Los Angeles. Steve Martin, Tom Hanks, Jack Nicholson and Michael Ovitz are notable collectors of modern and contemporary art. One observer remarks that collecting art has become a social competition for the new group of Hollywood collectors.

The contemporary art market has certainly changed since the 1950s and '60s when collectors such as Elyse Grinstein, Lenore Greenberg, Marcia Weisman and Joan Quinn patronized L.A.'s fledgling artists. As late as 1975,

Paul Kantor, a pioneering L.A. art dealer who sold multimillion-dollar Picassos and other major works privately, remarked about the Los Angeles art market, "The whole art community here operates at such a low level, they deserve galleries where they can pay a dollar down and a dollar a month for art." Perhaps not by the stroke of a brush but by a few phone calls and the whisk of a pen to a few large checks did the L.A. art world awaken to a fresh, giddy atmosphere.

It was the late Marcia Weisman, so-called mother of contemporary art in Los Angeles and the sister of Norton Simon, who pushed for the formation of MOCA. The L.A. County Museum of Art had modern and contemporary collections, but they were often given short shrift in the midst of the more traditional galleries. Lenore Greenberg remembers how an excited Weisman called her in the late 1970s to recount that she had just mentioned the idea of starting a contemporary art museum to Mayor Tom Bradley over lunch. Bradley jumped on the idea, urging the museum's completion by the 1984 Olympics in Los Angeles.

Weisman quickly got Arco President Robert Anderson, Eli Broad—then a budding collector but the eventual owner of a major contemporary collection and a Brentwood home designed by Frank Gehry—and Max Palevsky to contribute a cool one million each to the project. Emblematic of the high-stakes bickering that historically has occurred in the L.A. art market, Palevsky later sued to regain a portion of his gift because he disapproved of the museum's design. Bradley arranged for the museum to buy space for a token one dollar in a city-owned police building used to repair cars. Frank Gehry quickly redesigned the area provided. There were hopes that the downtown area would grow into a real downtown, a dream that has yet to be realized.

There was some rivalry with the Los Angeles County Museum of Art since Robert Anderson had also donated money there for a wing completed in 1986 to house modern and contemporary art. In keeping with L.A. style, the wing was scheduled to be torn down and replaced by a new design less than two decades later. But a lack of funding in the poor economy of 2002 halted plans to demolish the museum's buildings. MOCA opened initially in the Temporary Contemporary, which later became the Geffen Museum. The Getty Trust, the Ahmanson Foundation and Times Mirror contributed handsomely to MOCA, whose permanent home, designed by Japanese architect Arata Isozaki, was completed several years late but features an unusual truncated design and minimalist spaces. The museum has entered the new millennium riding a 10 million dollar gift from benefactor-trustee Dallas Price, co-owner of American Golf Corp. Major collector Audrey Irmas, former chair of MOCA, donated 3 million dollars to the museum as part of a capital campaign that totaled 25 million dollars by 2002. So far there are no plans to recast the MOCA structures.

With the stunning design of Disney Hall taking its place nearby, L.A.'s downtown may have the critical mass necessary to offer yet another point of attraction for the entire basin. A self-conscious L.A. could begin to realize its modernistic calling. L.A. was originally patterned after Midwestern towns, and until the 1960s it retained a Midwestern feel. But the city is now developing its own veritable image based on modernity that is simultaneously influencing Asian cultures and impacting the Old World style which provided much of L.A.'s past identity.

When you enter contemporary art collector Jane Nathanson's home filled with brilliant light and the best of modern and cutting-edge art, you get the feeling that she has it right: This is L.A., and this scene is what L.A. is all about. Old Hollywood had been too busy starting an industry to think much about surroundings. Its taste mimicked Old World taste. But a now grown-up L.A. is developing its own taste. Is it the Warhol portrait of Mao, Jane's delight in bringing back a barber's sign from Africa, or her Calder sculpture that is the key to the L.A. feel? Ultimately it's not the object per se nor even the type of art, but rather the attitude and expression, the willful playing with tradition, the radical mixing of haute with hip that Los Angeles is rapidly producing. A woman dressed in sleek black who collects top flight contemporary art and counsels AIDS patients does not fit the mold. She escapes the script historically reserved for upper class women.

And when you enter the home of Lenore Greenberg, whose father was an executive at MCA, a residence located on a street once inhabited by Stewart, Benny and Ball, and take in its relaxed spread and its contemporary art, you say to yourself, "Yes, she's got it right, too." Greenberg explains the natural affinity of L.A. and new art: "We live horizontally with big walls," providing ample space for the often large canvases of contemporary art; "We live in light." The entire rear wall of her home is glass, with an enticing view out to the sculpture garden and tennis court. This pioneer collector waited for the rest of the city to catch up with her. Meanwhile, besides starting MOCA, she helped form childcare centers in South-Central Los Angeles.

Los Angeles now boasts a nucleus of contemporary artists who no longer need to go to New York to make their name. Andrea Van de Kamp, West Coast President of Sotheby's, notes that a large group of young artists, the Venice school, hangs out in L.A., while artists such as David Hockney and Bob Graham have a large social circle. *L.A. Times* art critic Christopher Knight affirms that there are now too many new and established artists working out of L.A. to name. L.A. is among a handful of "internationally respected centers for the production of new art." In 1997 the renowned Louisiana Museum of Modern Art in Denmark became the first major museum to open an exhibition consisting exclusively of postwar art from Los Angeles. In 1998 the Santa Monica Museum of Art at Bergamot Station re-opened, housing the work of many Southern California artists and serving as a link between collectors, dealers and museums. Quality galleries and museums abound. *Art Forum*, the noted New York-based art magazine, has added an L.A. editor to its staff.

L.A. Architecture: A New Wave of Celebrity

With backing from Microsoft's Paul Allen, Frank Gehry, L.A.'s leading architect, designs a museum in Seattle. Christened the Experience Music Project, the Museum features chaotic, radical, flowing forms. It is as if the music is making the building sway. The Museum opens in 2000 with a gala including DreamWorks partners Steven Spielberg and Jeffrey Katzenberg. A few years earlier, Gehry had designed the acclaimed Guggenheim Museum in Bilbao, Spain. It is Gehry who designed the "abstract" or "deconstructivist" Disney Hall in Los Angeles. The Gehry phenomenon is not singular nor is it isolated: L.A. is now exporting not only its film, but its architecture as well. How incredible this may sound considering that Los Angeles architecture in any real sense is only a century old. Gehry was also slated to get the go-ahead for a proposed Guggenheim Museum along the East River off Wall Street, but plans have been put on hold due to a poor New York economy. The museum would have been a hopeful addition to the disaster-scarred Manhattan skyline.

Many early Los Angeles structures mimicked, for better or worse, architectural models from elsewhere, and perhaps it could not have been otherwise. Still, the brief flirtation with original and experimental designs by Greene and Greene and Frank Lloyd Wright hinted that greatness was on the horizon. The Victorian homes built initially in the 1880s seem incongruous in the Southern California landscape. But a second style of Southern California home, the Spanish Colonial Revival, inspired by Mexico and Southern Spain where there are similar hot and dry climates, has endured. Other Mediterranean derivative styles, such as the Italian villa with gardens, continue to inspire homeowners and architects. The much ballyhooed art deco style with its ornamental structures imported from Europe in the 1920s existed more in film, in sets created by Cedric Gibbens for Carol Lombard movies, for example, than on the real life Los Angeles panorama. There were surprisingly few structures built in Los Angeles with art deco; its profusion of artsy design seems too busy for L.A.'s desert landscape.

Richard Neutra and Rudolf Schindler brought modern architecture to the modern city in the 1920s. Using steel, concrete, redwood and glass with exposed structures that playfully flirted with the environment, they invited the exterior into the home with a sleek design that ridiculed the pomp and complexity of tradition. Schindler studied modern architecture in Vienna and found his way to America hoping to practice the new, progressive design forms. Frank Lloyd Wright sent him to Los Angeles to work on a house named "Hollyhock." L.A. became Schindler's home, its open lands free for experimental design. Perhaps it was L.A.'s lack of tradition in architecture that allowed the city to become a new showcase of form, a model of novel uses of materials. With nothing to tear down, everything is possible.

And when there is something significant there, such as the L.A. County Museum of Art, the plans are to tear most of it down anyway because they didn't get it right the first time as the museum wasn't, well, it wasn't L.A.-enough. And so the plans were to raze its four main buildings—the Ahmanson, Anderson, Bing and Hammer buildings—to erect a structure on stilts with a tent-like roof under the guidance of radical modernist or "deconstructivist" Rem Koolhaas. A lack of funding has put the plans on hold.

Surprisingly, the new modernistic forms did not take off like wildfire in the L.A. environment of openness and sunshine for which it seems they would have surely been destined. The 1950s saw the so-called "case study" homes of Charles and Ray Eames and others as part of a series of post-World War Two model homes commissioned by *Arts & Architecture* magazine to introduce modern design to the United States. But the 1960s brought an unwelcome modernist derivative: The proliferation of boxy, nondescript tract homes of the middle class, one cloned after another, that mocked the modern style, turning modernism into a caricature. David Brown, former president of the Art Center College of Design in Pasadena, sees the sleek geometric design of his college's structure, ensconced in its lush, hilly terrain, as a culmination of the first strong modernist thrust in L.A. The College was designed in 1969 and built by the mid-70s. In a touch of symbolism contrasting the emerging, modern L.A. with the city's past, the Center had been located in a Tudor building in Hancock Park that was once a girls' school.

Fast-forward to the year 2004, and Los Angeles architecture shows signs of finding its true calling, taking a leading role in the extreme modern form led by the world-renowned Frank Gehry and Eric Moss and Thom Mayne. Los Angeles has become a center for avant-garde architecture, architecture characterized by its free-flowing forms and its unusual, highly experimental designs. In design, everything becomes problematic and therefore interesting. Gehry's Disney Hall design evokes the feeling one gets in looking at an abstract expressionist painting. He changed plans for the building's exterior time and again, from limestone to titanium to stainless steel. L.A. is so in love with architecture as art that Professor Tim Vreeland of UCLA warns, "Los Angeles is a city with little or no tradition in comparison to much older cities like Paris, London, or Rome, and the danger is that rather than build up a tradition, we will settle for something which is superficially satisfying without ever reaching the depth that is necessary for a real culture. Being too satisfied with surface appearances affects our architecture also."

The city of Hollywood is a microcosm of what's happening in L.A. architecture. Hollywood's revival chic does not hinge just on the opening of the Kodak Theater as the venue for Oscar night. Tony restaurants such as Café des Artistes are interspersed in the Hollywood of touristy glitz, theatergoers at the Pantages, courtyard apartments, and yes, run-down buildings. This patchwork of rich man/poor man, of glories past and glories to come is beginning a new chapter. The Hollywood name was too precious to rest sullied for long. The historic Beaux Arts classical-style Broadway building at Hollywood and Vine is being restored to its 1927 glory. Broadway was then the department store where stars from Warner Bros. (now KTLA) and the old Columbia Pictures studio (now Sunset and Gower Studios) would shop between shoots.

Elsewhere in Los Angeles, the opening of the new Getty Center attracted worldwide attention. With a myriad of travel publishers and magazine editors sending writers to get the scoop on the Museum for a spread in their publications, the Getty immediately became another must-do for locals as well as tourists. Modernist architect Richard Meier made one billion dollars stand up and be seen on the image-conscious Westside when he created the decidedly contemporary yet majestic Getty Center. The Getty complex of buildings, gardens and corridors highlighted by creamy Italian travertine walls and sparkling glass rests high up on a Brentwood hill, smiling down on L.A.'s wealthiest enclaves. Guests ascend in a very un-L.A.-like way to the summit by tram, leaving their cars behind as they float gently up to heaven. Down below, the usual flurry of motorists wishes that they were up there, at the Museum, instead of stuck in the perennial traffic jam on the San Diego Freeway.

The Getty Museum's old world art would be but a co-attraction—almost a playful irony if the art weren't so first-rate—to the experience of imbibing the expanse of the city from the Getty's power perch. That the newly wealthy such as J. Paul Getty who came to the city in the 1920s, '30s and '40s collected old world art as did their counterparts back East is but a footnote to the very modern and oh-so-L.A. Getty buildings and hillside on which they are ensconced.

Architects are following chefs as the next media stars. Los Angeles real estate agents now expect sophisticated buyers to ask for the pedigree of a house. Director David Lynch, producer David Zander and producer Joel Silver bought Frank Lloyd Wright homes, and Gucci designer Tom Ford lives in a Neutra in Bel-Air, while architecture junkies scrutinize Greene and Greene homes in Pasadena. A home on Rockingham Drive in Brentwood designed by Frank Lloyd Wright's son is advertised in the *Hollywood Reporter* as a Lloyd Wright in an "exciting California style." Super Hollywood agent/manager Michael Ovitz hopes to have renowned architect I.M. Pei design a home for him on a lot he purchased in Beverly Hills. Realtor June Scott, whose clients have included David Geffen, Bob Daly and actor Henry Winkler, remarks, "Los Angeles is a different mentality from anywhere else . . . We want trees, land and grass. The taste level is extremely cutting-edge, not at all provincial. Angelenos are not afraid to mix architecture and style."

David Brown sees Los Angeles architecture as "a cultural and geographical focal point permitting the importation and mixing of styles and so what if it doesn't all fit." Take a stroll down Melrose Ave. during the day where a hodgepodge of bright colors gives older buildings modernistic overtones, where pop art meets street fashion, and move along on the street where ten inch heels vie for attention with designer T-shirts; look into the shops—The Retail Slut, The Last Wound-up, or Sacks 5th Avenue—and see dresses so slim and slinky that you marvel at the body form that will wear them. It all comes together in a short patch of an Avenue that could exist in only a few places in the world.

The artistic flowering in L.A. is not limited to a single art form, and L.A.'s artistic influence is developing a global reach. Mrs. Howard Ahmanson affirms that, "This is an artist's Mecca," adding that the performing arts have blossomed also—there is now more off-Broadway theatre here than in New York. Architecture professor Tim Vreeland explains that architecture and interior design in L.A. have had a tremendous influence on the rest of the country: "Talent throughout the country is influenced by the trendy element in L.A."

Just in time for the new millennium, the renovation of Pasadena's Norton Simon Museum was completed in 1999 by none other than Frank Gehry. Presided over by Jennifer Jones Simon, the museum's CEO and a former

Oscar winner, a stellar group of art patrons gave their approval to the Gehry redesign, including: Carrie Fisher, Eli Broad, Gregory Peck, Jack Lemmon, Sidney Sheinbaum, Diane Keaton, Jacqueline Bisset, Helena Bonham Carter, Angie Dickenson, Sally Kellerman, William Shatner and sculptor Robert Graham. Los Angeles County Museum of Art Director Andrea Rich came across town to be on hand for the ceremony in a somewhat historical gesture considering that there was bad blood between the two institutions in their early years when both Norton Simon and Armand Hammer established their own museums after "ego" clashes regarding the Los Angeles County Museum of Art— an incongruous bit of New York attitude in the laid-back land of sunshine. Lauren Bacall and Tom Brokaw, who used to broadcast news in L.A. for NBC, gave a New York nod of approval to the 5 million dollar revamp. Simon trustee and bi-coastal Candice Bergen quipped, "People are starting to think of L.A. as a cultural stop—if not a center." The joke used to be on L.A.: L.A. and art, L.A. and culture, P-L-E-A-S-E! But Los Angeles is no longer a joke. All the world watches the L.A. stage.

Los Angeles: A Star is Born

The year is 1989. The site is an empty parking lot next to the Music Center. This is not just any lot, however, but the proposed site of the Disney Concert Hall designed by Frank Gehry and spawned by a 50 million dollar gift from Lillian Disney. The occasion is the 25th anniversary of the Music Center. One thousand people gave 1,000 dollars to sit out in the night air and eat fettuccine with Sevruga caviar, chicken breasts with veal and spinach, and peach ice cream with chocolate sauce. What ever happened to chicken Cordon Bleu? It was an evening of triumph. Mike Medavoy, then with Orion Pictures, summed it up: "This is a celebration of a city culturally maturing . . . And it's international in scope, not just national." Los Angeles was well on its way to worldwide social stardom.

But the L.A. upper crust, with the most powerful lever of cultural dissemination, film production, in hand, has often shirked the historic opportunity to set the tone for social distinction in America. It has shed the middle class chains of mass production only to entrap itself in the yoke of haute-only products of the traditional aristocratic upper class. But L.A. has many more real possibilities of social expression. It can be both hip and haute, rich and unpretentious, au courant and individual. The L.A. upper crust must decide what will be its true face to the world. Los Angeles is new to the game of Society, but Society is perennial, for people emulate others even as they deny doing so. L.A., you have arrived. Now what will you do?

CHAPTER SIX

Fashion Discovers Hollywood

Selling Couture in Los Angeles

Great designers of the world opening their shops on Rodeo Drive in the 1980s and '90s meant that L.A. had arrived. Personal visits to L.A. to stage showings of their couture line meant that L.A. had climbed to the top of the social heap. In the mid-1980s, Chanel's designer Karl Lagerfeld put on a couture show complete with European and New York models in the Grand Hall of the Music Center's Dorothy Chandler Pavilion. With the show Lagerfeld became a benefactor of the Music Center. Savvy marketers that they are, the couturiers were the first group to recognize the social power of Los Angeles. The great couturiers are the ultimate social arbiters in upper class society, as they interpret and present what wealthy women wear from season to season and year to year. They are stars in their own right. Society women in turn coddle the top designers, displaying a kind of social symbiosis.

High-end retailers understand and facilitate the insatiable drive of the wealthy away from uniformity; as soon as one has an exclusively haute product, a creation, someone else may copy it, making it available in a patterned form for the masses. The product loses its exclusivity, its rarified air, and the upper crust then often ceases to be interested in it. Exclusivity cannot be captured because it metamorphoses and becomes blasé. This is especially true in the fashion industry where ready-to-wear clothing for the broader market copies the patterns of haute couture and the couture collections. As a given style trickles down the social ladder it becomes déclassé, and the couturiers are off to set another haute trend. So Armani's black label couture collection gives way to La Collezione, a watered-down version of last year's collection. Further down the product line is Armani Exchange and finally the copy-catters who pattern clothes after the Armani label.

At the 1996 MTV Movie Awards, the heightened attention bestowed on designers took an amusing turn as an Isaac Mizrahi imposter greeted Faye Dunaway and other celebrities, only to be unmasked by Whitney Houston, whose bodyguard failed to find the hoax amusing. The imposter recognized that designers act like stars. He surely got a thrill from his moment in the spotlight before paying the penalty of a likely jail term. The real top designers are continually jockeying for position, for the chance to dress the right people at the events that count. These designers must size up the exclusive social scene at the top to place the appropriate emphasis with the right people, and increasingly they look to L.A. Their decisions are not academic; the life of their fashion empires rests on interpreting the social hierarchy correctly, and they must be particularly attuned to the goings on in New York and Los Angeles.

Great L.A. designer and couturier Jimmy Galanos enjoyed an haute send-off into retirement in 1998 as the Los Angeles County Museum of Art hosted a party and showing of his couture clothes. For many years Galanos shone almost alone as an L.A.-based couturier. His career began at Columbia Pictures under noted costume designer Jean Louis, who had created Rita Hayworth's black strapless "Gilda" gown and designed the dress Marilyn Monroe wore to sing "Happy Birthday" to President Kennedy. In 1951 Galanos got a break selling to Saks Fifth Avenue in Beverly Hills at a time when L.A. was a fashion wasteland. He went on to dress Nancy Reagan when she was an MGM starlet. Mrs. Reagan wore Galanos creations to all of her husband's inaugurations. Marlene Dietrich was often seen in Galanos chiffon gowns, while Judy Garland wore his black leotard and chiffon skirt. In that era, Loretta Young, Rosalind Russell and Dorothy Lamour all wore Galanos. But so too did Diana Ross many years later, appearing in a purple-beaded Galanos at the 1985 Oscars. The L.A. designer lasted so long at the top because he understood the fashion game of which he was a part: "What I wanted to do is make the most beautiful and most expensive clothes . . . I look at the fabrics, and I feel I am sorry, and I just fall in love with them, and sometimes I don't even want to sell." But L.A. has become a fashion capital not because of its designers; the explanation lies elsewhere.

Like vinegar and oil, fashion and Hollywood have always mixed. Still, it is surprising so many decades passed before the connection was consciously cultivated. Notable actresses are now routinely invited to peruse the runways at the world's top fashion shows. Historically, the European couturiers connected with New York, the height of American fashion and a hotbed of design. But the couturiers discovered an interesting detail: While New York and San Francisco are fashionable cities, it is Los Angeles that sells fashion, whether at the high end or with the déclassé chic lines. And it is in L.A. that the trendy hip and the elegant haute lines meet and are displayed throughout the city: Hip Melrose, chic Sunset, haute Rodeo, and casual Malibu. Music industry types and street types too walk the open path of L.A. style. The world focuses in as platform shoes showcased on Melrose become the craze in Japan. Street fashion makes its way in L.A. or withers away. Far from being heathen or provincial, Los Angeles provides a bonanza for the fashion industry.

Nothing in fashion today takes the place of Hollywood. See what Julia Roberts is wearing in her latest film, and then see a version of it three months later at K-Mart. Armani was the first designer to grasp the value of having stars wear his clothes. He understood the intimate connection between stardom and fashion, establishing a presence in New York and Los Angeles long before other designers. Armani cultivated and exploited celebrity power. He courted Hollywood, dressing agent Michael Ovitz, Jodie Foster, Annette Bening, Glen Close, Anjelica Huston and so on. And then Armani went for a direct hit by gaining wardrobe credits in films such as *The Untouchables* and *Shaft*.

Much is made of the Paris fashion shows, but do any of them compare to Oscar night in L.A. as a marketing tool? "And here is Cher in her latest Bob Mackie creation," gush the announcers. The couturiers court the stars months in advance for the chance to shine on their backs on Oscar night. The pre-Oscar broadcast in L.A. is now half as long as the awards show itself, yet all it really includes are actresses floating by in their designer gowns as the whole world looks on.

Since music industry dress often borders on the outrageous, a musician can wear most anything to the music awards. But Oscar fashion has become too important to be left completely to whim. For the 2000 broadcast, telecast producer Lili Fini Zanuck hired L.A. stylist L' Wren Scott to coordinate the production's look. Scott traveled to New York and Europe to select gowns from the collections of Armani, Dior, Gucci and others. Even men's formal wear was on the checklist. The broadcast strove for an original, modern look.

Designers, like movie stars, have become the social elixir of top events. On one notable visit by Valentino to Los Angeles in 1990, vice-president of Valentino New York, Luciano Villarini, dubbed Los Angeles "the most important city in the United States today." It is "the atmosphere, wealth, climate, the concept of homes with gardens." Other noted retailers have chimed in on this melodic ode to the new queen. You know you're at the top when high-end retail managers such as Saks Fifth Avenue President Rose-Marie Bravo, upon visiting Beverly Hills, state, "If something is upscale and unique and expensive and it doesn't sell in Beverly Hills, well, chances are it's not going to sell anywhere . . . The ladies in L.A. want whatever's new, whatever's hot. They want it first. They want it now." Other clothes don't sell elsewhere not because wealthy women in Chicago or Atlanta make an appointment with the store and decide not to buy because the clothes don't look good. Rather, they have already surveyed what their counterparts in L.A. and New York are wearing through the pages of the fashion press, or have contacted their friends in L.A. and

New York to see what they are buying.

With couture in the United States, you first sell the L.A. and New York women, and then the rest of the upper class women follow suit, or should we say dress, since these women rarely wear pants even to do lunch because there is little social distinction in pants, the Armani line notwithstanding. The keen eye of the upper class, with its highly refined tastes, only accepts the testimonials of the top players. Their eye is honed to one thing: Whether or not the haute object is unique—whether its display will be a socially significant event.

It is only the female members of the upper class who can be spotted on sight, the women whom Tom Wolfe called "social X rays" in *The Bonfire of the Vanities*. There can be no mistaking the glow from the brilliant and unusual colors of their attire, the magnificent and alluring patterns of their Versaces or Chanels. Their exquisitely made-up faces with carefully pampered skin augmented by a facelift when necessary stop one in his tracks. The ever-present stone-sized jewels on their fingers attest to their status even as they go through the paces under the watchful eyes of their personal trainer. Their slender shapes testify to hours of painstaking care devoted to cultivating their bodies. When the American upper class shows itself to the public, it is in the style and manner of its women.

But the pressure to maintain the perfect face and figure, especially for L.A. upper crust women competing with a steady flow of Hollywood starlets, can have its down side as women feel they must defy gravity to fit the cultural ideal forever. The resulting huge plastic surgery industry has grown so lucrative in L.A. that it has even spawned offshoots such as the post-op hotel. Guests pay a premium for a few days of totally private recovery time in lavish surroundings where even the entrance is shielded from outside eyes. Apparently the reasons for choosing surgery are often more than meets the eye, so to speak. According to staff at the post-op havens, some clients have surgery to hold their marriages together: "As younger women use having a baby, older women [and men] use a facelift."

Searching elsewhere for upper crust women, we see them walking out in full splendor to the stables at Santa Anita racetrack in Southern California to view their horses before the Santa Anita Derby. Their colorful hats add a touch of elegance to the exciting, festive atmosphere, foreshadowing the winning family's trip to Louisville for the Kentucky Derby. They are dressed in the same manner as socialites who do lunch in Beverly Hills. The sheen from their dresses livens up an already brilliant mélange of horses and jockeys. Wealthy women who meet in the walking ring at Santa Anita may have horses competing with each other on the racetrack, and their family businesses may compete in the business arena; but standing there, gleaming, *en evidence* in the walking ring, they are of the same social circle.

From L.A. to New York, upper class mode looks the same. At an unveiling of Adolfo's Spring collection at the Beverly Hills Hotel attended by Nancy Reagan along with the crème de la crème of L.A.'s Society femmes, an *L.A. Times* journalist commented, "Surveying the crowd, it looked like a sea of Nancy Reagan sisters—women in red suits, ash-blond hair neatly poufed, and sensible heels." A half-dozen women had on slight variations of the same Adolfo jacket, among them the prominent Betsy Bloomingdale, widow of Alfred Bloomingdale and close friend of Mrs. Reagan. Why is this conformity present at the height of social distinction? One of the women who attended the Adolfo unveiling responded to a similar question, "I consider it to mean I have exquisite taste."

The purpose of haute dress is not to be unique among one's equals, that is, other upper crust women, but to be set apart from the other social groupings, marked by the distinction of one's style. L.A. designer Jill Richards was put on the map when Nancy Reagan and her friends began to buy her clothes. When Richards expanded her line in 1987, the label lost its cachet. If everyone can get it, it's not worth having. Only after she re-purchased the exclusive use of her name for a new line of clothes in the 1990s did she return to grace among L.A. upper crust women as her dresses began reappearing at Saks Fifth Avenue and Neiman Marcus stores in Beverly Hills.

In fact many of L.A.'s wealthy choose to shop down the street from Rodeo Drive on Wilshire Blvd. at Neiman Marcus, Barneys New York and Saks Fifth Avenue. There are fewer tourists here, and celebrities can make appointments to shop, even after store hours, and arrive easily without being detected. Neiman Marcus, which came to Beverly Hills in 1979 but knew a good thing when it saw one, has a large Hollywood clientele attracted to both its classic and avant-garde couture collections. The store even features a special facility upstairs where a top star or V.I.P. can shop in complete privacy. Because couture is largely a woman thing, there are no men's clothes in sight.

Neiman Marcus Beverly Hills displays its jewelry collections on the first floor amidst a backdrop of contemporary art. The bottom floor houses its own restaurant featuring light cuisine—remember, the women need to be able to slip into the gowns from the couture collections up on the second floor. Next to the fine crystal is an Estee Lauder Spa. After all, shopping can be so stressful these days with all those choices. L.A.'s top femmes can choose between de la Renta, Ungaro, Bill Blass, Lacroix and Misony. Society types also favor Chanel—thus the Chanel boutique location on Rodeo Drive.

The crossover designer is Armani, worn by Hollywood and non-Hollywood alike. In spite of Robin Williams' quip that "A man in drag is funny, but a woman in drag is Armani," the line maintains its popularity. The hip, now haute younger Hollywooders are more daring and cutting-edge in their choice of designers. Of course you have Versace and Richard Tyler, the latest darling of Hollywood women. Stella McCartney and Narciso Rodriguez often grace the figures of those sleek Hollywood ladies on those Hollywood nights in those Hollywood hills.

You find yourself in rarified air when you arrive on the second floor at Neiman Marcus. Blissful moments become delicious hours as you smile at the couture of the world's finest designers, each collection with its own piece of the stage, as so many galleries of contemporary artwork. You may think you've entered the Twilight Zone as you swear that the glistening gowns are winking back at you. You imagine seeing Rod Serling sans cigarette watching you as you roam the collections mesmerized. You know you're in a special place when the salespeople seem to outnumber the clothes. This is definitely not a scene from J.C. Penny, where you could barely squeeze through the aisles last week as you bought your socks.

Neiman Marcus is one of the few places in a media-driven society where photographers are not allowed. In fact there on the second floor there are none of those mass-produced elements of the world from which you retreated ten minutes before. The couture collections are not mass-produced; they are hand-woven, hearkening back to the excellence of craftsmen and artisans of an earlier time. This fashion-as-art notion has now so worked its way into the modern culture that the venerable Guggenheim Museum in New York honors Giorgio Armani with a retrospective exhibit of his clothes.

But on the second floor of Neiman Marcus, you get your own private exhibit, each designer's collection gracing a separate gallery as a distinct, unique experience. You blink to see if the colors are real. The fabrics are refined, but it is the finishes that jump out and shout, ever so gently, with fine, very fine tones. These are gowns crafted by a human hand in top form with the mark of the designer showing through down to the buttons. Minimum prices can range from $1,200 for a woman's suit up to $4,000 plus for formal evening attire.

You wonder how much better the gowns can get as you think about the handful of women, some 2,000 or so worldwide, who actually go to Paris to attend the fashion shows and private fittings, returning with creations costing as much as $50,000 a pop, or even more—possibly $250,000 for a beaded gown. A simple blouse to wear under a suit can cost $6,000. This true haute couture is not in the stores, and you need an invitation to see the creations in person on the Paris runways. But the couture collections with gowns costing several thousand dollars are statement enough for even the upper reaches of the L.A. upper class and Hollywood, for the women who dress to be seen in the ultimate entrance town, in the city where being seen may mean seen around the world.

The top designers are in L.A. because Hollywood is in L.A. Armani visits L.A. personally because Hollywood is in L.A., and Hollywood sells fashion as no other entity could. "The rest of America is trying to emulate what it sees in the movies or in *People* magazine," explains one fashion insider. Adds Kenneth Cole spokeswoman Kristin Hoppmann, "As much as we'd like to think all the fashion trends come out of New York, the people starting the trends are in L.A." So designers bend over backwards to give their gowns and accessories free to the top stars on Oscar night. What better way for their creations to be *en evidence*, as a presentation, a statement, as a work of art? The only part of their outfits that the big stars pay for is their shoes. "A buck is a buck" does not hold in Hollywood, where a buck spends louder and top stars need not even pay real dollars to make the sound.

The Hollywood/Rodeo Drive connection creates a kind of virtual shopping. A Midwestern woman sees a dress from Neiman Marcus on a soap opera star and the store gets a call that very day asking to buy it. If haute Hollywood doesn't whet your whistle, the L.A. day look probably will. Daytime attire is much more casual, with designer sunglasses on the celebrities and would-be stars, on the wannabes who just visit the city where every hip venue provides a backdrop for a photo shoot or a chance to be discovered by a Hollywood producer.

Neiman Marcus and Saks Fifth Avenue are also major venues for top social events, providing space and often a fashion show. Neiman Marcus has hosted Stop Cancer, headed by Paramount chief Sherry Lansing, and presented the Donna Karan Collection at the event. The Dallas-based store often serves as a venue for charity functions, from a black-tie dinner for the Fraternity of Friends, the men's support group for the Music Center, to a reception co-hosted by the Music Center's Blue Ribbon for the opening of the L.A. Opera. Sometimes jewelry takes center stage at Neiman Marcus in lieu of fashion, as with a fundraiser held for HELP, a group that raises money for troubled children. And events held elsewhere by charities such as the Alliance for Children's Rights may ask Neiman Marcus to contribute table favors to spice up the proceedings. But Neiman Marcus is not the only concern to have discovered L.A. as a fashion capital. Just up the road off of Wilshire Blvd. is where all eyes turn as everyone wants to ride the L.A. fashion express on that now famous and pretentious street: Rodeo Drive.

The Rodeo Show

L.A. attitude—"We love it." Listen to Hollywood socialite Dani Janssen, widow of late actor David Janssen, who jests, "I remember one time someone asked me to have lunch at a wonderful new place in the [San Fernando] Valley and I said, 'Sorry, my Rolls hits Mulholland and turns around automatically.'" The adjacent Valley, below the hills of Beverly, could have been Anytown, USA. Ms. Janssen's comments, while obviously stated with tongue in cheek, should not be taken lightly; they represent a culmination, a bringing to fruition of a social reality that took some fifty years to put in place.

The creation of an L.A. haute attitude is directly linked to the development of Rodeo Drive in Beverly Hills. Rodeo de las Aguas, as it was called when it was built in 1907, sat across from lima bean fields. The street was for locals to do their shopping, and at one time had a trolley running down the middle. A 1920 picture shows that Rodeo Drive was also used as a bridle path. Hollywood's first royal couple, Douglas Fairbanks and Mary Pickford, had by then established their home dubbed "Pickfair" in the hills and were entertaining all comers. The rest of Hollywood soon exited their apartments and followed the lead of the famous couple by moving to Beverly Hills. But meanwhile Hollywood landlords were also posting "No Actors Welcome" signs to keep the entertainment industry rabble out of their city. Hollywood was viewed as trashy at least as much as it was viewed as glamorous in those days. Show biz types were looked upon warily as being somewhat quirky. That the transplanted, "sleazy" Hollywooders arriving in Beverly Hills had set in motion a process in the 1920s that would produce the most exclusive real estate in the world in Beverly Hills by the latter half of the century and help to create one of the most fashionable streets in the world, Rodeo Drive, was simply unfathomable.

Even as late as the 1960s, humble Rodeo Drive had a hardware store, inexpensive restaurants and beauty salons, echoing Jack Lemmon's view of Beverly Hills as a small town. International chic did not arrive until Gucci opened in 1968, a time when the social scene in California was more dominated by the reverberations of the Monterey Pop Festival, the hippie movement and the social protests at Berkeley than by alligator shoes and Gucci handbags. But the social ambiance of the 1960s "blew away with the wind" as the pop group Peter, Paul and Mary would have said, and Rodeo Drive began a transformation.

In the 1980s Daryoush Mahboubi-Fardi, whose father had introduced chewing gum to the Middle East, built a large complex of fifty-five stores on Rodeo and then flew to Europe to sign up Louis Vuitton, Gianni Versace, Fendi and Ungaro as tenants. Mahboubi later stated, "At the time, a designer lent credibility to Rodeo Drive. Now [the 1990s] the same designer comes to Rodeo to borrow credibility." Turn about is fair play.

A sort of feeding frenzy ensued. A voracious consumption of haute products had been unleashed, unparalleled anywhere on earth. Mahboubi and the European retailers merely capitalized on a situation begging to be played out. There was so much money—locally, nationally or internationally derived—concentrated on L.A.'s Westside that the social stakes had to be raised. "I'll call your hand and raise you a million dollars" was the poker being played with the buying and selling of mansions in the hills above Rodeo Drive. Surely these poker players of the highest order should eat well at the restaurants below. They should dine and shop in an atmosphere where they could be seen, and they needed to wear the best—shoes, clothes, jewelry, make-up, and so on—doing it, as the whole country would be watching.

And so Hunter's bookstore closed its Rodeo doors in 1985 after the rent was raised; not doubled, not tripled, but raised thirty-fold! If you can't call your opponent's hand and raise him, then be so kind as to give up your seat, or in this case store, to someone who can. When you are at the pulse of one of the world's great battles for social distinction on Rodeo Drive in the 1980s, you had better be better than good. And so the contenders and pretenders were quickly sorted out.

And then there is Bijan, the store with locked doors, the store where you shop by appointment only, the store with an attitude on the street that created attitude, for the Rodeo revolution isn't merely about luxury and elegance, which also exist elsewhere; it is about attitude. And so when an *L.A. Times* reporter and photographer came to do a story on the Rodeo show, one shopper after another turned down the chance for an interview. "Who are these people?" one regular asked. Photographs belong on the charity circuit, not in private life. Everything at the proper social moment. Another shopper admonished, "Shopping is a very private thing. It's like going to your psychiatrist."

You pass your ordinary $6,000 cat suit, $800 cashmere sweaters and $1,300 sequined party dresses on sale (everyone in the United States likes sales, even the upper class) at Theodore's, and you remember seeing Carolyn Mahboubi selling Gianni Versace's line to a clientele that routinely spends $10,000 or $20,000 at a time. Mahboubi isn't a particular fan of the stargazers who also come to

143

Rodeo vacationing and sightseeing from Anytown, USA: "Here [the tourists] are noticeable because they look like they should be in Disneyland ... " Rodeo Drive is one of Southern California's top tourist attractions, domestic and international tourism fueling much of the business on the street. Everyone wants to say she bought something on Rodeo Drive, the shopping Mecca that captures the adult consumer's imagination.

You walk past Giorgio Armani and Ralph Lauren; you look down the street at Tiffany's. How do you tell the real Rodeo shoppers? It's not the shoes or the handbags— you look for the jewelry. A quick thought: Nothing like this scene was ever mentioned in your Sociology 101 class a few miles away at UCLA. And so you recall Herb Fink's statement at Theodore's, representing a real life version of Sociology 101: "I call a 'local' [shopper] anybody from New York who shops with us constantly, anybody from Chicago . . . People are out here maybe six times a year or more and they buy designer clothes but in different colors than they would buy in their rainy cities or in their dismal cities or in their filthy cities." Rude? That's attitude.

In somewhat nicer terms Andrea Van de Kamp, head of Sotheby's West Coast office, explains at tea upon returning from the East Coast: "In L.A. we're outside, we're casual. There's very little color at a New York party." Rodeo Drive's haute mode balances atop a mountain of hip designs and attitudes a short drive away on the streets of L.A. The city's culture cannot be understood without taking into account both its hip and haute strands which developed after 1960. And the impact of L.A. culture on American and global tastes cannot be grasped without recognizing the conveyor belt of culture and style that Hollywood has become.

You walk down the street to look through the glass at Bijan Pakzad in his store, Bijan. You remember his statement in the newspaper about his store: "My prices make a glass wall between me and those people outside, and I find out many of them have lots of taste but not that type of money." "'Quality' is one of my favorite words," he adds. Bijan does fly collections out to customers too busy to come by who might spend $100,000 on a season's wardrobe. After opening his boutique on Rodeo, he later opened a shop in Manhattan.

In 1997 all of Rodeo Drive celebrated twenty-five years of fashion as the entire street was blocked off, becoming a giant runway as models paraded from both directions. Called "A Tribute to Style," the affair was partially emceed by Sylvester Stallone and raised money for Hollywood charities and Teach for America. One of the founders of the Rodeo Drive Committee, which organized the event, left the street in 1998 for retirement. Fred Hayman had been on Rodeo since the 1960s, originally with Gucci. An innovator in the selling of haute products, Hayman had a pool table installed to give men something to do while their wives shopped. Gucci had a private second floor to which special customers had a key.

Hayman's then wife Gale started Giorgio Beverly Hills in 1981. Later Fred Hayman joined her and the business expanded, adding the perfume Giorgio and taking on the name Fred Hayman Beverly Hills in 1989. The fashion coordinator for the Academy Awards since 1988, Hayman relished dressing stars for Oscar night. Hayman was bought out in 1998 by Louis Vuitton—an example of international corporate ownership eroding the boutique owner as a distinct personality that Hayman so epitomized. Ex-wife Gale has since moved east—married to a prominent doctor, she is very much in the social swim in New York and Washington, D.C.

Although some Rodeo-watchers believe that the street has lost much of its entrepreneurial spirit, someone new always seems poised to step in on the street that is better than Fantasyland. Tommy Hilfiger, the new hot designer with the young crowd, opened a flagship store on Rodeo Drive in 1997 offering a special line of upscale clothing. But, as they say, you don't last long in L.A.—the Hilfiger store is no more. Easy come, easy go.

So you leave Rodeo and all its designers and drive down Sunset Boulevard toward the beach. But then you look up at a billboard and see Bijan giving you an haute smile. As you pass by UCLA you wonder just what you did study in Sociology 101.

Two Fashion Shows

You have arrived. 1988—it was a very good year. Valentino and Armani came to L.A. to pay their respects, to hold hands with the new queen. Scene. The Armani gathering, where even the rented chairs are covered with Armani fabric flown in from Italy for the event, takes place at the ultra-modern Los Angeles Museum of Contemporary Art. East Coaster Lee Radziwill, who works for Armani and is the sister of Jacqueline Kennedy Onassis, represents Armani in making a list of invitees. Radziwill was married to director Herb Ross; they owned a ranch in the Santa Ynez Valley near Hollywood producers Ray Stark and Doug Cramer before Cramer sold the ranch and refocused some of his social efforts in New York, becoming an official bi-coastal. Radziwill is joined in making the guest list by one of MOCA's founders, Jane Nathanson, whose husband Marc founded Falcon Cable TV and whose Holmby Hills home is a private little museum of contemporary art, including a Picasso and self-portraits by none other than Andy Warhol.

The conflict: You can't buy a ticket for this event. Lists? What does this mean? The L.A. upper crust had congealed. It had developed a hierarchy. It had real players. The ticket was hot: The event promised to be the most glamorous fashion show Armani had ever staged in the U.S., and since stars sell fashion, the designer wanted celebrities galore to highlight the bash, which coincided with the opening of Armani's L.A. boutique. Hollywood's premier chef, Wolfgang Puck, was slated to whet the haute palates. The Nathanson phone rang off the hook.

Who was there? Of course, you had Barbara Sinatra; Steven Spielberg; Jodie Foster; Doug Cramer; Betsy Bloomingdale; Barbara and Marvin Davis; Harriet Deutsch;

the late Dawn Steel, then head of Columbia Pictures; actresses Anjelica Huston and Victoria Principal; Lew and Edie Wasserman; David Geffen; the Eisners; movie mogul Jerry Weintraub; the Ovitzes; Jack Nicholson; Tom Cruise and Richard Gere. At the event one socialite asked another what a homeless man was doing there, pointing to a disheveled-looking guest across the room. The "homeless" man turned out to be Bob Dylan, who later sat next to Armani—at Armani's request.

The event was a perfect demonstration of social commentator Lewis Lapham's quip that the point of Society gatherings is to determine one's place or value in "the social equivalent of a stock market." Jane Nathanson recalls that the plan was to let guests roam the museum during a cocktail hour and then hold the Armani fashion show featuring European models with a dinner to follow. The evening proved a fabulous convergence of L.A. artists and others from the art world with Hollywood, topped off by a memorable couture show—L.A. at its hip and haute best.

Not to be outdone by his counterpart, Valentino staged a similar fashion show later that year using 20th Century Fox Studio as the setting. Neiman Marcus Beverly Hills and Valentino kicked in more than $700,000 to make the evening even more special. Same names, new names, more names were there, about 700, and all for a mere $250 tax deductible ticket, as the net proceeds of the event went to charity. New York socialite Nan Kempner flew out to give an East Coast stamp of approval. An *L.A. Times* Society columnist wrote, "And there was that tremendous feeling of satisfaction important people achieve only when they arrive at a party—and realize that everyone there is as famous as they are. Or even more so." Among L.A.'s top crowd that ate roasted Petaluma de-boned chicken and glazed chocolate tartufo balls with raspberry sorbet were Patti Skouras and Felisa Vanoff of the Hollywood set, who also found themselves in the November 1989 issue of *Town and Country*; and Marion Jorgensen, Giney Milner, Chardee Trainer and Betty Wilson of the Nancy and Ronald Reagan crowd.

Yet another Italian designer, Nino Cerutti, visited L.A. a year later and surveyed the L.A. scene: "American people are getting out of their cult of quantity and into a cult of quality. There is a very dramatic change going on. On my tour, there were none of those typical requests for lower prices or cheaper products. It's a completely different attitude here than five years ago." Of course Cerutti is not referring to just any people, certainly not to those who listen to "Attention K-Mart shoppers," but rather to the upper crust, the top dog in social distinction. In L.A., even a fashion arbiter like Cerutti had to blink and reflect on what he saw. But Cerutti quickly caught some L.A. haute attitude. When asked about some of his own clothes, he quickly responded in fitting L.A. style, "I am not a mass-produced man."

The changes Cerutti grasped, the demand for quality and innovation, have gone beyond the parameters of the upper crust, also becoming a consumer focus of many in the middle class. No greater influence on American consumption habits has surfaced over the last twenty-five years than that of L.A./Hollywood. Premier fashion magazines *Harper's Bazaar* and *Vanity Fair* come to Los Angeles to host parties and meet with retailers to take the L.A. fashion pulse. They look for that special something, not knowing what—perhaps a trend in designer sunglasses—that they will highlight as the new trend. The L.A. fashion impetus sells, and there is no more telling reality than that in the modern, consumer-driven culture where people are measured by what they buy.

Rumor has it around L.A. that the "Big One," meaning an earthquake, will eventually sink L.A.'s Westside into the Pacific Ocean. Soothsayers should take note. L.A. has already had its big explosion. Through its upper echelon situated on the Westside, L.A.'s wealth and social power have propelled it, not down, but up into the ultimate success in the American social arena. The L.A. upper crust has become a dual partner with the New York crowd as the twin peaks of the American upper class. If L.A.'s Westside were to sink, it would be because of the burden of its heavy bank accounts, or rather stocks and bonds, and the weight of its women's jewels.

Beverly Hills in 1921 with a population of 700.
Photo courtesy of Jeff Hyland of Hilton and Hyland.

UCLA and Westwood in 1931. No Westside real estate frenzy here.
Photo courtesy of Jeff Hyland of Hilton and Hyland.

The Goetz estate in the still rural Beverly Hills of 1928. Edie Goetz, as the eldest daughter of Louis B. Mayer, was Hollywood royalty.
Photo courtesy of Jeff Hyland of Hilton and Hyland.

Dorothy Chandler, accompanied by Mia Chandler, shines as the queen of L.A. Society at a Blue Ribbon Event in the late 1970s.
Photo copyright Berliner Studio/BEI.

Caroline Ahmanson, the *grande dame* of L.A. Society, with opera diva Dorothy Kirsten French at a 1985 reception at the Beverly Wilshire Hotel for H.R.H. Princess Stephanie of Monaco and the Princess Grace Foundation. Photo copyright Berliner Studio/BEI.

Nancy and Tim Vreeland at a 1983 Gala honoring renowned *Vogue*
editor Diana Vreeland. Nancy Vreeland was a force in L.A. charitable
causes in the 1980s and 1990s. Tim Vreeland, a professor of architecture,
is the son of Diana Vreeland. Photo copyright Berliner Studio/BEI.

Dennis and Terry Stanfill at a Charlton Heston Theater Event in the late
1970s. Dennis Stanfill was Chairman of 20th Century Fox. Terry Stanfill
is a novelist and is on the board of the L.A. Opera.
Photo copyright Berliner Studio/BEI.

Joan and John Hotchkis with cellist YoYo Ma and composer John Williams at an L.A. Philharmonic event in 2002. Joan Hotchkis is the President of the Blue Ribbon. John Hotchkis is the President of the Board of the L.A. Philharmonic. Photo courtesy of Joan Hotchkis. Photo copyright Lee Salem.

Larry Gagosian of Gagosian Galleries with Eli Broad and actor/artist Dennis Hopper—all key players on the L.A. contemporary art scene. Photo copyright Larry Hammerness/BEI.

Westsider and contemporary art collector Joan Quinn visits the King of Spain, Juan Carlos. Joan Quinn is the daughter of J.C. Agajanian, sponsor of two Indianapolis 500 winners. Photo courtesy of Joan Quinn.

Bob Tuttle and Jane Nathanson honor Susan Bay-Nimoy and actor
Leonard Nimoy at the Museum of Contemporary Art in 2003. Jane
Nathanson is a noted collector of contemporary art and has served on the
board of the Museum of Contemporary Art.
Photo copyright Alberto Rodriguez/BEImages.

Young executives at Paramount Studios in 1982: Producer Stanley Gaffe, Barry Diller, Sherry Lansing and Michael Eisner. Eisner would later head Disney, Lansing became chief of Paramount, and Diller later led Universal. Photo copyright Berliner Studio/BEI.

Hollywood female elite: Director Mimi Leder, Paramount's Sherry Lansing, Columbia Pictures President Amy Pascal, and producer Lili Zanuck at a 2001 Women in Hollywood luncheon.
Photo copyright Berliner Studio/BEI.

The last of the great moguls, Lew Wasserman, with Barry Gordy at a gala honoring Edgar Bronfman, Jr. in 1999. Wasserman headed MCA/Universal. Gordy founded Motown Records in Detroit before relocating, as many have done, to L.A.'s Westside.
Photo copyright Eric Charbonneau/Berliner Studio.

Frank and Barbara Sinatra paying tribute to the Beverly Hills Hotel at the hotel's 75th anniversary dinner. Photo courtesy of BEImages.

Guests at the 75th anniversary of the Beverly Hills Hotel included actors George Hamilton and Joan Collins. Photo copyright Berliner Studio/BEI.

Actor Charlton Heston with Lee Minnelli and his wife, Lydia Heston, at a Christmas party given by Mrs. Minnelli in 1988.
Photo copyright Berliner Studio/BEImages.

Producer Alan Ladd Jr. and wife Cindra at a reception for the Children's Diabetes Foundation at Sotheby's in 2002.
Photo copyright Alex Berliner/BEImages.net.

Oprah Winfrey and Barbara Davis at the 2002 Carousel of Hope Ball
benefiting childhood diabetes at the Beverly Hilton.
Photo copyright Berliner Studio/BEImages.

Lilly Tartikoff, wife of late NBC executive Brandon Tartikoff, hosts
the Fire and Ice Gala with Ron Perelman, New York investment
banker and head of Revlon, and actress Candice Bergen. The 1998
event benefited Revlon/UCLA Women's Cancer Research Program.
Photo copyright Berliner Studio.

Singer-actress Jennifer Lopez in front of Oscar at the 73rd Annual
Academy Awards Deadline Room in 2001.
Photo copyright Laurie Wierzbicki/BEImages.

Actress Angela Bassett at the *Vanity Fair* party at Morton's Restaurant for the 73rd Annual Academy Awards in 2001.
Photo copyright Eric Charbonneau/BEI.

Restaurant owner Patrick Terrail in 1982 in front of the many Rolls Royces at his little restaurant, Ma Maison, that helped start a food revolution in L.A. Photo copyright Alan Berliner/Berliner Studios/BEI.

From Ma Maison to Spago, Hollywood super chef Wolfgang Puck with actresses Alexandra Paul and Daryl Hannah at Spago in 1982. Photo copyright Berliner Studio/BEI.

Wolfgang Puck hosts Chefs Across America at his signature restaurant, Spago Beverly Hills, in 2002. Twenty years on and L.A. is now a major center of world-class cuisine. Photo copyright Alex Berliner/BEI.

Frank Gehry's scintillating design of the Disney Concert Hall. A true culmination of the L.A. sensation.
Photo courtesy of Frank Gehry of Gehry Partners.

Maria Shriver with Disney Hall architect Frank Gehry, both L.A. Westsiders, in 2000. Photo copyright Berliner Studio/BEI.

The Beverly Hills Hotel, built in 1912, is almost 100 years old and still going strong. Photo courtesy of the Beverly Hills Hotel.

2 Rodeo Drive in 2000, a far cry from the street's days as a bridal path. Photo courtesy of 2 Rodeo Drive.

PART FOUR

L.A. TODAY

CHAPTER SEVEN

The New Hollywood: A Global Player

"Everyone's avocation in America is show business."

—Buck Henry

The New Studio System

The L.A. panorama, the L.A. economy, L.A. power, L.A. style—all are inextricably tied to the entertainment industry. Hollywood is a series of business and social relationships that play out across the city. You can't point to it and say "I see it" as you could the Eiffel Tower in Paris, but Hollywood's influence in L.A. wafts throughout the basin, perceptible if you look for it and sometimes even when you don't. There is more to L.A. than the entertainment industry, but Hollywood is what makes Los Angeles such an important city.

The major American studios, though often owned by New York, French or Japanese firms, are all based in Los Angeles. They may be corporate controlled and ownership may be elsewhere, but the major players all live, socialize and make deals in L.A. The major studios are Sony, which bought out Columbia; Metro-Goldwyn-Mayer (owned principally by L.A. and Las Vegas-based Kirk Kerkorian); 20th Century Fox, owned by News Corp.; Warner Bros., which merged with Time Inc. to create Time Warner, which in turn merged with AOL; Universal; Disney Studios; and Paramount Pictures, owned by Viacom. Ownership and control change often and can take on complex forms. Walt Disney Studios is 100% owned by the Walt Disney Co., but the Walt Disney Co. has had a big chunk of its shares held by the Texas-based Bass family, which controlled as much as 25% of the stock in 1984 and finally sold off all of its Disney stock in 2001.

The top executives of the major studios have automatic social distinction when they step out in L.A. social life. After all, the studio heads have the power to give the final green light on a movie. Studio heads reap tens if not hundreds of millions of dollars from the deals they make for their studios, and they can choose to step out and play the game of L.A. high society at any time. Their power and clout draw America's brightest and most interesting talent, and their spending power ensures a breathtaking spectacle. In the recent past, if the late Lew Wasserman of Universal or Dennis Stanfill at 20th Century Fox were hosting a party on the studio lot, you found a way to show up. This formidable social power of studio heads has been a constant, going back to the Old Hollywood of the Warners, the Mayers, the Steins, and the Goldwyns.

What has changed is that the entertainment industry is no longer just a flashy enclave, but is now integral to the Southern California identity, influencing the entire city. L.A. cultural life oozes Hollywood. As you sit at a coffee house on Sunset Blvd., you can't help but notice the Directors Guild of America across the street. You can't help but take in the scene of would-be actors and actresses milling about the tables, or the man with the script.

The studios often underwrite the L.A. charities run by prominent women, and studio heads attend showings of the great designers such as Valentino and Armani. No studio head is bigger than Disney's Michael Eisner, who cashed in 5.4 million Disney shares worth 202 million dollars in income reported for 1993. No studio head is as socially active as Sherry Lansing of Paramount, who is personally affiliated with the Music Center and on the Board of Times Mirror Co., which controls the *L.A. Times*. But these names are interchangeable with other studio heads in terms of social clout. For example, Jane Semel, wife of Terry Semel, one of the Warner Bros. chiefs at the time, co-hosted the fabulous Fire and Ice Ball for cancer research in 1997. A high-level studio affiliation combined with the hosting of a premier charity event put the Semels very much in the social swim.

The Hollywood studio is actually a misnomer today. The studios are really entertainment companies owning television stations and cable. Studios hold interests in home video outlets, music companies, and even ticket-selling firms. One example of this broad studio reach is at Universal, where Edgar Bronfman led a takeover of Polygram in 1998. With control of Polygram, Universal— until then known for films—became the top-selling recording company in the world. AOL Time Warner is the largest Internet company and second-largest cable operator. Viacom Inc. and News Corp. have major broadcast interests, and Sony Pictures' parent company is the well-known electronics giant. The major studios are increasingly international in scope as foreign sales and rights to entertainment products have become critical to profit margins.

Economic power is still with the studios; they make the ultimate decision on what project goes and how money is spent. But Dennis Stanfill, President and CEO of 20th Century Fox from 1971 to 1981, points out that the studio heads generally stay out of the limelight and forego interviews. This gives the impression that Hollywood is run by actors, producers and directors, who are more visible.

Studio executives often change companies, giving the illusion of great flux in the Hollywood power structure, yet they are for the most part giving the same performance at a slightly different venue. So Frank Biondi goes from Chief Executive at Home Box Office to Viacom's No. 2 to Universal. Biondi's severance package for a short two and one-half year stint at Universal was 30 million dollars, paltry by Hollywood's now lofty levels. Jeffrey Katzenberg leaves Disney to become a major player at DreamWorks SKG. No one sheds any tears at these departures, and the players walk away with severance packages in the tens of millions of dollars.

Michael Ovitz leaves Creative Artists Agency for a stint at Disney and then forms his own management company, which handles Leonardo DiCaprio, Robin

Williams, Cameron Diaz, and author Michael Crichton. Nobody ever knew what role Ovitz played at Disney, but he cashed out after a year with a 90 million dollar package that was the talk of an envious Hollywood. Ovitz's partner Ron Meyer also left CAA to take over the presidency of then MCA Universal, while Mike Marcus, another partner, ran MGM for a time. The Creative Artists trio has followed in the tradition set by Lew Wasserman, who began as an agent but ran MCA Universal for decades.

Barry Diller, a key power player, left 20th Century Fox to head Universal, which bought a majority stake in Ticketmaster from Paul Allen of Microsoft. Diller started the Fox Network with Rupert Murdoch, pioneered the mini-series format at ABC, and was CEO at Paramount. Diller then headed Universal's movie, television and theme park divisions. And while the Universal staff was attending a retreat at the Winter Olympic Games in Utah, Diller was in New York with his wife, Diane von Furstenberg, for fashion week. The top, top players play above the corporate structure. Does Diller have a job description? It's doubtful, since his work changes from year to year, if not from month to month. He would need a full time secretary to continually update his résumé, but real players such as Diller don't need résumés.

When Sony Corp. bought Columbia Pictures Entertainment in 1989, it provided a special compensation package to Hollywooders Peter Guber and Jon Peters to run the corporation. Sony first paid 200 million dollars to acquire Guber-Peters Entertainment Co., as it needed Hollywood insiders to run Columbia to protect and enhance its investment. The Sony package for Guber, Peters and three other executives included 14 million dollars each in salary over five years with cost-of-living provisions for living in the L.A. area; a percentage of company profits that could total an additional several million dollars; and a 50 million dollar lump sum payment to be divided among the five officers that could reach as high as 80 million dollars depending upon the studio valuation after five years. Sony later took a whopping

2.7 billion dollar loss in the second quarter of 1994 due to losses at the studio. Of course Peters and Guber did not have to refund any of their earnings when they left Sony.

For the first time in decades, a new studio emerges. Mega-director Steven Spielberg, ex-Disney top executive Jeffrey Katzenberg and recording tycoon David Geffen have been joined by Microsoft co-founder Paul Allen in building DreamWorks SKG. The studio has 1000 employees at its animation division in Glendale and 500 workers in its live-action film and T.V. division on the Universal Studios lot. But with the paucity of quality real estate in L.A. today, even these movers and shakers have difficulty starting a major new project. After several years of negotiation the mega-moguls, with a 2 billion dollar capitalization and the unqualified backing of then Mayor Richard Riordan, were unable to build a studio-type work facility and campus on a piece of land in Playa Vista once used by Howard Hughes to build his Spruce Goose. The DreamWorks facility was to have been the first major studio built since the Great Depression, but much to the chagrin of the Hollywood community, the project fell through due to environmental and permitting concerns. Open land is increasingly a scarce commodity in the once expansive L.A. basin, and Los Angeles is becoming more structured as it matures into a major city with global reach.

Super agents perch at the top of the Hollywood power structure, the most noteworthy being Michael Ovitz. Creative Artists Agency was founded in 1975 by Ovitz, Ron Meyer and Bill Haber, and quickly changed the structure of Hollywood business by stabling a stunning number of directors, producers and actors under one roof. The rise of CAA and the power of talent agencies coincided with the growth of independent production (not strictly studio initiated) and the growing box office power of the top stars. In the old studio system, agents' maneuverability had been limited since most stars were under contract and the studios could assign them as they saw fit to the projects that came down through the pike, leaving less room for negotiation. By concentrating a large group of talent under one roof, CAA was able to fill and expand on the void opened up after the dissolution of the studio contract system.

CAA is still by far the largest talent agency in Hollywood, representing such top names as Tom Hanks, Nicolas Cage, Will Smith, Tom Cruise, Meryl Streep, Oprah Winfrey, Steven Spielberg, Brad Pitt, Al Pacino, Robert Redford and Madonna. Its extraordinarily long-lived reign at the top has been no small feat since Ovitz left CAA in 1995, especially considering the fact that both stars and agents hop around from agency to agency trying to judge just which way the wind of power in Hollywood is blowing. A case in point is Jim Wiatt, who headed International Creative Management, another top Hollywood talent agency, until his departure in 1999. Power in Hollywood is so tied to personal relationships that departures such as Wiatt's (his clients include Julia Roberts, Mel Gibson, Sylvester Stallone and Eddie Murphy) can send tremors throughout the industry. Hollywood cards get shuffled and re-shuffled, and so Wiatt (and most of his clients) wound up at the William Morris Agency, Hollywood's oldest agency, which built its name with such stars as Marilyn Monroe, Elvis Presley, Sammy Davis, Jr., Frank Sinatra and Mae West.

The role of the agent, fixed for decades—since MCA Universal was forced to divest itself of the talent agency business due to a perceived conflict of interest—is once again uncertain. Whether or not a star can be adequately represented by someone also working for the star's employer (the studio) is being brushed aside in the hap-happy Hollywood of movie deals and mega-stars. If a particular agent-star-studio alliance gets the wheels spinning, there seems to be plenty of money for all; and if a movie fails, sharing the risk is the new prudent thing to do anyway.

Ovitz's Artists Management Group may take on financial interests in a television or film project while also representing the artists. His firm thus takes on managerial/ownership roles as well as that of an agent. Ovitz creates both independent television and film production companies, and in 2000 quickly had seven shows in production for the networks. He signs up Tom Clancy to represent writers as well as actors while negotiating movie and television deals. But in the fickle, what-have-you-done-for-me-lately Hollywood, where success rests squarely with television ratings and box office numbers, Ovitz is forced to lay off half his staff in 2002 as many of the company's shows are cancelled. Then he has to sell the profitable parts of his company to an upstart music industry company called the Firm. Part of the sale agreement is that Ovitz would sever all ties to his company. But shed no tears for Ovitz—the Hollywood players come back again from the dead and near dead more often than an Egyptian mummy in a horror film.

In the meantime, the penchant for independent movies has also opened up the agenting game. Agencies such as Endeavor and UTA have pushed their way into the heart of Hollywood deal-making, with UTA representing Jim Carrey, Martin Lawrence and young filmmaker M. Night Shyamalan of *The Sixth Sense* fame. Following Ovitz's lead, other agencies are engaged in fierce competition to finance and produce shows. Agencies want financial interest rules relaxed so they can also sell off part of their agency business to outside entities. In other words, they want equity in their business, whose revenue has traditionally been based solely on their 10% commission for deals. Actors, seeing the conflict of interest, cry foul where the agencies see only dollar signs.

The ever-powerful CAA has a budding contingent of younger stars: Gwyneth Paltrow, Neve Campbell, Matt Damon and Ben Affleck among others. When CAA flexes its muscle, the agency has the ability to shop scripts to its bevy of stars and directors and then look around for studio financing. *Saving Private Ryan* was one such "in-house" production with director Steven Spielberg and actor Tom Hanks. By controlling the talent, the agency has a surprising amount of power. As CAA's Bob Bookman explains, "We can cast a script before we go to the studio. In other words, we can determine what gets made and who is in it." To illustrate, Bookman, who along with CAA President Richard Lovett represents Steven Spielberg, can take a script turned down by Spielberg to another one of the Agency's clients who may be more suitable for the film before anyone else outside of CAA has a crack at it.

Yet the studios also have alliances that are constantly changing. The Hollywood movie complex embraces a whole slew of independent producers and distributors who are unknown to the public but who are significant Hollywood players. Producers are independent contractors who are generally in hot pursuit of that famed studio "deal": An office with staff on a studio lot and money to buy scripts in the so-called development stage of a film. Exceptions are major producers such as Alan Ladd, Jr. and the venerable Richard Zanuck and his wife Lili Fini Zanuck, producers of *Driving Miss Daisy*, who maintain their own offices. Alan Ladd, Jr., however, did for some time have his offices on the Paramount lot.

Few producers would be so bold as to put up their own money to make a film. George Lucas of *Star Wars* fame has done so, yet even a major figure such as Steven Spielberg, who can afford to finance projects, almost always works on somebody else's money, either studio corporate funds or bank loans. Scores of happy amateurs flock to Hollywood with millions to invest in a picture, but they don't last. Even Hollywood veterans cannot really tell if a film will be a hit. And it only takes one film going bust to knock out the amateur investor. Hollywood is the grave of many a would-be movie mogul.

But still the money keeps pouring in. Ted Turner spends $90 million on *Gods and Generals*. Jeff Skoll, co-founder of E-bay, pays $10 million for completion costs on *Eulogy* and finds himself on a set for the first time in Pasadena watching co-stars Ray Romano and Debra Winger, presumably hoping that the two actors can pull out all the stops and make the film a hit. Gateway Computers founder Norman Waitt, Jr. shows up at the famous Cannes Film Festival in 2001 to do what? To finance movies, of course.

Waitt meets with William Morris Agency representatives to explore new projects. "The idea is to have fun, make money and do productions we're proud of," Waitt says, outlining his business plan. And it only takes one unforeseen hit to shake the pillars of Hollywood, which are a lot easier to shake than an outsider may imagine. The 2002 hit *My Big Fat Greek Wedding*, which grossed over 350 million dollars, was passed over by the top players, and even after it was filmed most distributors shunned the film. Who gave the movie the go-ahead? None other than Norm Waitt through his Beverly Hills-based Gold Circle production company. Tom Hanks, his wife Rita Wilson, and Gary Goetzman produced the movie, with Hanks getting Home Box Office to help with the financing as a "favor."

Producer Alan Ladd, Jr. explains that the person who has the power in Hollywood is the one who controls a good script, whether independent producer, actor, director, agent or studio. *L.A. Times* show business columnist James Bates does not like to dwell too much on questions of power in Hollywood: "I don't go much for power lists—they are only a snapshot at a given time and/or the obvious names. Power in Hollywood is transitory. I have seen people high up on magazine lists only a few years ago who are not even working in the industry. Positional power is also elusive since people in high level positions change jobs frequently." No matter who winds up controlling the script, the producers act as the arbiters, the power brokers. They try to attach a director and stars to a script in the developmental phase and to secure the all-important financing for the project. Each project is unique, and a producer's last success will go only so far in selling the next venture. Nobody will put up tens of millions of dollars for an iffy story line. The constant positioning and repositioning of players, the perpetual need to look one or two steps ahead for the next project, keeps Hollywood in a state of frenetic activity. Producers work with agents who juggle their stars' schedules, attempting to line up their next picture. Former studio head Dennis Stanfill estimates that there are anywhere from twenty to forty top Hollywood producers who are constantly working.

The Hollywood establishment also includes the highest paid directors and of course the actors. While the top movie stars have increasing power in making a project viable, their power is highly ephemeral. Today they may be hot, tomorrow not. It only takes one box office bust to lose some luster. In Hollywood two questions are always at the forefront: "Are you working?" and "What have you done lately?" It is hard to be content in Hollywood no matter how much money you have made in the past. However much in demand today, a movie star is always replaceable. As Robin Williams acknowledged the night he received his Academy Award for *Good Will Hunting*, " . . . all this has a half-life of about a day. And then all of a sudden, people go, 'Yeah, O.K., Robin, now you gotta go back to work.'" Oscar party hostess Dani Janssen explains that, "While a star is big today, he can get 20 million a picture. So during that 20 million, 20 million, 20 million period, he's a power. But he's out there on his own—nobody's backing him. Nobody's secure. You can be the biggest star, but the minute they stop working, they wonder what they're doing next."

While new talent has always been integrated into the Hollywood structure, the cast is continually replenished from within, as Hollywood is very much a family affair. The children of Fonda, Huston, Curtis, Spelling, and Douglas are all well known examples of those carrying on the Hollywood tradition for their families. Former MGM/UA and 20th Century Fox chief Alan Ladd, Jr., now an Academy Award-winning producer, is the son of actor Alan Ladd. The past President of Paramount Pictures, John Goldwyn, is the grandson of one of the original studio moguls, Samuel Goldwyn. Other children of Hollywood work as producers or in behind-the-scene capacities. When Peter Guber was chairman of Sony Pictures Entertainment, his wife Lynda had a development and production deal at Sony-owned TriStar Pictures. Guber's niece has been a producer at TriStar as well.

Hollywood is also replenished from the outside as money flows toward its gates in a perpetual tidal wave. Edgar Bronfman, Jr., using a portion of his family's Seagram liquor fortune, purchased MCA Universal. Later, Vivendi took a controlling interest, bringing the French into the picture. Everyone, it seems, wants to own a studio. The Bronfmans, while holding a big stake in Universal, still controlled a large chunk of Seagram, which was founded by Edgar's grandfather in 1928. In a not atypical twist, the Seagram shares' major earnings came not from liquor but from the company's holdings in Du Pont Co. These holdings in turn were sold to finance the MCA Universal deal. Bronfman had previously hung out with the Hollywood crowd, taking a stab at the action by investing Bronfman money in various movies. But a studio is much more à propos if one wishes to make a splash among the Hollywood hierarchy who wheel and deal as if suspended in mid-air, fully air-conditioned, phone in hand, in the Southern California sunshine.

Every Hollywood story line gets told at least five times, be it in sequels or plots re-packaged under another movie title. That's Hollywood formula. Well, Vivendi bought a controlling interest in Universal. Through Seagram, Bronfman still remained Universal's largest single shareholder, but unceremoniously stepped down from Universal's daily management. Universal was then bought by NBC. The bet is Bronfman will not leave Hollywood. To bide his time, he led a 2.6 billion dollar purchase of Warner Music in 2003. Once you get bitten by the Hollywood bug, running a company with a run-of-the-mill product line pales as an alternative. Ultimately, Hollywood's greatest story is itself.

Hollywood and High Society

Surprisingly, the social impact of Hollywood is not a frequently discussed topic in L.A.'s top circles. The *L.A. Times* runs a column on the business of Hollywood as if

Hollywood's influence in the city and elsewhere were only economic. But the cultural values of Hollywood developed during the studio period deemed the social realm outside show business important. Society with a capital S represented a higher plane for many stars that today rank as classic, or Hollywood royalty. No such inherent social responsibility exists today, creating somewhat of a social vacuum. Who on today's scene can replace the Jimmy Stewarts, the Henry Fondas, the Cary Grants, the Fred Astaires? Who is taking up the social banner of the Gregory Pecks and the Kirk Douglases?

Prior to his death in 2003, Gregory Peck had organized a reading series at the L.A. Public Library in which actors read a portion of a favorite work. Peck's work with the library continued a lifetime of dedication to social causes. Yet even Peck would sometimes go through a P.R. person when calling on actors to participate in his reading series and, incredibly, at times got a "No." It is hard to imagine a similar faux pas in the Old Hollywood. Those who said "Yes" to Peck included Beau Bridges, Richard Dreyfus, Sally Field, Morgan Freeman, Charlton Heston, Anjelica Huston, Lynn Redgrave, Shirley MacLaine and Kevin Spacey. There are still some in Hollywood who honor social responsibility.

Anne and Kirk Douglas have taken it upon themselves to revamp many of the abysmal school playgrounds in Los Angeles area schools. Anne Douglas, having read about the playground problem in the *L.A. Times*, immediately met with then Mayor Richard Riordan and set about raising 2.5 million dollars for the playgrounds, one million of which was the Douglases' own money funded through the Anne and Kirk Douglas Foundation. The legendary Lew Wasserman, long-time head of Universal, pledged one million dollars for the Los Angeles Library Foundation during a New Year's Eve millennium celebration at Paramount Studios.

One Hollywood insider speaks of a "gulf" between L.A. Society and Hollywood and of the lack of significant

Hollywood participation in L.A.'s prime cultural institutions as a "problem." The gulf was always there historically, as Old Hollywood and L.A. Society socialized separately. But the mainly Jewish moguls understood that the social realm outside the glamour of Hollywood was an even greater prize than purely Hollywood clout. Ironically, Hollywood celebrities, often snubbed in L.A. and deemed "low class" by Society standards, were readily embraced by the New York upper class and Café Society.

Associated Press reporter Bob Thomas, who has written on Hollywood for over six decades and has known the likes of Louis B. Mayer, Jack Warner, Darryl F. Zanuck and Harry Cohn, comments on the huge studio publicity departments of yesteryear which cultivated stars and left little to chance: "Everything was very well-organized and no star ever refused to do interviews. Everyone was available, because the studios insisted on it." Perhaps long-time L.A. designer Jimmy Galanos, who has dressed the likes of Rosalind Russell and Loretta Young, went a bit too far when he stated in 1999 upon his retirement from a forty-year career, "The stars look no better than the average person on the street today. You want to talk about the '40s? Those were movie stars whose whole thing was to look magnificent and glamorous. This is the way they were promoted, this was the way the studios wanted to see them." Old Hollywood seemed to understand the social calling inherent in true stardom. Being social was a studio mandate in Hollywood's golden days, and the penchant for Society became second nature to stars weaned on the studio system.

Despite the ubiquitous appearance of stars on television shows today such as "Access Hollywood," "Extra" and "Entertainment Tonight," the current crop of movie stars seems to be less in tune with the larger social obligation that is Society, Hollywood charities notwithstanding. The Old Hollywood studios groomed their stars for the Business, yes, but for much more. Who does the grooming today? Publicists, managers, lawyers and stylists all throw in their two cents and cross their fingers, and stars' images flood magazines and T.V. screens, but to what avail? Entertainment news is as deep and porous as a slice of Wonder bread. T.V. entertainment news shows have become vacuous, tabulating the dollar amounts movies have made as if everyone is a studio stockholder looking at the bottom line, with less and less discussion about the artistic quality of a movie. The *L.A. Times* devotes considerable space to coverage of entertainment industry economics, tediously pouring over dollar figures of the latest releases. Yet in today's media-driven culture, Hollywood has come paradoxically to represent that which it no longer seems to covet: The social realm of American life.

Newspaper no longer has the depth in readership to provide the daily social link in politics or culture for the majority of citizens. Network television, the one cultural link everyone shared in the '50s and '60s even with all its inadequacies, has been blown out of the water by cable and a host of other media. Event movies such as *Titanic* fill this void by happenstance, providing some material that is a shared common experience in American culture. But event movies are inevitably shallow. Hollywood is called upon to take on the role of Society—a role it often shuns—as it unashamedly declares to the media that it is simply a business. The television news media step into the social vacuum, trying to pump up events and experiences to capture public attention. Everything on the 11:00 o'clock news is advertised as "shocking" or "chilling" in a pathetic attempt to satiate the social hunger of the audience.

News on Hollywood exists simply to promote the next movie. While big publicity firms such as PMK control huge lists of stars, there is little substance to their publicity. AP's Bob Thomas comments that press agents are really "suppress agents": "Mostly they say, 'no' and try to keep their clients out of print. If they are in print, they might say the wrong thing, set off some controversy . . . So the only time you will ever get an interview with a star these days is when they have a movie to promote, or something specific to sell." Social obligation has ever so quietly and shamelessly given way to self-promotion and self-aggrandizement. Overall, the end of the studio system has left a social void in Hollywood. Hollywood is part of Society because it is an industry that eats publicity for lunch, an industry that captures the social imagination. But as long as it remains within itself as just an industry, it can only be a faux Society.

A few stars such as Candice Bergen, Tom Hanks and Anjelica Huston do make individual efforts here and there and find their way into top social circles or politics. Henry Winkler has long supported L.A.'s children and was active in establishing Children's Action Network, an entertainment industry organization that focuses on children's issues. Sharon Stone served as fundraising chair for AMFAR and raised $1 million for AIDS research. Although it was not well known before his successful run for Governor of California, Arnold Schwarzenegger is chairman of the Inner-City Games Foundation, taking a half-dozen big city mayors to East L.A. to watch minority children in athletic and academic competitions. He also donated $1 million for a state ballot initiative to provide an after school program for teenagers.

Actor-director Rob Reiner, best known for his "Meathead" role as Archie Bunker's son-in-law in the 1970s television show "All in the Family," was instrumental in convincing Steven Spielberg, Robin Williams, and his father, Carl Reiner, to contribute heavily to the 1998 California campaign for the passage of a fifty cent tax on tobacco. Reiner was also appointed to head a commission to provide health and education services to pre-schoolers in California. Media In Action, a group started by *New York Times* and *Vanity Fair* writer Cliff Rothman, boasts an array of Hollywood and Society supporters of funding for the arts. Noted activist and filmmaker Tim Robbins presided over a 2003 press conference to protest cuts in California arts funding and was cheered on by studio executives, movie stars and L.A. socialites alike.

And then there is Warren Beatty. Normally content to be on the sidelines doing political work behind the scenes,

Beatty held a Beverly Hills press conference in 1999 amid buzz that he would be a presidential candidate. In perhaps a symbolic first sign of the post-Clinton era, Beatty exhorted the Democratic Party to move to the left. Besides some 150 reporters from all over the world, others in the audience included Dustin Hoffman, Jack Nicholson, Michael Ovitz, Penny Marshall, Garry Shandling, Courtney Love, Hollywood publicist Pat Kingsley and Faye Dunaway. Beatty was introduced by producer Norman Lear and received a video message from Barbra Streisand. Clinton, though often the darling of Hollywood, left a thirst for more liberal politics among Hollywood activists.

But despite honest attempts to leverage the power of Hollywood for altruistic pursuits, faux society events persist. The 1998 Artists' Rights Foundation honored a deserving actor, Tom Cruise. The event brought out a big chunk of Hollywood including Michael Ovitz, Jodie Foster, and Dustin Hoffman. On television the function came off as a Society event. It was, but then again, not really. An industry event honoring one of its own is not a Society function because its aspirations are self-contained rather than serving as an outreach to benefit others. Although the honoring of artistic freedom is broader than many other Industry awards, supporting a children's charity, school, or hospital it is not. Caroline Ahmanson, perhaps the most prominent woman in L.A. Society and a major stockholder in Walt Disney Corp., states pointedly, "There's not enough thinking of the whole community. The new money, especially the entertainment money, has not been trained. The new money comes in so fast and in such big amounts, there isn't the sense of its coming from this city."

One Hollywooder is privately embarrassed at the current penchant for self-aggrandizement in the Business, where everyone honors everyone else and everyone has to attend an honoree's dinner because they just may need the favor back sometime. The whole process becomes a merry-go-round of prestige seeking. "Some people will do anything just to get their name on the doorknob of say their child's local private school, and be quick to point out that one of the Eisner children had attended the same school." This Hollywooder questions the authenticity of purpose of some fellow Hollywooders thrust into the giving role. Hollywood has become Society by default because it is so intertwined with publicity, but Hollywood's mandate is to be genuine Society, to fulfill the role cast upon it by circumstance. The Old Hollywood studio heads understood the relationship between Hollywood and Society, and perhaps social acceptance was ultimately the final goal of the early, mainly Jewish pioneers.

But the new Hollywood is like the new Coke—it is suspect. People still prefer the Coke Classic of Old Hollywood. The feeling is more than nostalgia. Watching "Entertainment Tonight" or "Access Hollywood" is like eating a candy bar when you're hungry: It leaves an empty feeling. It is not a coincidence that Richard Zanuck's home displays pictures of him with virtually every past U.S. President and with Princess Diana. Zanuck, son of noted Hollywood studio mogul Darryl F. Zanuck, grew up in the tradition of Hollywood royalty. The Oscars for *Driving Miss Daisy* and *Jaws* are there too, but alongside the photos showing a linkage with established wealth and position that may well be worth more in the social arena.

A Glimpse of the New Hollywood

If we must be critical of Hollywood for its spotty social track record and self-laudatory style, surely Hollywood's strengths are its work ethic and creativity. Reams have been written about the creative Hollywood, but Hollywood as a role model for work culture? We visited a top drawer studio executive, an Oscar-winning producer and a top agent to glimpse how Hollywooders carry on their work on a daily basis. The film fantasies about the Business in movies such as *The Player* and the endless glamour of Hollywood ensconced in the popular imagination give way to this real Hollywood, to the grueling schedules of Industry executives, to a world where glamour does indeed exist, but alongside a daily regimen of hard work.

*   *   *

Bob Bookman, relaxing in a chair in the sitting area of his office in the ultra-sleek, I.M. Pei-designed Creative Artists Agency building in Beverly Hills, surely represents the positive side of what Hollywood and Industry people have to offer modern culture. Entering the building that is seemingly without a name, one is greeted by a huge Lichtenstein on the front wall reigning over a large, half-dome reception area that allows a generous amount of Southern California sunshine to beam down from the high glass ceilings. The offices, laid out in circular fashion conforming to the dome-like structure, occupy the upper levels and are almost an afterthought to the spacious reception area that sets the tone for the entire building. Stairway access to the upper-tier offices on each side of the reception area is strictly guarded. One does not just walk into Hollywood these days. On the guest table in the middle of the lobby are copies of the current *Hollywood Reporter* and *Daily Variety*, the two major Hollywood trade publications. A secretary comes down to greet us, takes us up the elevator and then directly to the Bookman office. The door is quickly closed behind us.

Bookman wears a white shirt without the jacket. His tie is in place but not in any obligatory sense as one would expect in the IBM-cloned business world. The tie is there more out of choice, in a daring, colorfully mixed reddish hue, because Hollywood style is individual and self-expressive. In this world, you leave your dress-for-success business suits in the closet. Surprisingly, rather than talk about the Business, Bookman seems eager to discuss the L.A. upper crust generally. "The Presidency of the Fraternity of Friends [of the Music Center]," the smiling Bookman explains, "seems to be rotated each year from downtown to the Westside, meaning from gentile to Jew. I wanted to get involved with the city because of the upbringing of my family. My grandparents were founders of the Music Center, and my grandfather was also a founder of the Hillcrest Country Club." Bookman himself is a former Fraternity of Friends president and continues to be active in Music Center affairs, having recently had lunch with L.A. Opera board member Terry Stanfill. At one time he co-chaired an entertainment industry fundraising drive for the Music Center. The afternoon we see him, Bookman, one of Steven Spielberg's agents, has just returned from a meeting with Peter Schneider. Schneider was working under Disney's head of the motion picture division, Joe Roth, and later inherited Roth's position after Roth left to form his own company. Schneider has gone on to be a Broadway producer.

Bookman, after patiently explaining the evolving role of agents in the Industry, is eager to talk more about the L.A. social scene and Jewish involvement in the city: "I still don't think there is a real mix in the city socially [between Hollywood and Society and between Jewish and non-Jewish]. Of course, the motion picture industry is so insular. It is hard to make friends outside of the Business." Ironically, Hollywood's insular structure mimics the old closed-in structure of Society and even takes it one step further, since traditional Society in L.A., while known for exclusivity, is much more accessible today than is Hollywood.

Hollywood producers often have not one but two secretaries to wade through to set up an appointment. You hope you get put on the producer's "calling log" so that you will be assured a return call—from the secretary—to assure that you are there and ready to speak so that not a precious minute is lost. Then and only then do you get a producer on the phone. You may circumvent the process by getting a home phone number. Now you are in—sort of. You will still be referred back to the secretary at the producer's office to set up an appointment and work over details. And for all that fuss, consider yourself lucky. Anything is better than having to go through the publicity department and/or send a letter.

With the publicity department, your chances of making contact are very slim. With a letter the chance for an interview is slightly better, but when you call back to follow up, you hope the response is not "It is on the top of his/her desk." This usually means "No," although the word "No" is almost never used. But the beauty of Hollywood is that you're never really out since any "No" can and has turned into a "Yes" later on. Yet for an Industry that lives on publicity, you get the sneaking suspicion, poking around Hollywood, that even the major players are incredibly insecure, usually dodging publicity not strictly tied to their latest movie. Now contrast calling Hollywood—agents, managers, producers, studio executives and the like—with calling someone at the very top of L.A. Society, Caroline Ahmanson. With Mrs. Ahmanson you get the social secretary but one who, although understandably protective, actually is active in promoting the woman she works for, a lady who in fact really doesn't need the promotion at all.

Relaxing on the sofa in his office, Bookman continues without pause, speaking animatedly on L.A. Society. "In the past, the WASP upper class hardly extended open arms to Jews. It is true that Dorothy Chandler went after and got Jewish involvement in the Music Center. But what is overlooked is that that involvement, at the time, didn't mean mixing socially." Indeed the *L.A. Times* Society page in the early 1960s hardly carried pictures of Jews, and few of the original founders of the Music Center were Jewish. One prominent Jewish physician who knew Mrs. Chandler well enough to call her "Buff" privately balked when invited to her Hancock Park home for one of the many fundraising dinners that she initiated to get the project built. The physician called up Mrs. Chandler about the guest list and quickly surmised that the dinner would be a largely Jewish grouping. He politely declined the invitation, pointing out that if Jewish money were to be mixed with all the other money, then too should the donors mix socially. Having made his point, the physician did later contribute to the Music Center.

Traditional L.A. Society has historically not held Hollywood, Jewish or otherwise, in high esteem. Unlike today's top players, few early Hollywood leaders had college educations. Bookman remarks that as late as the 1970s, when Dennis Stanfill, a Rhodes scholar, left the *L.A. Times* to head 20th Century Fox, many in the traditional upper class wondered, "What is he doing there?" While today Hollywood money is sought everywhere in the city, many Society institutions still remain closed in subtle ways. "Just try to get into the Bel-Air Bay Club," Bookman remarks pointedly. "There is a long waiting list."

Turning next to Hollywood, as if moving from appetizer to entrée, Bookman explains how the dissolution of the contract system opened up the agenting world. More Hollywood talk: Bookman boasts how CAA can cast a movie with script, stars and director all in-house. He teases about the self-promotion of his fellow Hollywooders, and refuses an exclusive on his Hancock Park home (once owned by Howard Hughes, who lived there with Katharine Hepburn) for the book ("I want privacy for my son."). At the same time, he proudly recounts CAA's charitable efforts and, as if chiding himself, states that "I am only one of Spielberg's agents. He will probably get mad if I state that I am his only agent." Still smiling, and careful not to mention his contribution of $100,000 for Disney Hall, this affable young Hollywood executive has his secretary escort us down to the first floor as he looks over his messages from the actors and directors he represents, lining them up for that one script that breaks through and becomes a motion picture ten months later.

*   *   *

It is hard to classify Alan Ladd, Jr. as either new or Old Hollywood. For the son of '40s and '50s Paramount star Alan Ladd and producer of films spanning over four decades, such a dichotomy is meaningless. Ladd, having grown up through studio system days, continues his flourishing career at the center of the various power structures that make up the new Hollywood and today's filmmaking. Sitting in the spacious office of his Ladd Co. on the Paramount lot, Ladd is simply beaming at the script sent to his home over the weekend by Paramount studio chiefs Sherry Lansing and John Goldwyn. "They told me that I just had to read it." Ladd just a few years earlier won an Academy Award for producing *Braveheart*, and has several projects in the fire as usual, working his 9 to 8 shift at the office. That leaves Saturdays at home for script reading. When one speaks of Hollywood families, the Ladd family invariably comes to mind. Alan Ladd, Jr.'s mother was his father's agent before the two married. His brother, David Ladd, was a child actor and is a producer. David Ladd's former wife is actress Cheryl Ladd and their daughter, Jordan, is also an actress. Alan Ladd, Jr. has four daughters, two of whom are in the Business—one is a producer like her father, the other a studio accountant.

The Ladd family history was on our minds as we drove along adjacent to the Paramount lot, gazing out at the Hollywood sign in the distance. Thinking of the Hollywood sign and what it symbolizes, and marveling at the huge compound that is the Paramount studio, one cannot help but be mesmerized with the thought that less than a century ago, sign, studio and the Industry which captures the world's imagination did not exist. The Hollywood sign and the sprawling Paramount lot that spans several city blocks sprouted almost out of nowhere. Both are now part of the world's greatest metropolis that is the L.A. basin.

Paramount has two major gates on Melrose in Hollywood, and you will not be cheated entering either one. When you pass through the massive wrought-iron gates under the classic California Spanish stucco arch, you step into the magic world of Hollywood where everyone looks at you inquisitively as you walk by. And why not? All seems possible in this Hollywood. But the Hollywood dream world is full of real people. The lot is home to the actors, set designers, cooks, technicians, cameramen, producers, make-up artists, directors, delivery people, security people and the like who mix in a fabulous blend of people and cars and bicycles which together meander through the Spanish-style architecture of the studio that promises genuinely, without fingers crossed, that you can be nowhere else in the world except Southern California. The pace of the studio seems surprisingly relaxed considering the frenetic reputation of Hollywood.

We walk by the Roddenbury building dear to the (Star) Trekkies, pass the Marx brothers building and the myriad of sound stages to the Lucille Ball courtyard that leads to the Maurice Chevalier building where the Ladd Co. is located. Paramount Studios is a place with a sense of its own history, as the names of other buildings—Cooper, Crosby, DeMille, Valentino and Zukor—make clear. The foyer of the Ladd Co. office is highlighted by posters of some of the notable movies that Alan Ladd, Jr. either produced himself or authorized to be produced when heading MGM/UA or 20th Century Fox. Again, a surprise as to the relaxed atmosphere: No one is sitting at the desk in the foyer. You are quickly greeted by one of the assistants, however, and offered something to drink as you marvel at the range of movie posters on display: *Star Wars, Blade Runner, The Right Stuff, Julia, Thelma and Louise, The Turning Point* and *Chariots of Fire.* You gobble up the famous names of the actors and directors as you peruse the walls and then stop by the Oscar-winning *Chariots of Fire*, which gives you an eerie feeling as you notice the name of its producer, Dodi Al-Fayed, who died in the car crash with Princess Diana.

Ladd is an L.A. boy, having grown up in Holmby Hills when he wasn't on the studio lot playing games, pretending to be a cowboy on a Paramount set while his father was making one of his classic westerns. Ladd is an Industry child and grew up with other Hollywood children: "Richard Zanuck has been my best friend for over forty years. All of my friends work in the business." He is what Lee Minnelli would call "Hollywood Hollywood." "I never felt part of the Society world," says Ladd. Still, the modest

Ladd hosted a fundraiser at his home for the children's charity I Love Children in June 2000 that raised $500,000. But most of Ladd's adult life has been devoted to making pictures—over 200 of them. He is a movie aficionado par excellence. And this unpretentious man offers another worthy face of a Hollywood that rarely gets the headlines, explaining that he would never make a picture that was gory or showed children in danger. But the former studio executive is political enough not to chastise those who do make such films.

Ladd reminisces about his youth—of driving around a much safer L.A. with the top down. "My father was a quiet man and did not really enjoy the Hollywood parties. But in those days, if the studio wanted you to go, you had to go. My mother was more outgoing." "Paramount then was one big family. I knew everyone on the lot: The technicians, the transportation people—everyone. They even used to work regularly on Saturdays." The quiet-like-his-father and respectful-beyond-his-position Ladd started out as an agent. "I got lucky in those early years. I had Redford." Ladd went to a public high school, University High, in Santa Monica, and Robert Redford was one of his classmates. He moved to London in the 1960s to produce movies: "I often had several pictures in production at one time and with actors like Brando, Burton, Taylor and Caine, and I would frantically move around the city checking on each one." A move back to L.A. and a stint with 20th Century Fox led to a new role as President of Fox at a time when a little movie called *Star Wars* was released. "It is my most significant accomplishment besides the Oscars for *Braveheart* and *Chariots of Fire*. Here is a movie that is still number two to *Titanic* in overall box office proceeds. But more than that, I get a kick out of watching a new generation of youth getting fascinated by the film. It is the type of movie where people still remember where they saw it twenty years ago." Ladd went on to head MGM/UA, and his Ladd Co. completed a six-year contract with Paramount. Ladd then left the Paramount lot and set up his own office.

Politely asking the authors if he may light a cigarette in his own office, Ladd, dressed simply in black jeans and a light blue shirt, relaxes and talks about the Business he thoroughly enjoys and of which he has so long been a part. "I even go watch the movies that have bombed—you want to see what went wrong so you don't make the same mistake. I can never put a tedious script down; some people can, but I always wonder if there is something at the end that may be worthwhile. My younger daughter helps me to stay current. When I go home, she will have on a youth-oriented television show, something that I would never watch, and I watch it with her and get her reactions." "I recently had an idea for a movie and heard that Robert Evans was also thinking about a film along the same lines. So I called him up and said, 'Bob, wouldn't it be fun to do it together . . .' And Harrison Ford just called me about another script . . ." This son of Hollywood is off again as we leave his office, on his way to the next film that just may be another blockbuster.

*　　*　　*

Authors' Note: Thomas Schumacher was head of animation at Disney from 1999-2003.

The Disney name is one of the few things revered in irreverent L.A. Hollywood happened before Walt Disney started producing animated films, but it is hard to imagine Hollywood today without Disney productions. As we drove onto the Disney lot and looked up at the center tower complete with a picture of Mickey Mouse, we thought of some of the animated films in Disney's past such as *Fantasia* and *Snow White*, and what the animation department means to the company. Box office proceeds from animated films are only part of the picture; animation drives the entire company, from Disney products to theme parks to the most precious of commodities: The Disney image.

The animation building, topped by a sorcerer's hat modeled after the one Mickey Mouse wears in *The*

Sorcerer's Apprentice, attests to the continuing legacy of Disney animation. We pass posters for *Mulan, A Bug's Life* and *Toy Story*. The reception area, complete with Mickey Mouse logos, sits amidst an elongated, slightly slanted cylindrical dome reaching some forty feet in the air, ascending to the heavens and imparting a space-age feel. Workers pass us to and fro in a relaxed atmosphere. There isn't a man in the building with a tie save one of the authors. On the second floor, a lively game of ping-pong is in progress.

We are about to greet the head of animation, Thomas Schumacher. We ascend to the third floor—the brain center and development floor for Disney animation—to meet him. The modernistic floor's open warehouse effect, complete with art deco touches and faux skin furniture, as well as the space-age lobby below obscure the fact that we are in a major profit center of a major corporation. Roy E. Disney, Walt Disney's nephew, devoted much of his time to animation. Jeffrey Katzenberg's 2%-of-the-profits clause that produced his $100 million-plus settlement with Disney years after his departure from the company was largely attributed to animation dollars. Schumacher, presiding over such successes as *Lion King, Tarzan*, and *Toy Story*, would be viewed as a *wunderkind* approaching the acclaim of a Steven Spielberg as a producer/executive in any area of Hollywood other than animation. But animation is mistakenly seen by the viewing public as somewhere on the sidelines of the Industry, and does not take on the patina of glamour. Still, animation dollars are real, and more and more actors such as Tom Hanks and Tim Allen, who do voice-overs in the *Toy Story* features, want in on the animation gravy train. At least *Première* magazine has taken notice, as Schumacher, producer of two of the top ten 1999 movies (*Toy Story 2* and *Tarzan*), made their elusive and exclusive power list two years running.

Schumacher greets us sans tie and eagerly talks about L.A. and New York culture in his spacious office done in soft beige and brown with padded upholstered walls. "I need soft colors and tranquility in my office since my schedule is so hectic and I am always dealing in the bright visuals of animation," he explains, pointing out the total absence of animation in his office. Schumacher is just back from New York, where the musical *Lion King* had a successful run on Broadway, and had just premiered *Toy Story 2* at the El Capitan theater in Hollywood. "It is a mistake to compare L.A. and New York—they have two different power bases. In New York, if you are on certain boards you have power and if you contribute to an institution like Lincoln Center. In L.A., being on a board is somewhat meaningless, especially for Hollywood people whose names look good on the board but who generally are not very efficient in bringing in money for the institution. I mean people start up their own charities in L.A.; we don't have definite charities where people feel that this is the right one, whereas in New York [you donate] to be a part of a club." Schumacher adds, "The last great wave of social activity in L.A. was at the time of the 1984 Olympics when MOCA was created and Robert J. Fitzpatrick left his post at Cal Arts to run the Olympic Arts Festival. L.A. Society people were hosting parties around the city for all of the artists. The lack of cohesiveness in L.A. Society today is why the Disney Hall has taken so long to be built."

Schumacher, perhaps all of 40, a rare fourth-generation Californian and a UCLA graduate who has lived both in Los Angeles and San Francisco, continues to talk freely about L.A. Society: "Besides, in Hollywood, if you are working, you just don't have time for the social part. The geography of the city—of being so spread out—prevents a varied social life. My own social life is based in Pasadena. The other night Matthew [Matthew White, a noted interior designer] and I held a dinner party. Terry and Dennis Stanfill, [artist] Glenn Keanne and [CAA agent] Brian Siberell attended. But while there are obvious Hollywood connections there, I really did not meet any of the guests while working in Hollywood. I met Terry Stanfill because we both travel so much to Italy. Occasionally I get out elsewhere in L.A. I just came from a dinner party at the home of Sting where I met Lili Zanuck. I work in Hollywood but I wouldn't necessarily know her."

Schumacher continues discussing the time he spent in New York overseeing Disney's Broadway production of *Lion King*: "In New York, I can meet with someone for drinks and then someone else for dinner because it is so compact. I mean I ran into Caroline Ahmanson, the venerable Los Angeles matron, in New York at a production of *Lion King*. I do see her from time to time in L.A. because she is on the Disney Board, but I often see my L.A. friends more in New York than in Los Angeles. Of course, I get invited to affairs of New York Society as the producer of *Lion King* because the show is hot and people want access. But I observed at a restaurant in New York recently that everyone ignored Mikhail Baryshnikov and Steve Martin to talk to Robert Fuller, the producer of *Death of a Salesman*. Movie people walking down the street with me in New York hardly get noticed. Now perhaps when I was walking with Elton John—then New Yorkers paid some attention."

As we ask Schumacher to recount a typical workday out of his 6-day-a-week, 11-hour-per-day schedule, we marvel that this Disney executive has given us close to an hour of his time. "Well, we have theatrical productions going on today in Chicago, New York, London, Berlin and Tokyo—so I do a lot of flying back and forth. I was on the phone today from 8 to 9. I screened a cut of a movie with Pixar's John Lassiter [Disney has a contract with Pixar to produce animated movies] for two hours, taking extensive notes. I ask myself, does this scene work, is the voice-over right. Then I spent another hour with Lassiter [creator of *Toy Story*]. I had half a sandwich, returned phone calls, read a script, reviewed twenty minutes of another movie in development and talked to a storyboard artist. I had an interview with an *L.A. Times* reporter and just heard a pitch for another movie. It is now 4:30 and I have another meeting to go to, a script to read tonight and a plane to Chicago in the morning." When Schumacher returned the call of one of the authors on a Sunday from New York he couldn't immediately set a date to meet. "You have to call my office; they set up my schedule. I don't know what I'm even doing next week."

Before leaving, we ask Schumacher to name his most cherished achievements. "Before coming to Disney, it had to be working as associate director of the Los Angeles Festival that grew out of the Olympic Arts Festival held during the 1984 Olympic games in Los Angeles. Southern Californians were exposed to so many varied art forms in that heady time. I am still on the Education Council of the Music Center where I worked." Schumacher produced a number of plays for the Music Center's Mark Taper Forum. Also in his pre-Disney days, Schumacher brought *Cirque du Soleil* to the U.S. from Canada in spite of warnings that the show wouldn't fly here. "At Disney, it would have to be getting *Lion King* on Broadway. I had actually started out as a producer of the movie. Later, Eisner came to me and kept insisting that it could make a successful play. I was doubtful at first. Then I brought in producer Julie Taymor and later Elton John, and it began to happen." Schumacher is already off to his next meeting.

CHAPTER EIGHT

The L.A. Upper Crust Mosaic

Social Fault Lines at the Top

Exclusivity is a peculiar term in the new millennium, in the midst of a 300-year wave of democracy worldwide. In L.A., you cannot afford to be too exclusive either geographically or socially, because in the city that harbors Hollywood, where glitz and glamour twinkle about the edges, you run the risk of excluding yourself from the game of honor. Honor accrues from the right kind of publicity, and publicity is the triumphant modern social phenomenon. The L.A. upper crust is exclusive but not in the New York upper class sense of exclusivity. Geographically, L.A.'s wealthy enclaves are surprisingly open and increasingly spread out across the basin. A retreat such as the East Coast's Martha's Vineyard would be impossible to imagine in California. So would any obligatory weekend getaway such as the Hamptons. Southern California is too diverse, and people are too comfortable in their homes to trek any one way for pleasure. The East Coast enclaves are a continuation of aristocratic petulance. Socially, L.A. exclusivity is exclusivity with a caveat: If you take yourself too seriously you risk appearing foolish. Cutting edge and over the edge run deceptively down what appears to be the same path, but perceiving the difference determines whether you're hot or you're not on the L.A. social scene.

The top social circles in L.A. are more complicated than in any other city in the world because of the presence of Hollywood. The usual sources of wealth found in many cities are present—the Dohenys (oil), the Ahmansons and Tapers (banking), the Jorgensens (steel), and the Chandlers (publishing)—but Hollywood is the wild card that makes the L.A. upper crust unique. The Music Center's Blue Ribbon is the key social grouping and shows who's who among the social set in Los Angeles. Most members of the much smaller and more private Colleagues group also belong to the Blue Ribbon.

Many Blue Ribbon women also volunteer elsewhere, such as with the L.A. County Art Museum's Costume Council, which puts on a monthly program related to fashion and raises money for the Museum's costume collection. Some take direct action, such as Iris Cantor, who donated one million dollars in 2003 to the L.A. County Museum of Art for an exhibit through a family foundation. Besides holding up the banner in the art world, society women may do charitable work for organizations such as St. John's Hospital in Santa Monica, once heavily supported by actress Irene Dunne and friends; the Cedars Sinai Medical Center; the City of Hope; for USC or UCLA; for the Jules Stein Eye Institute, founded by Doris and Jules Stein; for various children's groups or for AIDS or other medical research. Pasadena's Huntington Library and Norton Simon Museum number among the few institutions that bring Westsiders across town for philanthropic work.

But the Blue Ribbon, the ultimate social group for women in Los Angeles, is still unsure of its role. Some thirty-five years after its inception, the group seems unable to decide whether to be a private "Society" club, or something more—a full-fledged community organization with social goals related to the Music Center and its outreach programs. The stigma of Society is that it is undemocratic—the reason L.A. Times coverage of the top social circles has waned since the retirement of the much-loved Jody Jacobs in 1986. The Blue Ribbon faces another conundrum as well. The group surpasses by far the other notable women's group in L.A., the Colleagues, in terms of social importance. Yet the Colleagues is a more exclusive group and is based almost entirely on the Westside. The Colleagues could be likened to a sorority except that the group raises several hundred thousand dollars a year for children's causes, including the prevention of child abuse, by selling the used designer gowns and housewares of L.A.'s wealthiest women. The work takes place in a boutique at the trendy Bergamot Station in Santa Monica, where the members staff the store themselves.

The first Colleagues benefit, dubbed "A Ribbon Party" and led by group founder Lucy Toberman, took place in 1951, with stars such as Irene Dunne, Lana Turner and Ava Gardner modeling. More recently the Colleagues teamed up with Saks Fifth Avenue Beverly Hills to salute former First Lady Betty Ford at a luncheon and presentation of an Adolfo collection. It has been said that there's not a Colleague who doesn't own an Adolfo.

The Colleagues can also bring out Republican firepower. Nancy Reagan served as honorary chair for the 1998 luncheon culminating the season's fundraising efforts. Then California Governor Pete Wilson was in attendance. The Reagan Kitchen Cabinet wives are a special grouping within the Colleagues: Jean French Smith, Betsy Bloomingdale and Marion Jorgensen all attended the luncheon. One L.A. insider commented that when you have a former First Lady, your group automatically garners considerable prestige. Yet others dismiss the group as a clique and passé.

But the Colleagues definitely touches a bit of Hollywood, with Rosemary Stack, Mary Ann Mobley, Lee Minnelli, and Joan Collins attending the 1998 Bill Blass fashion show. Ricardo Montalban and Gary Collins were on hand to show support, and key Blue Ribbon members Joni Smith and Joan Hotchkis participated as well. In the L.A. upper crust, the few who cross over easily from one grouping to another—from the art world into traditional enclaves or from Hollywood into established circles and vice versa—are ultimately the top players.

Paradoxically, the super-exclusive Colleagues, limited to a membership of sixty-five, does at least publish a private directory of members, unlike the Blue Ribbon. Past directories reflect undeniable social power. Mrs. Clark Gable was an earlier president, and Mrs. Arnold Kirkeby, whose husband once owned the Beverly Wilshire Hotel, was a member. One of the Kirkeby mansions served as the home of the Beverly Hillbillies of television fame. Some in top circles say that the Colleagues see themselves as holding up the face of traditional Society. Others complain that the group takes itself too seriously. But filling the role of Society in L.A. requires greater accessibility and a broader-based focus than the Colleagues alone can provide. When Ronald Reagan became governor of California and then President, there was some need for this social grouping to close ranks for privacy and security. But the insularity that has resulted from the closeness of many key Colleagues members to a President has retarded the full flowering of the L.A. upper crust as a more cohesive group.

The famous debutante balls of upper class lore, another traditionally exclusive venue, have dwindled in the democratic age. In Los Angeles, the Las Madrinas debutantes began coming out in the 1930s as parents donated to Children's Hospital for the right to launch their daughters into the social realm. The ball still exists, but its social consequence is almost unnoticed. Dressed comfortably in a light beige pantsuit and sporting a little summer sun in her bright Pasadena home, Alyce Williamson, herself presented at a Las Madrinas ball in the 1940s, remarks some fifty years later, "The debutante ball has declined because you don't want to be exclusive now." But Mrs. Williamson quickly notes that while the old-style exclusivity is an affront to the democratic purpose, doing away with Society as such represents a loss: "There is nothing more uplifting than getting together with others and helping the community." As if to accentuate her point, Mrs. Williamson is preparing to host a dinner at her Pasadena home for the trustees of the Art Center College of Design, to which her family has donated one million dollars. She carefully oversees flowering trees being put in place and tables set up outside on the lawn leading to the pool and tennis court and graced by a life-size statue of a race horse. She previously hosted a costume dance for the Center where the art students themselves dressed up and participated in a contest for best costume, the winners being four students who came jointly as a chair.

But the question remains: What is it that appropriately fills the social realm of honor? Mrs. Williamson herself wouldn't expect the *L.A. Times* to cover her marriage to Warren Williamson, a member of the Chandler family that long had controlled the paper, today as the paper did decades ago with a full page spread, photos and hoopla. One wonders whether the last great Society editor of the *L.A. Times*, Jody Jacobs, would even get hired to cover the L.A. social scene were she to step out of retirement and return to L.A. Has the coming of the democratic age meant the dissolution of social calling, of the honor and glory that is part of the human fabric?

There are many who say simply that there is no L.A. Society, but rather a moneyed upper class based not on lineage but on wealth and accomplishment. On the surface this appears partially true. Producer Lili Zanuck remarks that in L.A. there is no real social calendar. David Brown, who co-produces with Zanuck's husband Richard, lives in New York and has yearly events he must attend with his wife, Helen Gurley Brown of Cosmopolitan fame. Mrs. Zanuck, on the other hand, could not follow a social calendar even if there were one. Echoing the predicament of most producers, directors and stars, Zanuck says she does not know where she will be six months or even six weeks from now. She might well be on location, since much filming occurs outside the L.A. area. Another insider who crosses over from Hollywood to more established social circles and back says that because there are few regular, must-attend affairs in L.A., there is no occasion where one can do a tally, so to speak, to see just who the major players are and determine a pecking order. But there is an order or perhaps multiple orders, and people generally know who is "way up there," in one socialite's words.

Society photographer Alan Berliner remarks that by definition, Society people are the social individuals in the city who go out all the time. You can have a lot of money, but if you stay home in obscurity, you have chosen to remain outside of Society. There are always exceptions such as the Doheny family, which has been in L.A. for generations but whose members generally shy away from publicity. The Dohenys are nonetheless very well known in the ranks of L.A.'s top circles.

Since Hollywood tends to close in on its own ranks, preferring its own social gatherings centered around movie premières, choice restaurants and the private screening of movies in homes, the L.A. social scene is quite fragmented even though institutions such as the Music Center have grown and developed over thirty years. Terry Stanfill, one of the few who truly crosses over from traditional circles to Hollywood and back, laments privately that the Music Center has not spawned the hoped-for strong city core. Perhaps the Disney Hall will.

The authors themselves have experienced the social fragmentation of L.A.'s top social groups firsthand, being invited and then uninvited to a Blue Ribbon function. Many a prominent player has explained that Mrs. Chandler, née Buffum of the Buffum's retail family and called "Buff" by her friends, held all the top groupings together with an iron will, much respect, and when all else failed, with the power of the family-controlled *L. A. Times* in hand. One Blue Ribbon member remembers feeling appropriately intimidated upon being called into Mrs. Chandler's office and given the once-over when she wished to resign her Blue Ribbon membership. And Mrs. Chandler's ability to maintain cohesion extended into upper echelons far beyond the Blue Ribbon. No comparable force exists in the L.A. upper crust today.

Party Animals: Who's In and Who's Not

Two prominent families had both invited the Ricardo Montalbans to separate parties on the same night. The Montalbans made it to one party that evening without a problem, since they had heard that the other one had been cancelled. Not so. Apparently the hostess of the party they attended had called the Montalbans to graciously let them know that the rival party would not take place, thereby ensuring their prime arrival for **her** party. The "cancelled" party stumbled on without the Montalbans, hardly a story from Fantasy Island but perhaps a new version of Star Wars: Party Wars. Needless to say, the two party hostesses no longer acknowledge each other.

L.A. plays in a serious way. No player is more serious than Candy Spelling, wife of television producer Aaron Spelling. Mrs. Spelling's jewels for big events take second place only to those of Barbara Davis. It seems Candy leaves home sans jewels, which travel to the party in a Brinks security truck. She and the truck arrive simultaneously, and she puts the jewels on before entering the party. After the jewels play their glittery part for the evening, they are whisked back to the vault by Brinks.

More Party Wars stories. Former *L.A. Times* Society editor Jody Jacobs recalls how one Colleagues member was hit in the face with a cream pie thrown by her son's disgruntled friend as she entered the grand Beverly Wilshire ballroom for an event. On another occasion a socialite invited Jacobs to a party on an evening the columnist already had an engagement booked. The socialite kept pestering Jacobs, saying that she was being specially invited and simply must attend. When the lady finally understood from the ultra-polite Jacobs that she would not be able to attend, she burst out: "Well, can you [*The Times*] send someone else?" Jacobs' husband, author Barney Leason, remembers how his wife could be spotted at events by the line of people near her wishing to make their presence known and hopefully noted in the *Times* write-up. A little publicity, just a tidbit in the Society column, never hurts.

Perhaps only in L.A. are parties important enough to paint signs, call the press, get out the bullhorns, and organize the troops for a protest. That's just what happened at a party thrown to mark the 1998 reopening of Italian jeweler Bulgari's Rodeo Drive shop. The Benedict Canyon estate in the hills above Beverly Hills where the Bulgari party took place had also been used for several film shoots, including scenes from *Indecent Proposal*. Sheryl Crow had performed a concert in the backyard, and on one occasion rap music blasted away at a record label function. The chagrined neighbors took notice of a continual stream of parties and noise at the mansion and mounted a protest at the Bulgari affair. The steadfast and not-too-polite protesters shouted at the elegantly dressed guests in limos entering the estate's gates. The scene prompted the owner of the home, Mark Slotkin, to storm outside, challenging the protesters and grabbing a sign from one of them. Slotkin said he grabbed the sign in self-defense from the woman, who had brandished it over his head. For his trouble Slotkin was taken away from his multimillion-dollar home in handcuffs as the event unfolded inside, and booked on suspicion of misdemeanor battery.

Ever defiant of the protesters, Slotkin exclaimed, "When you have a house like this, you have a social obligation." He concluded, "This is an outrageous violation of our personal property. These people are just jealous. They're not my neighbors . . . they live 1,500 feet away." Slotkin built his 20,000 square-foot chateau in 1991 on a lot once owned by Elton John. Despite the unexpected scene, the party proved successful as the tennis court was transformed into a Roman garden, and each of the 240 guests was treated to a personal portrait by celebrity photographer Firooz Zahedi. The event raised a "generous" amount of money for the Starbright Foundation, which helps ill children. All's well that ends well. Or, maybe not. The Slotkin home, all 20,000 square feet of it, went on the market a few years later after going into foreclosure. Originally listed at $14 million, it was reduced to $8.9 million. There was no comment from the neighbors.

Tinseltown parties can get just as hairy. Since Hollywood is a closed set of business relationships that evolve into personal ties, one cannot just walk into the Hollywood party scene. People receive invites to A-list parties based on what they can do for each other or each other's clients in the business of Hollywood. Career and money talk. So if a Hollywood couple divorces, who comes to the party? Super agent Ed Limato sends his Oscar party invite to an A-list film director, but unwittingly mails it to the Brentwood home of the director's estranged wife, who also works in the Business as a producer. Though the couple is getting a divorce, she accepts the invitation. And why not? An assistant at Limato's office calls, pointedly asking her if she will be attending with her husband, to which she answers "No." Limato's office calls back later asking her *not to come*. Life can be cold in the Hollywood spotlight, and something as supposedly innocuous as a party can measure one's social position. Hollywood runs 24 hours a day: Tinseltown has no down time.

So who are the top L.A. party givers? It depends on the era and whom you ask. Jody Jacobs recalls Dolly Green, whose father developed Bel-Air, and Virginia Robinson as great hostesses. In Old Hollywood Doris Stein would be at the top of the list. Lee Minnelli, a party queen in her own right, is sure she knows who are the top, top party givers of today and yesterday. Minnelli rattles off in no particular order nor specific time period: Frances Bergen, mother of Candice; Henry and Ginny Mancini; Dana Broccoli, widow of Cubby Broccoli, who owns the rights to the James Bond films; Betsy Bloomingdale and Marvin and Barbara Davis. But the New Hollywood to some extent would disagree. That's in part what makes the L.A. upper crust unique—its power groupings can be so disparate and so diverse.

And what about super crossover couple Terry and Dennis Stanfill, who tend to be more private these days socially? The couple was highlighted in an exclusive brochure put out by the Beverly Wilshire Hotel in the early '80s when Dennis Stanfill headed 20th Century Fox. Who else appeared in the brochure? Only Prince Rainier III of Monaco, Cary Grant, John Wayne, Mr. and Mrs. Jimmy Stewart, Kirk Douglas, Gregory Peck, Mr. and Mrs. Billy Wilder, Truman Capote, and L.A. business moguls Ed

Carter, Dr. Franklin Murphy and Harry Volk. In those days Terry threw parties for the Blue Ribbon on the studio lot of Fox and studio parties at the Los Angeles County Museum of Art. She organized a party for Plácido Domingo and the whole opera cast after the debut of the L.A. Opera, and a super party for Princess Grace and Prince Albert at her home in Pasadena. While the Stanfills go mainly to small house parties or to events at the Music Center these days, their social standing remains impeccable. The couple attended the 1998 Music Center tribute to Caroline Ahmanson. And unofficially, when you call someone in the L.A. upper crust, the Stanfill name carries weight. One constant is present in all this partying and jockeying for social standing. If you hold a key position, the most obvious being the head of a studio, your party will be a happening. Position, not just wealth, is coveted in L.A. A prominent name will get you, well, a train ticket to New York.

Most top party giving today ties in with a charity and takes place at a major venue. Lilly Tartikoff's 1997 Fire and Ice Ball for cancer research unfolded in a tent the size of a football field above a makeshift lagoon in such a way that guests actually felt they were walking on water. Isaac Mizrahi's Spring Collection was unveiled by models gliding down a runway literally on water. Half the Hollywood top brass attended, including Steve Tisch, Ron Meyer, Sherry Lansing, Frank Biondi, and stars Anjelica Huston, Sidney Poitier, Jaclyn Smith, Tom Hanks and Rita Wilson. Caroline Ahmanson exclaimed, "It's like something you'd see in an old Hollywood musical." Then there are the political events, usually fundraisers and usually for Democrats. Former Clinton backers David Geffen, Ron Burkle, and contemporary art super collectors Marc and Jane Nathanson have all hosted parties which brought in big bucks for Clinton and the Democrats. Whether for a charity, for a political cause, or just for having fun, these party spectacles do really count. They show who's in and who's not. Author Barney Leason observes that the top party givers usually change every ten years—if they last that long. And in L.A. if you last for more than just a scene or two, you are for real in a town where the social reality changes almost faster than the flash of a camera.

New Faces on the Westside

Few cities are as culturally diverse as L.A., and few have as significant a Jewish grouping. It is well known that Jews were instrumental in the formation of Hollywood studios. Paramount's Adolf Zukor, Carl Laemmle of Universal, the Warner brothers, Louis B. Mayer of MGM, Fox's William Fox and Columbia's Harry Cohn were the early pioneers. But before 1950 Hollywood Jews and the traditional L.A. upper class existed almost in separate realms. After 1960 Jews began playing a major role in the Music Center and in the L.A. art scene, both as collectors and as supporters of museums. Since then Jews have done more crossing over between Hollywood and the more traditional crowds than any other grouping. MOCA board member Jane Nathanson remarks, "There is more cross-mingling [between Jews, Anglos and others] here in L.A. than anywhere else." Lenore Greenberg confirms that those Jews who mix "are very much accepted in the heart of things."

In addition to the longstanding Jewish grouping, there is a budding Asian element on today's Westside, not surprising considering the amount of investment that has come in from Pacific Rim nations. And although wealthy Arabs have garnered media attention in Beverly Hills, from the infamous statues with highlighted genitalia on Saudi Sheik Mohammed al-Fassi's estate facing Sunset Blvd. (the home was eventually burned to the ground), to the Sultan of Brunei's purchase and lavish renovation of the landmark Beverly Hills Hotel, many insiders consider recently arrived Arabs to be on the fringe of the L.A. upper crust. No matter how vast their fortunes, cultural differences remain. Iranians, ethnically Persian or Jewish rather than Arab, are quite a different matter, having made an impression selling haute products from couture to furniture to the wealthiest Angelenos. The influx of Iranian wealth to the Westside during the 1970s and '80s now has established roots. One Beverly Hills resident remarks, "The Iranians will follow the same pattern that the mainstream Jewish community followed. The Jews' first interest was in education, and their first political impact was felt on the schools and through the Board of Education... inevitably, there will be an Iranian on the (Beverly Hills) city council."

Historically, the L.A. upper crust was, along with the American upper class generally, WASP. Although there is now a vital Jewish grouping, the quintessential multicultural city still has top social circles that are almost exclusively white. Exceptions do exist: African-American Hollywooders Quincy Jones, Denzel Washington, Eddie Murphy and Will Smith are major players in the Business. Longtime star Sidney Poitier is often spotted at Society events. Sherry Belafonte and Whitney Houston have attended the Carousel of Hope Ball. Denzel Washington focuses on the city's youth, giving one million dollars to the Boys and Girls Club. The music industry, whether white or black, has always been slightly adjacent to high society. So too major sports figures who command a world apart.

One sports personality, former L.A. Lakers star Magic Johnson, has branched out and become a major wheeler-dealer around town. He had a talk show and made a deal with 20th Century Fox to produce films. A partial owner of the Lakers basketball team, Johnson cut a deal for a 100 million dollar shopping center in an area of Los Angeles in need of commercial development. Johnson is one who is putting his money back into the black community, having already built his Magic Johnson Theaters and Starbucks there. Johnson notes, "The people in our community haven't had a place to hang out. They shouldn't have to drive 20 to 30 minutes to get a salad and a cup of coffee." Johnson also served as the event chair with Elizabeth Taylor and Carrie Fisher in Passport 99, a fashion show in Santa Monica that featured hip clothing lines and attracted the broad middle class with many modestly priced seats. The "fashion for compassion" show is an annual event, with proceeds benefiting AIDS groups. The Johnson "magic" continues as his Magic Johnson Foundation helped to fund a computer center in inner city South Los Angeles in 2001.

Society magazine *Beverly Hills 90212*, once described by one insider as the magazine some of the richest women in L.A. were trying to outdo one another to get into, is run by a black woman, LaVetta Forbes ("Call me LaVetta.") LaVetta, a dress designer whose clothes found their way into stores such as Fred Hayman on Rodeo Drive and Bendels in New York, felt her calling was in writing. Since no one would hire her as a writer, she mortgaged her home to start a Society magazine in 1990. Her first issue featured Mr. Blackwell on the cover and showed wealthy women at charity events and parties. LaVetta's focus is ladies who can raise 1 to 5 million dollars at a single event. She has reportedly been offered as much as $50,000 by upper crust women pining for their picture on the cover. The magazine's publication has been erratic, however.

The black middle class normally moves to areas of the city that are predominantly white or racially mixed. The few in the black upper class usually find their way to the Westside. One African-American insider told us bluntly, "Wouldn't you move into a nicer house if you could afford it?" In a way, L.A.'s wealthy enclaves are now more fluid racially than middle class suburbs. Money is the only criterion for entry and acceptance. Did anyone complain when actor Will Smith and his actress wife, Jada Pinkett Smith, moved into their 100-acre ranch in the Malibu-Santa Monica Mountains that they paid $7.5 million for in 1999? Certainly many attitudes have changed since Hancock Park was established in 1920 with covenants of ownership allowing for the "Caucasian race" only. The many current Asian, especially Korean, residents of Hancock Park certainly wouldn't have qualified. It is hard to imagine a group of homeowners in Hancock Park today hiring an attorney and protesting the purchase of a home by a black person as they did in 1948 when a singer by the name of Nat King Cole moved into the neighborhood. Here was an entertainer who was a regular performer up the road at the famous Hollywood night spot, Ciro's, being told by the Hancock Park homeowners' attorney that "We don't want undesirables here." Cole adeptly replied, "Neither do I, and if I see anybody undesirable coming into this neighborhood, I'll be the first to complain."

Los Angeles in the 1930s, '40s and '50s replicated the culture and racial attitudes of the East Coast and the Midwest. Well-known black architect Paul Williams often encountered the usual "black people not allowed" routine, by no means limited to Southern culture, as he helped to design such storied structures around the city as the Beverly Hills Hotel and the theme restaurant at the Los Angeles International Airport. Williams knew that his own family could neither live in nor even visit many of the homes he designed in the Los Angeles basin in Hancock Park, Bel-Air and other tony enclaves. Despite this "handicap," he still managed to design homes for Cary Grant, Frank Sinatra, William Holden, and Lucille Ball and Desi Arnaz. It is hard to imagine Williams getting such a client list in New York, and perhaps that is what was different about L.A. even in those early years. To win over many clients who Williams says would "freeze" when they found out at a meeting that he was black and would then look for "a convenient exit," Williams would coyly offer free advice, do an on-the-spot design and carefully keep a "safe" distance from his potential white clients. Today, says realtor Jeff Hyland, "people claim their homes are designed by him [Williams] even though they are not." Actress Michelle Pfeiffer and her husband, David E. Kelley, paid $15 million for a real Paul Williams house in Brentwood. The home was built in the 1940s for a Kansas City oilman.

But can the L.A. upper crust shoulder the blame for a minority exclusion problem that spans the spectrum of American society? Surely Hollywood must be criticized as a business for the virtual disappearance of minority groups on the television screen. The lack of minority stars for the Fall 1999 television line-up was so glaring that the NAACP launched a vehement protest, calling for Congressional hearings. NAACP President Kweisi Mfume called the Fall programs a total "whitewash." ABC Entertainment President Jaimie Tarses conceded that her network lacks diversity. From 1990-1999, only 19 non-whites (including Asians, Native Americans, African Americans and Latinos), or about 8% of nominees were contenders for the top Oscar awards: Best actor/actress, best supporting actor/actress, and best director.

Yet the 2002 Oscars saw Denzel Washington and Halle Berry win the Best Actor and Best Actress awards, which could signal increased access to the Hollywood power structure for all minority actors. It is also often overlooked that Hollywood as a business is more integrated than society at large and has more opportunities for advancement for minorities at many (lower) levels than do other industries. The minority issue at the top of L.A. society is economic and one of numbers.

In the 1990s, there were only three Latino directors with whom the studios made significant films: Gregory Nava, who made *Selena*; Robert Rodriguez, who wrote and directed *Spy Kids* and made *From Dusk till Dawn*; and Luis Valdez, who made *La Bamba*. Nava, who also made *El Norte*, struck a deal with New Line Cinema allowing him to make several Latino-themed films with his partner, Susana Zepeda. Still, a study by the Screen Actors Guild found that—surprise—Latino actors work less often and are ranked near the bottom in earnings when compared to their non-Hispanic counterparts. However, with the film success of Jennifer Lopez along with the musical splash made by Ricky Martin, the cultural scope in the entertainment industry is broadening. Creative Artists Agency's Emmanuel Nunez handles clients Robert De Niro, Al Pacino and Neve Cambell along with Gloria Estefan and Antonio Banderas. Julio Caro produced *The Cell*, and David Valdes co-produced *The Green Mile*.

Latinos and Asians as a group have tended to remain close-knit sociologically. An ethnic group sometimes has a tendency to remain insular. But that will change, as the social limelight is as powerful a lure as most anything in the human make-up. The call of Society breaks down the strongest ethnic bonds. Many Russian Armenians who had found their way to L.A. by the 1960s and who took great pride in their Armenian roots often strayed socially into American culture at large upon becoming successful in business. The top level of a purely Armenian grouping, centered around weddings and other social gatherings, paled next to the greater glory of the more universal forum of American public honor. Over time assimilation will always win out over tribalism. The obstacle is economic, not social. The L.A. social doors are open.

Hollywood and the Charity Circuit

The opening of the opera season each September kicks off the social year as the normally hard-to-get Hollywooders show up and mix with the Music Center crowd. Jodie Foster, Drew Barrymore, Tom Cruise, Nicole Kidman, Michael York and Anjelica Huston have all attended opera openings. Candice Bergen, Michael Eisner and Tom Hanks are regulars. The 1999-2000 kickoff to hear Plácido Domingo and Denyce Graves sing for $1,000 per ticket included Jacqueline Bisset, Sidney Poitier, Angie Dickinson, Faye Dunaway and Harry Hamlin among the Hollywood portion of the throng. Wendy Stark Morrissey, daughter of the late Hollywood producer Ray Stark, was responsible for getting out the Hollywood crowd, and she chimes in that the event could be even more successful if the opening were moved from mid-week to a Saturday evening. The Wednesday evening opening is inconvenient for the Hollywood crowd, says Morrissey: "A Disney executive, say, has to go home and change and be at the opera by seven." Actress Faye Dunaway chirps, "I think it's wonderful what Wendy Stark Morrissey [chair of the opera gala] is doing. She gives the best parties in the world. I sat between Oliver Stone and Gore Vidal one night—it was historic." The 2003 L.A. Opera benefit at Staples Center raised one million dollars and was attended by Michael Caine, Don Rickles, Dom DeLouise and Dustin Hoffman along with Barbara Sinatra and author Jackie Collins. Media mogul A. Jerrold Perenchio underwrote the event.

So Hollywood is not always invisible on the established L.A. social scene. But Hollywood, being Hollywood, usually does its own thing when it comes to charitable giving. One top Hollywood insider who asked to remain anonymous stated that Hollywood mainly contributes to AIDS charities, reflecting an attitude, correct or incorrect, found throughout the city that the entertainment industry shirks much of its social responsibility. Certainly Hollywood has stepped up to the plate for AIDS causes. The first AIDS walk in the country took place in L.A. in 1985 starting at the Paramount gates, and was encouraged by then Mayor Tom Bradley. The thousands of walkers have since symbolically paraded around Hollywood, year after year, and a long list of Hollywooders have spoken to or performed for the throngs of walkers and observers: Ann-Margret, Lynn Redgrave, Linda Lavin, Mike Farrell, Christine Lahti, Marlee Matlin, Rhea Perlman, Angela Lansbury, Eartha Kitt, Kelsey Grammar, Sarah Jessica Parker, Jamie Lee Curtis, Sandra Bullock, and Madonna—to name a few.

Sharon Stone worked the auction floor at Cannes in 1998 for the American Foundation for AIDS Research. She put on expensive jewelry and mingled as bids were solicited for auction items. She even danced to Elton John and Ringo Starr as the event raised a quick one million dollars. Stone later presided over an AIDS research benefit and art auction in Dallas called "Modern Art and AIDS in Texas," which took in $750,000. Barry Diller, David Geffen and Barbra Streisand have donated gifts for a new kitchen for Project Angel Food, which brings meals to sick AIDS patients in the L.A. area. Elizabeth Taylor's AIDS Foundation also donated to the Project. But there are many non-AIDS Hollywood causes as well.

SHARE is an organization founded decades ago by women executives and wives of executives or stars in the entertainment industry. In 1953 several women, including Janet Leigh and Mrs. Dean Martin, put on a dance show called Boomtown. The dance show has become SHARE's annual fundraising event. In earlier years Dean Martin, Frank Sinatra and Milton Berle performed for the event. During 1997 and 1998 SHARE distributed over one million dollars to various charities including Cedars Sinai Medical Center and Kids Café, an organization founded by Steven Spielberg and Henry Winkler that brings after-school meals to poor children. Kids Café is supported by other Hollywooders such as Norman Lear, Robin Williams, Danny DeVito, the Zanucks and former MCA president Sidney Sheinberg.

Hollywood also helps its own—those who worked in the Industry but are experiencing tough times—through the Motion Picture Relief Home. Michael Douglas hosted a celebrity golf event for the Motion Picture & Television Fund in 1999 that brought out an ample Hollywood crowd including Kevin Costner, Andy Garcia, Will Smith, Jack Nicholson and Cuba Gooding, Jr. The dinner for the event, which brought in half a million dollars, took place at Universal Studios and was attended by James Garner, Anne and Kirk Douglas, Lew Wasserman, Jeffrey Katzenberg and Ron Meyer.

In an Industry where everyone is on his own, Hollywood has managed to fund the Entertainment Industry Foundation, which channels money to various charities and works with Revlon/UCLA Walk/Run for cancer research. The Foundation is funded by a payroll deduction maintained by the studios and networks, and raised $14.8 million in 1998 for Southern California charities. One example of Foundation involvement was a jewelry and fashion show celebrating the new millennium. Rodeo Drive was blocked off for the outdoor runway, and Andrea Bocelli performed. Tiffany & Co., Giorgio Armani, Gucci, and Hermes were among the many participating retailers. The $1,000-a-head dinner benefited the California State Summer School for the Arts, the Museum of Contemporary Art and Teach for America. Jennifer Tilly, Natalie Cole, Catherine Zeta-Jones with Michael Douglas, Bo Derek, Elizabeth Taylor, Bai Ling, and Peri Gilpin, Kelsey Grammar and David Hyde Pierce of "Frasier" were among the many stars attending the event. As the Southern California skies offered a rare threat of rain to the outdoor proceedings, actor Martin Landau remarked, "I guess we could all go into Bijan . . . I don't think he'd welcome everyone coming in though. You have to make an appointment," referring to Bijan's policy of being open with locked doors. The Rodeo Drive street scene event raised 3/4 of a million dollars. The Foundation has also backed one of Michael Milken's foundations, Cap CURE, which seeks a cure for prostate cancer. But the Entertainment Industry Foundation is not widely known and uses a P.R. firm to handle its publicity, as if it were selling a movie instead of doing charitable giving. Nonetheless, the Foundation has raised 150 million dollars through direct donations or fundraisers since its inception as the Motion Pictures Permanent Charities Committee founded by movie mogul Samuel Goldwyn in 1942.

Creative Artists Agency has created its own foundation and has adopted Venice High School, offering a mentoring program for students. In the past, the CAA Foundation has worked with Colin Powell, who came to speak to the Agency about charitable work. About 25% of CAA executives have contributed to the CAA Foundation. The pattern of establishing one's own charity seems to be the rule in Hollywood. And the people you do business with— agents, producers, actors, executives—your clients—are asked to give. When Hollywood executive Tom Sherak needed fundraising help on a charity dinner for the National Multiple Sclerosis Society, he turned to his friend Joe Roth, head of Revolution Studios. Roth helped Sherak get out the troops and buy up tables—which ran from $3,000 to a cool $100,000—for the event held at the Century Plaza Hotel.

Some Hollywooders do not consider this pattern true charity since the motivations for giving are so strictly tied to business. But other industries tend toward similar behavior. Bankers and real estate developers, wholesalers and retailers—all follow the simple notion that "One hand washes the other." American business has been done that way for a long time.

In Hollywood, as far as raising money for charities goes, the key is to get the studios to pick up the cost of an event so the charity can collect all the proceeds. If a name or two gets involved at the outset, such as Barry Diller and David Geffen with AMFAR, the charity will reap huge benefits. But nothing is cut in stone on the Hollywood charity circuit. One well-known charity started up in L.A. and quickly got top Hollywood names involved by hosting a dinner for Richard Donner, producer of *Lethal Weapon* and *The Omen*. The event brought out the likes of then Warner studio head Terry Semel and David Geffen, and pulled in many significant Hollywood contributions, one from actress Meg Ryan. The charity quickly gathered in half a million dollars. But relations between the organization and the participants quickly became strained, and Hollywood support was just as quickly withdrawn.

The difficulty of maintaining Hollywood start-up charities is no doubt due to the demanding nature of the Business itself. Willing and active Hollywooders later focus in on other interests or simply become more involved in their careers. A food bank called Life started by actor Dennis Weaver and actress Valerie Harper that once fed almost 200,000 people a week through 200 participating agencies ran out of funding in 1999 after a successful sixteen-year run. The food bank would salvage edible but not saleable food from supermarkets. At its start, Life quickly gathered steam with corporate contributions flowing in on the crest of a wave of Hollywood star power that included Whoopi Goldberg, Bette Midler, Shirley MacLaine, singer Garth Brooks, David Geffen and many others from film and television. Life had been in some competition for food with the already existing Los Angeles Regional Food Bank, which continues to feed needy people in L.A. The inconsistent nature of Hollywood charitable giving also springs from this penchant to start one's own organization rather than channel energies into existing institutions.

Getting and keeping Hollywood support for an existing institution continues to be a precarious endeavor. CAA agent Bob Bookman recalls that when he was chairing a drive to get entertainment industry contributions for the Music Center, he called for a fundraising meeting: "It had to be a breakfast or I knew no one would come." Still, only three people showed up: Producer Tom Polluck, who ran Universal for many years; Russell Goldsmith, who heads Beverly Hills-based City National Bank; and Larry Turman, producer of *The Graduate*. Bookman says the three all had existing ties to the Southern California community. Polluck, who is now President of the American Film Institute (AFI) and runs his own production company, Montecito Pictures, out of Santa Barbara, grew up in L.A. Polluck recalls how he came to be appointed to the Music Center Board of Governors: "Buffy Chandler asked me to try and bring in new, young faces to the Music Center especially from the entertainment industry. She was tired of just seeing the same people all the time. And, if Mrs. Chandler asked you to do something, you did it."

Stars are ubiquitous on the charity circuit and are often used as a lure to bring in donors. Charities even pay finder's fees to celebrity brokers to help line up a star. Charities are often set up to combat a disease: AIDS, Muscular Dystrophy (Jerry Lewis has hosted a telethon for muscular dystrophy for many years), breast cancer, diabetes, etc. Someone in a wealthy family may have contracted the disease, giving the impulse to set up the charity to bring in dollars for further research. Nancy Davis, daughter of L.A. studio, oil and real estate tycoon Marvin Davis, has Multiple Sclerosis. She has organized a charity, Race to Erase MS, to combat the disease and was instrumental in getting doctors who do MS research to meet every three months in L.A. to compare notes. Race to Erase MS events are glitzy: From a rock concert in Aspen to a Las Vegas show in 1999 at the Hard Rock Hotel where Tommy Hilfiger put on a fashion show.

A typical scenario for a Hollywood charity event? Actress Rita Wilson was honored at the Regency Beverly Wilshire in 1999 at a benefit for research on women's cancer for the Cedars-Sinai Medical Center. Bette Midler, Martin Short and Glenn Frey performed. One of the prestigious co-chairs of the event, those who sell the tables and bring in the crowd, was Anne Douglas, the socially active wife of actor Kirk Douglas. Honorary chairs were Kate Capshaw and Steven Spielberg. Candice Bergen is a national spokesperson for the organization. Other co-chairs for the Cedars-Sinai event came from the non-Hollywood upper crust. Margie and Robert E. Petersen, who run a publishing empire, joined Mrs. Douglas in spearheading the drive to sell tables. If the event is big, and an event honoring Rita Wilson for Cedars Sinai was fairly high up the scale of importance on the L.A. social ladder, stars and major social players will show up. The Cedars-Sinai event was underwritten by Saks Fifth Avenue, and Tiffany gave guests engraved crystal water decanters.

If a Hollywood charity event has both agent power and studio power on the organizing committee, the turnout may be extraordinary. Ron Meyer, Doug Morris, Kate Capshaw, Steven Spielberg and William Morris Agency's Jim Wiatt co-chaired the 1999 Fulfillment Fund's Stars of Tomorrow benefit for L.A. youth at the Beverly Wilshire. Somewhat unusual with the Fulfillment Fund event is the addition of music industry power, which is not always part of the scene at film industry affairs. Stevie Wonder performed at the event, which drew much of the Hollywood top brass including Rupert Murdoch, Barbara and Marvin Davis and Jeffrey Katzenberg. Then Universal chief Edgar Bronfman, Jr. was the honoree. Of course, Universal is now also the largest music company in the world. During the charity auction, Courtney Love outbid Murdoch for a trip to Paris to see the Spring show of Christian Dior; and Motown's Barry

Gordy won the bidding on the Winston diamond and jawbreaker pearl earrings for $42,000. The event raised 2.5 million dollars. Entertainment industry people are like everybody else, only more so. The question of whether or not to attend an event or support a cause usually hinges on the response to "Who is going to be there?" and/or "How important is it?"

Does Hollywood Do Enough?

How does one weigh philanthropic contributions? Tax considerations that may have prompted the gift and the amount of one's personal wealth must be taken into account. Very wealthy non-Hollywooders' donations can be substantial and yet go relatively unnoticed by the Industry and high society crowds. Before succumbing to cancer, Ann Nickoll, with her husband John, donated one million dollars to the educational foundation of the Beverly Hills school district. The couple had previously contributed another million to Planned Parenthood in Los Angeles. When we asked a prominent socialite who they were, she responded, "I don't know. My own family got much more publicity for giving than they did and for a lot less money." Or take businessman Richard D. Colburn, an unknown outside art circles who funded the Colburn School of Performing Arts in downtown L.A. to the tune of 25 million dollars and with prospects for 100 million more. Alfred A. Mann, a physicist who made a fortune in pacemakers, contributed 100 million dollars each to UCLA and USC. Mann also is not a regular on the social circuit. Then there's the high-tech money. Former UCLA professor Henry Samueli, who founded Broadcom Corp., a communications chip maker in Irvine, California, gave 50 million dollars to UCLA and UC Irvine. Samueli had a net worth of 4 billion dollars at the time.

With regard to Hollywood generosity in particular, is the philanthropic glass half empty or half full? It is difficult to gauge Hollywood charitable giving. The mother of one well-known television actress asked the authors over the phone not to mention the family trust that she controls. "I contribute to a lot of lesser known causes for the most part and I do not want to be hounded for donations." While Kirk Douglas and his wife Anne move from funding the rebuilding of L.A. school playgrounds to donating $2.5 million to revamp the Culver Theatre in Culver City for young actors, our overall impression is that Hollywood does not do enough for the city to which it is inextricably tied. But Hollywood does more than most people think.

Hollywood does not get a great deal of bang, publicity-wise, for its charitable buck—strange for an Industry where promotion often wins out over substance. This anomaly is due to Hollywood's own secretive business demeanor that strictly separates the world into insiders and outsiders. Everyone knows someone in L.A. who unsuccessfully spent his or her youth trying to get a foot in the Hollywood door for a career. And so Hollywood insiders conduct business as if to avoid the throngs of wannabes banging on their doors. Many in the Hollywood establishment are just plain fearful of publicity, especially if it is publicity that they can't control. Better no publicity than bad publicity. A kind of schizophrenia runs the gamut of Hollywood: The key players want and even crave publicity for validation and to promote new business, but they are equally fearful of publicity because a faux pas could bring them down.

But Hollywooders, like anyone else, do have their pet projects. Steven Spielberg established the Righteous Persons Foundation with profits from the movie *Schindler's List*, setting aside some 50 million dollars for a grant-making organization dedicated to strengthening Jewish life. Producer Lili Zanuck emphasizes that Hollywood is very political, contributing heavily to campaigns and women's rights groups. Children's causes are also popular. Prior to our interview, Zanuck had just donated to the Starlight Foundation, which grants wishes to seriously ill children. On the political side, former "Cheers" star Ted Danson funded American Oceans to the tune of one million dollars to help clean up the U.S. coastline. Barbra Streisand has done private concerts on the grounds of her Malibu estate to raise money for Democratic candidates. And despite Clinton's chastising of Hollywood for making violent films, during his presidency movie moguls and entertainers flocked to a Democratic fundraiser at Greystone Mansion, built in 1928 by one of the Doheny clan. The infamous history of the mansion, now owned by the city of Beverly Hills but once the scene of a murder-suicide, did not deter the illustrious guests. The April 1999 event at the Mansion, called Majority 2000, was hosted by the DreamWorks team of David Geffen, Jeffrey Katzenberg and Steven Spielberg and brought in 2 million dollars. Attending the event, which required a per couple donation of between $25,000 and $100,000, were Meg Ryan, Dennis Quaid, Goldie Hawn, Kurt Russell and Whoopi Goldberg.

Political differences also run through the heart of L.A. upper crust giving. L.A.'s traditional social groups are generally Republican. Hollywood is largely Democratic. The current, hipper Hollywood social scene tends to be younger and boasts a large Jewish contingent. The players in the New Hollywood relish the political role. The late Dawn Steel, head of Columbia in the 1980s and the first woman studio chief, was an early supporter of President Clinton before she died of cancer at age fifty-one. Spielberg, Streisand, Tom Hanks, Rita Wilson and Barry Diller all attended the White House reception for British Prime Minister Tony Blair in 1998, showing support for a beleaguered Clinton during the Monica Lewinsky scandal. Rob Reiner, Oliver Stone, Tom Cruise, Nicole Kidman, Michael Douglas, Jeffrey Katzenberg, Ted Danson and Mary Steenburgen all put up the $10,000 price for an L.A. fundraiser for House Democrats attended by President Clinton in 1998.

One Hollywood insider related that the Music Center is Republican (and rich): "They will get their money anyway. Some of the groups that Hollywood contributes to are underprivileged and not as glamorous." Disney president Michael Eisner says that, "Whether they [the entertainment community] support specifically the Music Center is not to be attributed as anything negative; they support a lot of other fabulous things." Eisner and his wife Jane donated 89 million dollars worth of Disney stock to a private family foundation in 1997 to be used for education and medical care mainly in Southern California. The Eisner Foundation pledged one million dollars of scholarship money to students in poorer sections of the San Fernando Valley if they graduate from high school and go on to college. An inside source states that Eisner and late Universal Studios chief Lew Wasserman each donated substantial sums for the new cathedral of the Catholic Archdiocese built in the cultural corridor in downtown Los Angeles near the Music Center and the new Disney Hall. Wasserman's donation was reportedly in the 1 million dollar range, while Eisner's sum was directed at the project's courtyard. Eisner also donated 7 million dollars for a teacher education program at California State University, Northridge.

The Walt Disney Co. did contribute to Disney Hall, but it was the first entertainment company to do so, and that too several years after Lillian Disney's 50 million dollar gift. The project lay dormant until then SunAmerica chief Eli Broad took it under his wing, encouraged by his good friend, then Mayor Richard Riordan. Lillian Disney's daughter, Diane Disney Miller, and Music Center Chairwoman Andrea Van de Kamp also played crucial roles in the long years that the project lay dormant. For a time, Disney Hall had a huge parking lot built, but no hall. Entertainment money came for the Disney Hall from Ginny Mancini, widow of composer Henry Mancini; and from composer John Williams. Each gave one million dollars. Still, the bulk of the non-Disney money for Disney Hall came from business and L.A. Society, led by the $7.5 million donated by Ron Burkle. Now complete, the Frank Gehry-designed, ultra-modernistic, abstract structure will surely become a major cultural focal point and architectural symbol in Los Angeles life, surpassing even the new Getty Center in Brentwood that received so much international attention.

Yet corporate Hollywood's commitment to the community is real and reflects successful executives' gratitude to the Industry that has made their dreams of "making it" in L.A. a reality. DreamWorks has pledged 5 million dollars to JobLink, an entertainment industry training program for disadvantaged students. One of the studio founders, Jeffrey Katzenberg, stated the purpose of the donation: "We want to create opportunities and provide training for people who normally don't have access to the entertainment industry." DreamWorks executives also helped Los Angeles Community College design a program in entertainment studies.

All of this generosity aside, it is clear that Hollywood has not followed in the tradition of the American upper class by supporting the **existing** social institutions and charities on a regular basis. One socialite privately offered her opinion of Hollywood charitable giving to one of the authors: "We don't need them [Hollywood]." But then again, it may not be fair to blame just Hollywood for its freewheeling style. Gagosian Gallery's Robert Shapazian notes that the reverence felt by the average New Yorker for local cultural institutions such as the Metropolitan Museum of Art hardly exists in L.A.—not surprising considering that L.A. is the city where new is king. Past MOCA President Lenore Greenberg notices that L.A. does not have the tradition of patronage established in New York. She cites the difficulty in bringing the Disney Hall project to fruition as an example.

A notable exception to Hollywood's reticence in funding established causes has been the support garnered for the L.A. Public Library. Both the Huntington Library in San Marino and the Los Angeles Public Library draw supporters from Pasadena, the Westside and Hollywood. In 1998 Blue Ribbon President Joni Smith and Nancy Vreeland organized a series of dinners celebrating the 125th anniversary of the L.A. Public Library. Flora Thorton, whose late husband Charles Tex Thorton was the CEO of Litton Industries, was instrumental in starting the project. She later donated one million dollars to a foundation set up for the Library.

The 77 dinners took place mostly at private homes throughout the city and featured guest authors and heavy attendance from all social groupings including a cross-section of Hollywooders. Jane Seymour, Dennis Hopper, Carrie Fisher, Steve Martin, Charlton Heston, T.V. producer Steven Cannell, Hal David, Ginny Mancini and the Gregory Pecks graced the proceedings. Featured authors included the late Cleveland Amory, Dominick Dunne, and Susan Faludi.

Lew and Edie Wasserman's philanthropy has had an unusually broad reach, as the family's Wasserman Foundation, started over forty years ago, supports multiple causes, including the Motion Picture and Television Fund, the entertainment industry's retirement organization; the Music Center; the Jules Stein Eye Institute and the Geffen Playhouse, both adjacent to UCLA; and numerous universities and libraries. Son Casey Wasserman runs the Foundation, distributing several million dollars each year. Casey Wasserman points out that the Wasserman charity was set up in 1952, "long before it was fashionable."

Two of the hottest new charity events on the L.A. scene are both more or less exclusively Hollywood: The Davises' Carousel of Hope Ball in support of the Barbara Davis Center for Juvenile Diabetes in Denver (their younger daughter has diabetes), and Lilly Tartikoff's Fire and Ice Ball. Hollywood charity events draw few people from outside the entertainment industry. This is an anomaly, as no other industry is so self-contained. Of course there are exceptions. Paramount studio head Sherry Lansing organized a movie première for Stop Cancer that did attract non-entertainment players. But Lansing is one of a select few from the New Hollywood affiliated with the Music Center, so there is some natural reciprocity involved. Another exception was the première reception of the 1999 Paramount hit *Runaway Bride*, starring Richard Gere and Julia Roberts, at the Armand Hammer Museum in Westwood. The night's proceeds went to the Music Center, no doubt due to the influence of Lansing. Other chairs for the evening were the Colleagues' Anne Johnson and Jim Waitt, then heading

International Creative Management (ICM), a top talent agency; patrons included producer Ted Field, Elaine and Bram Goldsmith, whose wealth came from Beverly Hills banking; and Denise Rich, who co-wrote the film's song, "You're the Only One for Me." But with the proliferation of film releases and the film industry's laissez-faire attitude about social responsibility, many film premières are not tied to charities at all.

Hollywood premières, with or without ties to charitable causes, garner the television hoopla and press coverage and are packaged to the public as something more than just another phase of an advertising blitz that is part of a business plan—which is basically what they are. Television coverage of movie premières and the Hollywood scene in general are selling a piece of high society to the public, however contrived, surreal, or self-congratulatory it may be. Viewers experience spectacle through the screen. Inauthentic because of their self-promoting nature, the nightly Hollywood tidbits on "Entertainment Tonight" and all the cloned Hollywood news shows that have followed play to a basic human need to experience the social realm.

Hollywood today has belatedly discovered L.A. as a city, just as in turn Los Angeles finds itself inextricably connected to the entertainment industry in myriad ways. Entertainment mogul Haim Saban and his wife Cheryl pledge $40 million to the Children's Hospital in Los Angeles in 2003. In doing so, Saban proclaims his commitment to L.A. and admonishes Hollywooders who have made a lot of money but have been reticent to embrace social causes. Again, Old Hollywood has stepped forward with a $5 million dollar gift in 2003 to the UCLA Hammer Museum from Audrey L. Wilder, wife of famous director Billy Wilder of *Sunset Boulevard* fame. The Wilder gift will be used to build a theater to showcase international film. But Hollywood's fit with the L.A. social realm is far from perfect. Hollywood needs to rediscover a formula lost in its glorious past that highlighted the Industry's social responsibilities. With the unique mix of the traditional L.A.

upper crust, transplanted wealth from around the world, and the new Hollywood/music industry money, no other top social grouping in any American city is as divided socially as the Los Angeles upper crust. No grouping outside New York is as powerful in any sense of the word.

CHAPTER NINE
A Tour of L.A. Residential Chic

Where and How the L.A. Upper Crust Lives

The L.A. upper crust has congealed into several identifiable groupings, with the key people from each group often coming together at the top at major charitable events. Top designers such as Armani are particularly talented at bringing the various groupings together for collection unveilings. Still, it is surprising how little crossover occurs between the traditional upper crust and Hollywood. Hollywooders are viewed by traditional Society types either with antipathy, fondly—yet at a distance—or simply as from another world. Many in L.A.'s old-line families simply refuse to consider Hollywood in the context of high society. One daughter of generations-old L.A. Society royalty found to her chagrin that her traditional parents balked when she brought home her "A List" movie star boyfriend: "He has no education and frankly, he's just NOKD (Not Our Kind, Dear)." This traditional view of Hollywood seems destined to go the way of the rotary telephone, however. But it is up to the new Hollywooders to enter the social opening in L.A. Society. While some Old Hollywood couples such as the Kirk Douglases and Gregory Pecks have crossed over easily into non-Hollywood groups, the question remains whether or not Hollywood is up to the task of taking on high society. Peck's passing in 2003 only highlights the persistent gulf between Hollywood and the rest of L.A. Society. Those in Hollywood who had closed the gap for a generation must hand off the torch, but to whom?

The range of viewpoints within the L.A. upper crust is as wide as the San Andreas Fault. Equally surprising is the geographical isolation of the super wealthy: Pasadena people hang with Pasadena people, Malibu residents with Malibu residents and so on. The ubiquitous car and the too numerous freeways do little to provide connectedness as traffic jams torpedo any and all designs of the social planners for a more unified whole. In this disparate L.A. upper crust, perhaps the most powerful in the world vis-à-vis the modern culture, it is the few who do cross the various social divides who are at the top of everyone's "A" list.

The Pasadena/San Marino area has its own top circles, consisting mostly of those who consider themselves "established," or close to it. To be established may mean being on the L.A. scene only since the 1960s. Pasadena culture tends to be more conservative, often following European aristocratic patterns in decor and decorum. Historically much of the support for the Music Center and other traditional cultural endeavors has come from this side of town. As to why there are few strong personal friendships between the Pasadena crowd and the Hollywood group based mainly on the Westside, Pasadena resident Andrea Van de Kamp, past chairwoman and chief executive of the Music Center explains: "If I get a letter signed by entertainment people to attend a Hollywood function, I generally throw it out because there won't be anyone there I'll know." Joan Hotchkis, longtime resident of Pasadena and neighbor of Andrea Van de Kamp, sees the Hollywood scene as "very introverted"—they socialize with each other, and even as they socialize they're doing business. The late Nancy Vreeland offered an interesting perspective on this behavior: "Hollywood executives feel somehow disenfranchised from L.A.—this is where they sleep, but their audience is elsewhere."

Yet Hollywood and traditional L.A. Society are more intertwined today than was the case in the 1950s. Publicist Dale Olson, whose clients have included Steve McQueen, Gene Kelly and Shirley MacLaine, explains that "Movie stars have never been considered members of high society," mainly due to the lack of a prominent family background. Many come from elsewhere and may or may not establish strong ties with the city. Now more Industry people are living in Pasadena and San Marino, Warner Bros. and Walt

Disney Studios are in nearby Burbank, yet few non-Hollywooders from San Marino or the culturally similar Hancock Park have Hollywooders as their primary friends. The Stanfills of Pasadena are an exception as they cross easily back and forth between established circles and Hollywood. Active with the L.A. Opera and the Huntington Library, Terry Stanfill has also hosted American Film Institute dinners for Jimmy Stewart and Bette Davis. With time, L.A. Society, never as fixed as that of New York anyway, is losing remnants of its aloofness toward Hollywood. The new generations of established families look at the social scene with designer sunglasses: The more hip lifestyles of Hollywood can now be Society too.

The non-Hollywood L. A. upper crust is much more casual today. The pretense of established "Society" is fading, and traditional social circles attach themselves more and more to the sleek sophistication of Hollywood and the open playground it encourages. Children of older families tend to live more private lives, happily driving the kids around in a sports utility vehicle attending to family matters. Terry Stanfill explains that there is a great mixture of people now except for those in their seventies and eighties: "Everyone in L.A. is into doing things. There are not too many people making careers of doing lunch." The more open L.A. attitude results in large part from the Industry that dominates the city, and Hollywood culture values work, creativity, and merit—not lineage.

Pasadena and San Marino: Two Top L.A. Families

There are Pasadena families such as the Stanfills and the Hotchkises who, contrary to the pattern, have strong ties to Hollywood. A Rhodes scholar and board member at the California Institute of Technology, Dennis Stanfill headed 20th Century Fox from 1971 until 1981, when Marvin Davis bought the studio and decided to run it himself, at which time Stanfill took over at KCET, the local PBS station. The station was near bankruptcy, and Stanfill had to ask for donations to make the payroll. Working pro bono, he helped save KCET from imminent closure. Over the many years her husband was a studio head, Terry Stanfill hosted lavish Hollywood parties at the couple's home or on studio lots. In the late '70s she threw a party for the première of *Julia* and one to benefit the L.A. County Museum of Art. Mrs. Stanfill maintains her contacts across the various upper crust groups in part due to her work for Christie's. She is also on the L.A. Opera board, the advisory board of the Costume Council for the L.A. County Museum of Art, and an overseer at the Huntington Library in San Marino, where she did research for her latest historical novel.

Behind high walls off the winding roads of opulent San Marino at the Pasadena border lies the Stanfill home. Just across the street is the residence of Disney executive Thomas Schumacher, producer of *Lion King*. Two perfect rows of lemon trees line the path from the massive front security gate to the entrance. Mrs. Stanfill, fresh from the treadmill, is eager to discuss the L.A. social scene while serving tea and cookies. With her dark shoulder-length hair and lovely features, she cuts an exceptionally attractive figure. The house, designed by David Farquhar as California country in the Beaux Arts style, is decorated largely in the traditional mode, with the classical European art gracing each room and the library serving as the core of the home. Most tables are covered with costly porcelain and other *objets d'art*. Fragrant flowering bulbs lend a final elegance to the living room.

The Stanfill home dates from 1913 and features the hardwood floors standard for these lavish older residences. The dining room is an actual room rather than an appendage to the living room as in many middle class homes. The kitchen is out of view where the cook or caterers can work undisturbed and cooking odors can remain contained rather than wafting throughout the house and onto guests. No kitchen as household centerpiece or on-the-run dining room here—the room's location delineates it as a place mainly for staff, not the lady of the house. A kitchen separated from living quarters dates back to colonial times, when the kitchen was often in a different building. Mr. Stanfill has an office in a quaint room behind the main home, a not uncommon arrangement in L.A. upper crust families where much of the family business is conducted out of the residence. The Stanfills have resided in the lush San Marino area for over thirty years, where they have raised their three children and hosted parties in the 1980s for V.I.P.s such as the late Princess Grace and Prince Albert.

What's it like sitting with a lady who has hosted royalty and planned many a studio party? Terry Stanfill is remarkably down-to-earth and candid about herself and the city. She is less active socially, now an author, an unabashed Italiophile and surprisingly modest. At home, the Stanfills seem very much in tune with the relaxed Southern California lifestyle.

The Stanfills' good friend John Hotchkis is from an old-line Southern California family, his mother being a Bixby of the once huge Bixby land holding. He says that in order for his family to occupy an older place in L.A. history, it would need to have a Spanish surname. His wife Joan has strong ties to Hollywood because of a previous marriage to super agent Phil Berg, prominent in movie circles from the early days of Hollywood and handler of Clark Gable and Edward G. Robinson. After Berg, thirty-seven years her senior, died at the age of eighty, Joan married Hotchkis, whose wife had also passed away. Joan is now President of the prestigious Blue Ribbon support group for the Music Center.

Before heeding the "call of the Westside" and establishing a home in Bel-Air, John and Joan Hotchkis lived for nearly two decades in an exclusive enclave of Pasadena in the Hoover House, built in 1963 by Herbert Hoover's son. The home rests atop a hill behind security gates at the end of a long, lushly landscaped drive. The layout of the house is the trademark California spread, with living quarters on a single floor. The one level structure was the result of Herbert Hoover, Jr. and his wife's desire to have the former

President, by then confined to a wheelchair, live with them. The exceedingly low, wheelchair-accessible doorknobs throughout the home are further testimony to this desire of the original owners. Sadly, President Hoover died before this dream could be realized.

The home's gallery is long and stately, flanked by two rows of large Oriental vases perched on pedestals. Living areas are elegant yet comfortable, and the art is a blend of classic and contemporary styles. Books, increasingly absent in high-end homes according to Westside realtor Jeff Hyland, abound at the Hotchkis residence. Joan Hotchkis, just in from a tea and dressed tightly in black with a hot pink blazer, is undeniably stunning in garb that highlights her light blond hair and near perfect features. Add to this her exuberant personality and one couldn't ask for a more delightful person with whom to sip some tea, brought by a maid but served by Joan herself.

Joan narrates a bit of her husband's family history, explaining that the Bixby family came out from Maine during the Gold Rush and sold provisions to miners. The three Bixby brothers married the three Hathaway sisters, and the family bought the ranch, a Spanish land grant once stretching from the ocean to the mountains, around 1870. The couple often entertains at the ranch; John Hotchkis enjoyed one such bash celebrating his sixty-fifth birthday with the Governor of California and other notables in attendance.

Both Hotchkises are active at the Music Center— Mr. Hotchkis is President of the Board of the L.A. Philharmonic and wears several other hats as well, while Mrs. Hotchkis joined the Blue Ribbon after her marriage and chaired the group's 30th anniversary celebration committee before she became the group's President. The Hotchkises were honored at a 2000 auction gathering held at Ron Burkle's Green Acres estate in Beverly Hills for their work on behalf of the Music Center. Ebullient as always, Joan Hotchkis quipped, ". . . I think the real reason we are being honored is that they wanted to make sure we'd be here because we always bid on so much." Sure enough, the event raised one million dollars.

Mrs. Hotchkis also has a strong penchant for art, having helped to open Sotheby's auction house in Los Angeles in 1971. The first auction she arranged featured props from 20th Century Fox productions. Originally from San Francisco and a former resident of New York, Mrs. Hotchkis likes L.A. because everything is wide open, not stratified or inbred, and the emphasis is on merit. There is no landed gentry to speak of, since the Spanish land grant families such as the Sepulvedas and the Figueroas have been diluted.

Hancock Park Roots

Similar in many ways to the Pasadena crowd, the Hancock Park group tends toward a longer family history in the L.A. area and support for civic and cultural causes. Hancock Park homes, many of which date from the 1920s, often remain in the family and are passed down from generation to generation. The Chandler family of *L.A. Times* fame still maintains a Hancock Park home. As with much of Southern California, originally Hancock Park land was a part of one of the many Mexican rancheros. A member of the "Gringo" Hancock family bought the land, then part of Rancho La Brea, in 1860. After yielding up much oil, the land was finally developed many decades later.

Hancock Park was the L.A. answer to Pasadena and San Marino, and families from the two locales comprised what was L.A. Society before the social explosion of the Westside and the coming out party of Hollywood that occurred in the 1980s and '90s, when Oscar parties and the mega-mansions of the Westside permanently altered the L.A. social scene. But change in L.A. is a constant, so in addition to members of the business elite who want to be close to downtown, along with a growing Korean presence, the entertainment industry has discovered Hancock Park. Among the enclave's new Hollywood residents are Melanie Griffith and Antonio Banderas, who bought a Mediterranean-style house there complete with a ballroom, wine vault and greenhouse. The noted Hollywood couple converted a few of their nine bedrooms to create a music studio, sauna and gym and regularly host high-ticket fundraisers there to benefit favorite charities such as the Sabera Foundation, an Indian orphanage whose patrons include Tom Cruise, Christian Slater and Sting. L.A. today is difficult to classify, hard and fast, in terms of neighborhoods, with Hancock Park being a case in point. One can only speak in soft generalities.

Caroline Ahmanson, widow of banking tycoon Howard Ahmanson, lived with her husband in Hancock Park until his death in 1968, at which time she set up permanent residence in a Regency Beverly Wilshire presidential suite in the heart of Beverly Hills. She has continued to be active in promoting the Music Center and in her role as unofficial ambassador to China. Hotel employees have seen the American flag posted outside her suite during an unofficial "State" dinner.

Waiting for a signal from the Hotel's front desk for permission to take the elevator up to the Ahmanson suite, we inevitably feel jittery about meeting this top L.A. Society lady. We know that a visit with Mrs. Ahmanson is not routine. While waiting, we learn that Mrs. Ahmanson is also a major stockholder at Disney and has served on the Disney board. Minutes later, as her assistant Victoria opens the door to the suite of rooms, Caroline Leonetti Ahmanson, dubbed by some the "grande dame" of L.A., walks down the long, antique-filled entry hall to welcome us. Chinese incense wafts through the air, and Mrs. Ahmanson's incredible warmth immediately envelops us—this is clearly a lady who truly loves people. The residence features classical European decor and objets d'art, and boasts enviable bird's-eye views in three directions—up Rodeo Drive toward the hills, down Wilshire Blvd. toward the city center, and out toward Santa Monica and the sea. Clad in deep purple pants and top with a high-collared blouse and jewelry to match, Mrs. Ahmanson appears radiant. Hers is the face of a person satisfied with a life well lived. She ushers us into a library brimming with volumes on art and culture, where we will enjoy Chinese tea and delectable cookies for the next few hours while engaging Mrs. Ahmanson in a lively discussion about Los Angeles civic and cultural life.

Caroline Ahmanson's accomplishments are too numerous to discuss in the detail they deserve. She has received some thirty awards from all across the nation for her many years of service, including two honorary doctoral degrees. She is particularly proud of her work in the Education Division at the Music Center and her relations with China. Mrs. Ahmanson's interest in China began in the days she used to spend time wandering through Chinatown. She first traveled to China in 1973, before such a trip was in vogue. She has returned some fourteen times since, and has served as Vice-Chairman of the Board of the National Committee on U.S.-China Relations.

Her business career included the founding of a thriving self-improvement/modeling school, Caroline Leonetti Ltd., in 1945. Her daughter, Margo O'Connell, took over operations of the firm upon her mother's marriage to Howard Ahmanson. Mrs. Ahmanson is also a former Chairman of the twelfth district Federal Reserve Bank, which serves nine states. Of her Federal Reserve days she says, "Of all the public service, that was the most exciting and most rewarding—in the eye of the storm, so to speak."

At the Music Center Caroline Ahmanson serves as Vice-Chairman of the Board of Governors and continues her involvement with the Education Division, a collection of community outreach programs for the arts which she developed. She is also Vice-Chairman of the Los Angeles County High School for the Arts, which she helped to found in 1985 on the Cal State L.A. campus. The school educates artistically gifted students from around Southern California. Disney head of animation Thomas Schumacher, who has met Mrs. Ahmanson during the course of her work on Disney's Board of Directors, describes her as "the last of her kind, from the generation of Dorothy Chandler, who understood what social commitment to the city was all about."

Referring to L.A.'s "unique character," Mrs. Ahmanson points to the influx of diverse populations as contributing to the special flavor of the city, noting that the area boasts the largest Vietnamese, Japanese, and Korean communities outside of the Far East. As New York was the melting pot of Europe, so L.A. has become the melting pot of Latin America and the Pacific Rim. She believes that Los Angeles lacks a developed city center because the expanse of Southern California pulls businesses away from the downtown area. But with or without a city center, "We're the leaders in practically everything," she affirms. "There's a vitality and an energy here that doesn't exist in any other city today." As we left Mrs. Ahmanson's suite so she could prepare to attend a play that evening, another title came to mind to add to her seemingly endless list of accomplishments: Caroline Leonetti Ahmanson, Ambassador of Los Angeles to the world.

The Westside: Prime of the Prime

The development of the Westside as a social and cultural magnet goes hand in hand with what we call the "L.A. sensation." Beverly Hills, Brentwood, Bel-Air, and Malibu are magical names everywhere. It is the ubiquitous Hollywooders—actors, producers, directors, agents and writers—whose names have become synonymous with the Westside. By leaning toward modernist trends and contemporary art, the Hollywood element has moved the city toward its inevitable modern calling. This new social force does not include the remaining Old Hollywood element on the Westside, where the Fred MacMurrays and Charlton Hestons mix with the Reagans, who have spawned their own social circle including Betsy Bloomingdale, among other notables.

Up from Santa Monica Blvd. in the Beverly Hills Flats sits the classic Spanish-style home of Mr. and Mrs.

John Quinn. Mr. Quinn is a prominent attorney, and his wife is a well-known collector of contemporary California art. Joan Quinn is the daughter of J.C. Agajanian of auto racing fame, and grew up in wealthy L.A. circles. She attended Westlake and USC, and has been a Blue Ribbon member since 1973.

The Quinn residence rests unguarded by gates, characteristic of the openness that still prevails in the Beverly Hills Flats. The traditional Southern California architecture evokes the bygone era of Spanish land grants. Oriental rugs and antique furnishings abound, and the rooms are heavily draped in the classic European mode. But when it comes to art, this house is anything but traditional.

The numerous portraits of Joan by a variety of California artists remind one of Frida Kahlo, who painted herself almost exclusively. Still strikingly beautiful, Joan's stunning good looks are most dramatically highlighted in an early portrait which graces the fireplace. Her exotic beauty is depicted in characteristic L.A. style beside a cactus. Native American and Mexican elements of Southern California art shine through her image.

Mrs. Quinn began collecting contemporary L.A. art because she knew many of the artists. A writer herself, she still prefers socializing with creative types because they are usually working on something interesting, even cutting-edge; whereas many of the socialites talk about how large their most recent hotel room was or other topics which don't interest her.

Mrs. Quinn's 10-page bio reveals accomplishments in journalism, television and film. She was the West Coast Correspondent for Andy Warhol's *Interview* magazine: "I drove Andy around when he came to L.A." She was also the Society editor for the *Los Angeles Herald-Examiner*. Joan has hosted her own interview series on cable T.V. and has made numerous appearances on various news and information programs. She was involved in the making of three films, one on the life of Andy Warhol. And of course her Quinn Collection of California Art has been on view at major museums across the country and in Japan. This seems to be a lady who never sleeps.

When asked about her Armenian heritage, Joan says she has never felt excluded in top L.A. social circles. She continues to socialize with a group of Armenian ladies and is well respected in her own extended family as someone who has made the big time yet remains close to her roots. As relative Stella Marashlian says, "We're very proud of her."

*   *   *

Further toward the ocean, on South Mapleton Drive live Marc and Jane Nathanson, major forces on the Westside without being Hollywood players per se. Mr. Nathanson founded Falcon Cable T.V., which was sold in 1999 to Microsoft billionaire Paul Allen for 3.6 billion dollars. Nathanson began the company in 1975 with $25,000. Nathanson was also named by President Clinton to head the Broadcast Board of Governors of the United States, which oversees the Voice of America. His wife Jane has a reputation as a contemporary art collector of some note. She is a member of the Music Center's Blue Ribbon, but devotes most of her volunteer time to AIDS Project Los Angeles; AMFAR, which does research on AIDS; and the Museum of Contemporary Art, which she helped to found. She sits on boards of organizations benefiting AIDS patients along with names such as Elizabeth Taylor, David Geffen, Barry Diller, and Steve Tisch. Jane is also a practicing psychologist who spends much of her professional life on grief and bereavement counseling of AIDS patients and their loved ones. Another part of her practice involves celebrity individual and marital counseling. The Nathansons are heavily involved in Democratic politics and have hosted fundraisers for no less a Democratic celebrity than President Clinton. The President remembered his benefactors: Jane and Marc Nathanson were right behind Barbra Streisand and James Brolin in the line to greet British Prime Minister Tony Blair at the official 1998 White House dinner in his honor.

Down South Mapleton Drive away from the bustling energy of Sunset Blvd. lies a different world, a world of estates and great fortunes on the street one high-end realtor refers to as "the prime of the prime"—the most exclusive street in the most exclusive neighborhood in the world, Holmby Hills. Just how exclusive? One gets the feeling that the no parking signs up and down the street will also appear on the driveways. Adjacent to Beverly Hills and not far from UCLA, South Mapleton Drive is undeniably a place apart, the ultimate cut. High walls and dense foliage obscure many mansions, but one gets the picture from fleeting glimpses of grand homes seemingly hidden from the rest of the planet. Besides the speeding cars that all but run one over, this street has been graced by names such as Hefner, Keck and Spelling. Some homes are new, a result of teardowns, but perhaps the more interesting ones, such as that of Marc and Jane Nathanson, have watched over this exclusive street for many years.

The Nathanson home rises in white glory above the street, ensconced behind high walls, its entrance guarded by the huge gates so characteristic of the homes of the super wealthy. But the classic exterior is misleading. The door opens to reveal the ultra-modern world within, a scene that takes one's breath away. The perfectly polished blond hardwood floor extends throughout the first floor in an almost unlimited expanse. Elegant mats cradle the gatherings of furniture that is contemporary to the hilt. As Jane Nathanson explains, the home's classic architectural style, complete with stunning moldings and a wrought iron staircase reminiscent of *Sunset Blvd.*, provides an elegant backdrop for the contemporary art and furnishings. And sometimes the two are one in the same—consider the "Jane" chairs and ottoman designed for the lady of the house by none other than Frank Gehry. K-Mart is the last place that would come to mind here, yet the house was built in 1927 by the Kresge family, five-and-dime store tycoons and founders of K-Mart.

The living room includes a massive fireplace, 20 ft.

plus ceilings, zebra-skin furniture, and pictures of V.I.P.s galore, including one showing Mrs. Nathanson in an embrace with President Clinton. "Just like Monica," quips Jane. The floral arrangement is tall enough to tower over most mortals, and for the final mark of distinction, a Picasso presides over the room. The Picasso is there, on the Nathanson wall—not in a museum.

And all around the house, art and more art—Warhol self-portraits here, a Calder sculpture there, even a Mao portrait. The many reception areas, all graced by notable contemporary art, indicate that this home was built with entertaining on a grand scale in mind. The media room attests to the area's dominant Industry. The dining area alone is larger than most middle class living rooms, kitchens, dining rooms and entryways combined and boasts a massive table with multiple flowers vased separately but placed in a distinct arrangement.

The card room evokes a more intimate feel and remains largely in its original state. Fully paneled with the top row of paneling sporting card faces, the room testifies to an earlier era and contains a full bar. This jewel reminds one that in spite of its grand scale, felt especially in the sprawling entry hall and living room, this home consists largely of intimate spaces, and yet could accommodate a party of hundreds.

The lady matches her house. Perfectly. Tall and sleek, Jane Nathanson descends the stairs, sporting a black leather jacket, tight black pants and black boots. A long day with patients has taken nothing away from her considerable presence. A quick interview, a little tour of the mansion, and Mrs. Nathanson will be on her way to join her husband and another couple for dinner at a Westside restaurant. This striking woman is elegant, contemporary, and, regardless of her New York roots, totally L.A. Her black outfit highlights her long blond hair the way the home's classic walls provide the optimal setting for the display of contemporary art. This is the new face of the L.A. upper crust—chic, definitely, but also strong, independent, engaged in productive labor, and quintessentially contemporary with a touch of '60s hip thrown in.

Mrs. Nathanson grew up in the '60s liking modern art and started collecting pieces she could afford in her early twenties. Her family was big on collecting the much more costly Impressionist pieces. She was a key player in the formation of the Museum of Contemporary Art, where she remains on the Board. Jane moved to Los Angeles in 1975 from New York and says of her adoptive home, "It's a hot city now." She adds, "People don't last here"—you don't get into Society for a lifetime as by birth. As long as you're creative, an exciting face, you're in; when that ends, you're out. "The home of Ted and Suzie Fields was the place to be for five minutes when they were giving parties and donating money." Is this really high society, Nathanson wonders, or a kind of "faux Society"? The Fields divorced and the home has been sold to a new up-and-coming player, Ron Burkle, who contributes heavily to MOCA and through his supermarket firm donated to Disney Hall. Not to worry. In L.A. there are as many social comebacks as there are movie sequels.

*   *   *

Authors' Note: The authors greatly regret the untimely death of Nancy Vreeland but are proud to present an exclusive interview with her.

Still on the Westside, ensconced behind those trademark massive gates in Century City is the Vreeland residence. Newcomers to L.A. tend to imagine only mansions as characteristic of the city's haute lifestyle. But on the pricey Westside, luxury condos such as the Vreelands' are part of the residential mix. Tim Vreeland possesses a notable background, and Nancy's fundraising skills were well known. Mr. Vreeland is a professor of architecture at nearby UCLA and the son of the late *Vogue* editor Diana Vreeland, the legendary arbiter of New York fashion and a sought-after guest from Manhattan penthouses to the White House.

Having grown up on the East Coast among the Beautiful People (a term coined by his mother) and a graduate of Groton, Mr. Vreeland feels a bit mystified about social standing in L.A. because he doesn't have the reference points that he would have in New York. He explains that in the East, "Society" consisted of those he went to school with and saw socially—the delineations were fairly well drawn. Out in L.A., however, he often has no clear idea of the social standing of the person sitting next to him at an event because the historical context is lacking. As Mr. Vreeland points out, "An attraction of L.A. is that you can establish yourself quickly without worrying about who was already here." Vreeland and his wife consider the founders of the city and those whose families have been part of the community over generations to be "Society" in the purest sense.

The late Nancy Vreeland, that day dressed comfortably in a golden linen shift highlighting her generous blond hair, hailed from the affluent North Shore of Chicago. In the 1970s, before marrying Tim Vreeland, she owned her own fashion business under her maiden name of Stolkin. In L.A. she supported the Otis College of Art and Design, chairing the school's annual School of Fashion Design fundraiser that offers students an opportunity to show their work. Mrs. Vreeland also co-chaired the 1997 celebration of the 125th anniversary of the L.A. Public Library with then Blue Ribbon President Joni Smith.

A Blue Ribbon member, Nancy was very active in the Music Center in the 1980s and recalled three events she organized which were particularly spectacular. In the mid-'80s the Chanel couture show took place in the Dorothy Chandler Pavilion, scene of many an Oscar event, where the stage was built in the sumptuous Grand Hall entrance. Mrs. Vreeland remembered the event as "a beautifully elegant evening—they spared no expense." Everyone on the Music Center benefactor list received invites, and Chanel became a benefactor of the Music Center as well. She also recalled the gala opening of *The Phantom of the Opera* at the Ahmanson Theatre, when a tent decorated with dark tapestries similar to those of the Phantom set was put up opposite the Theatre. Top artists and designers such as Bob Mackie made a total of eight masks to raise funds. Lexus, just introducing their cars, was the major underwriter for the event. And then there was the *La Traviata* opening with Plácido Domingo, an outdoor dinner gala L.A.-style. The weather was perfect, and the area was decorated with lanterns.

Before departing, we asked Mrs. Vreeland what makes the L.A. charity circuit tick. She noted that in the 1980s the Music Center held together an exclusive list of supporters. With the explosion of new charities in the 1990s, the Music Center must compete with other causes. New charities vie with established charities to procure the top people for their fundraising committees. The competition can get fierce. Mrs. Vreeland continues our crash course on L.A. fundraising: The fundraising committees organize the events and shoulder the responsibility of selling whole tables and bringing in their friends to help sell the up to 1500 tickets required to reach the fundraising goal. That is why the prestige of who is on the fundraising committee is so important. People buy in not just because of the event, but also for the association with L.A.'s top players. A star or a studio head lending his name to a committee sells tickets. While celebrities are not critical for turning out a crowd, big names do guarantee national media attention.

*   *   *

Turning onto a quiet street off fabled Sunset Blvd. near the Beverly Hills Hotel lands one in territory well marked on star maps. Lucille Ball and Jack Benny once called this street home. You think back a half century and marvel at the thought of Hollywood stars outside waving to each other from their lawns. Jimmy Stewart lived here for over 40 years. Peter Falk owns a home here now, and Diane Keaton owned and refurbished the Spanish-style home down the street before Madonna bought it in 2000. The "star-struck" home was put on the market again in 2003 by Madonna for over 10 million dollars. Across from the Falk residence stands the house one top contemporary art collector and her husband have called home for over 30 years. The property is a Spanish-style spread the couple bought from a Hollywood playboy of sorts. Now the home sits calmly yet marvelously as an ode to modern, open-air design.

The expansive home features stunning black oak floors set off by groupings of off-white sofas and chairs resting on large woven mats in the living area. Our hostess, Lenore Greenberg, is dressed smartly but sensibly in beige, and coincidentally blends nicely with the home's soft colors. Wally, the resident sheepdog, matches the furniture. An art book on Brancusi graces the coffee table, and orchids supply the final touch of elegance. This modern home features a wall of glass that looks out enticingly into extensive gardens complete with sculpture and tennis court. This is Southern California living scripted for a movie, but better because it is real. The ample light coupled with the decor's dramatic contrasts of black and off-white offer the perfect setting for some stunning contemporary art. The dining room provided a venue for one of the exclusive dinners held in celebration of the L.A. Public Library's 125th anniversary. *L.A. Times* art critic Christopher Knight was the featured author at the dinner.

This particular Beverly Hills resident is one of those rare birds—a native Angeleno. Lenore Greenberg grew up in posh Hancock Park in one of the few Jewish families in the then WASP enclave. After attending public school and then boarding school, she studied art history in college. Her parents were major collectors of modern art ranging from the end of the 19th century up through the 1950s. She in turn began collecting contemporary art because it was the art of her time and more affordable. She is a past president of MOCA ("I was involved with it when it was only an idea"), for which she continues to volunteer, along with the Music

Center and children's charities. One gets the feeling that social responsibility is a given with Mrs. Greenberg.

The couple used to make frequent trips to New York to taste some culture and cuisine. They still go east, but without the previous sense of urgency, as now they can get everything in L.A. that they used to get in New York. They no longer feel deprived. When it comes to food these days, going to the Big Apple is like coming home: "Now all the food in New York is California Cuisine." But this Beverly Hills resident strikes one as a calm, low-key person possessed of an excellent sense of proportion, not likely to take food or like matters too seriously. As she walks us to the door she recalls the time she herself, as part of a birthday party, went on one of the many tour buses that frequent her famous neighborhood. Although she says the guide was "full of misinformation," she isn't bothered by the tour groups. One has the feeling that it would take much more than a few tourists to ruffle this serene lady's feathers.

Hollywood Then and Now

And finally we reach the Hollywood circle, the Westside personified, that most famous element of the L.A. upper crust. They are directors, producers, agents, studio heads and stars. They live almost exclusively on the Westside—in Beverly Hills, Bel-Air, Holmby Hills, Brentwood, Pacific Palisades, and Malibu. They have a strong Jewish contingent and frequent the Hillcrest and Bel-Air Country Clubs.

If there is Old Hollywood royalty, the Minnellis are it. Lee Minnelli, widow of Vincente Minnelli and stepmother of Liza Minnelli, has lived across from the Beverly Hills Hotel on the family estate that she shared with her husband until his death in 1986. Vincente Minnelli met Liza's mother, Judy Garland, as her director in *Meet Me in St. Louis*. Both were under contract to MGM. They married in 1945 to the approving nod of studio mogul Louis B. Mayer and set up residence elsewhere in L.A. Vincente Minnelli went on to direct *An American in Paris* and *Gigi*, for which he won an Oscar.

Prior to marrying Lee Minnelli, Vincente Minnelli lived in the home with another wife, Denise, who had mastered the skills of party-giving while living in Italy, and who later became Mrs. Prentis Cobb Hale of Broadway department store fame and won a prime place in top San Francisco circles. Liza Minnelli lived here for a time as a young woman. Down the street once lived novelist Dominick Dunne before the tragedy of his daughter's murder drove him from Los Angeles.

We had that special feeling of excitement and anticipation as we parked near Sunset and approached the Minnelli home. Mrs. Minnelli greeted us outside as she was discussing the maintenance of her classic Mercedes with her assistant. We walked in the side entrance and into another world—of Hollywood past, of pictures on the wall chronicling Hollywood's glory days. To touch the wall was as if to touch Hollywood itself and capture that elusive patina of celebrity we all see on the screen but can never garner.

The Minnelli home, designed in Italian Villa style and almost modest by current Westside standards, was built in 1925 and is nestled on 2.5 acres of prime Beverly Hills land. It features four bedrooms and over 6,000 square feet of living space. The garden boasts the requisite L.A. pool (put in by Liza Minnelli for her father), a rose garden and statuary. Both house and garden are elegant and well maintained without being pretentious or so perfect as to be uncomfortable. The decor, Mrs. Minnelli notes, was not done by an interior designer. This is a classic Old Hollywood home.

The formal entry facing Sunset Blvd. remains closed for security reasons except during parties, when Chuck Pick, valet to the stars, provides parking and security services. The foyer sports python skin wallpaper, and the huge living area contains an array of photos of the Minnellis with various celebrities, including President and Mrs. Reagan, Barbra

Streisand and Cary Grant. A precious family photo of Liza sits on another table. Memorabilia from Mr. Minnelli's films dots the interior landscape, and a separate Oscar room contains all of his awards earned during a career spanning four decades, including his 1958 Best Director Oscar for *Gigi*. The art throughout the house is a mixture of modern and classic styles, an unplanned mélange of whatever caught the Minnellis' eyes.

The large dining room features a giant priceless Japanese screen bought by Mr. Minnelli. One can only imagine the legendary Hollywood figures—Jules and Doris Stein, Barbara and Frank Sinatra, Gregory and Veronique Peck—who have relaxed in this classic setting that could double as a set for any Old Hollywood movie. Who wouldn't have cherished an invite to the Minnelli home for dinner in those days? Off the dining area is the entertainment-style kitchen, somewhat removed from the rest of the home. The kitchen area includes a separate room for china storage and display, and it is to this room that Mrs. Minnelli takes us to select a bottle of wine to share with her. The kitchen is also the abode of Mrs. Minnelli's cat and seemingly the headquarters of her live-in housekeeper Maria, who has been with her for over twelve years.

The upstairs rooms include Mr. Minnelli's suite, his study/library, and Mrs. Minnelli's suite, which she explains doubles as her library and study. It is acceptable and even commonplace in residences of the upper crust for husband and wife to have separate bedroom suites. And no, it doesn't mean that their marriage is on the rocks. In the Minnellis' case, the widow still beams when talking about her late husband. Mr. Minnelli's study is done all in red and has the appearance of having remained much as the late great director must have left it. It is to this most comfortable room that we repair to sip Chianti and chat with Mrs. Minnelli about life with Vincente and the Hollywood social scene today.

Lee Minnelli, a known party hostess and former professional social guide for those wanting to make a splash in L.A., recalls the many parties she has given over the years. What some people would give for her little book filled with the phone numbers of L.A.'s social elite. Mrs. Minnelli explains that for a party to be memorable, there must be a mix of Hollywood and non-Hollywood types so the conversation isn't one-dimensional, along with good food and wine. Renaissance (formerly Rococo) Catering has done Mrs. Minnelli's parties and has earned the trust of many Hollywooders. Since security is always a concern, caterers and others providing in-home services must be above reproach. Some who have chosen to go with other than tried and true service providers have lived to regret it when their houses were burglarized soon after their party.

Parties given by Mrs. Minnelli at her home have included a bash for Liza in 1994 and one for the late Vere Harmsworth, Viscount Rothamere, the British publishing tycoon, and his wife Lady Rothamere in 1996. Lee Minnelli herself is originally from Scotland and has had other titled friends, such as Lady Corda, better known as Merle Oberon. Mrs. Minnelli recalls that the party honoring Liza included the Frank Sinatras, Jack Haley, the Robert Stacks, Cyd Charrise and her husband Tony Martin, the Gregory Pecks, producer George Schlatter and his wife Jolene, and the Kirk Douglases. The event honoring the Rothameres drew guests such as Alejandro Helga Orfila, Ambassador of Argentina; Betsy Bloomingdale; Henry and Jane Berger; and the usual Minnelli pals: The Stacks, the Pecks, the Douglases and Cyd Charrise.

Authors' Note: The Minnelli interview was done in 1999, at a time when Lee Minnelli and Liza Minnelli were apparently on good terms. Pictures of Liza were ubiquitously placed all over the house. But their relationship deteriorated as Liza, the executor of the estate, sold the home, on prime Westside real estate, for a price in excess of 2 million dollars. She offered to buy Lee Minnelli a condo. Liza was wed to music producer-concert promoter David Guest in the "marriage of the year," a scintillating affair much ballyhooed on programs such as "Entertainment Tonight" in March 2002. The New York wedding was attended by such entertainment notables as Michael Jackson, Elizabeth Taylor, Diana Ross, Dionne Warwick, Rosie O'Donnell and Joan Collins and other prominent names such as Donald Trump and Martha Stewart. While Lee Minnelli attended Liza's engagement party in L.A., her invitation to the New York wedding was withdrawn as she filed suit against Liza in Los Angeles Superior Court. Lee Minnelli claimed that her late husband, producer Vincente Minnelli, Liza's father from his marriage to Judy Garland, had left her the house to use in her lifetime. Liza had apparently refused to continue paying Lee Minnelli's staff or her utilities and house maintenance. The pool we had observed purportedly became a green swamp kind to breeding insects. The lawsuit was later dropped and Liza was set to have dinner with her stepmother on a swing out to L.A. We make this note only as a news item addendum to our interview with Lee Minnelli. The L.A. story is not about its scandal but about its cultural ascendance. Let the reader speculate about the Minnellis. Perhaps the upkeep of the house was prohibitive, or perhaps it was something else quite innocuous that prompted Liza's actions. The Minnelli home will be missed because it represented yet another vestige of the old and glamorous Hollywood that is slipping away.

*   *   *

Producers of the 2000 Oscar television broadcast, Richard and Lili Fini Zanuck are a mixture of Old Hollywood and new. Both are major Hollywood players. Richard Zanuck, the former head of 20th Century Fox, is the son of legendary Old Hollywood producer Darryl F. Zanuck and has a coveted star on the Hollywood Walk of Fame. He won an Oscar for *Jaws* and has produced *Deep Impact* and *Rules of Engagement* among a host of film credits.

Lili Fini Zanuck, now a brash, daring producer in the New Hollywood, drove to L.A. in her Mustang in 1977 looking for some adventure after growing up on the East

Coast and in Europe. The adventure took the form of Richard Zanuck, some twenty years her senior, whom she married in 1978. Thus began her notable Hollywood career, which has included the production of hits such as *Cocoon* and 1989's Best Picture, *Driving Miss Daisy*. Between them these films garnered six Oscars and led to two Producer of the Year awards for Zanuck, placing her in the top flight of the current crop of Hollywood producers. She has appeared in the annual edition of *Vanity Fair* that features the new wave of Hollywood stars and producers.

The Zanucks live in Beverly Park, an enclave of estates at the end of a long, winding drive through Benedict Canyon. A gated entrance fit for a palace signals your arrival at these custom residences far above central Beverly Hills. Residents have included Rod Stewart, Magic Johnson and Denzel Washington. Association dues are over $1,000 a month, a mere drop in the bucket compared to the 10 plus million-dollar price tags of many homes here. The Zanuck estate, built in 1992 on land the Zanucks bought from Kenny Rogers for $2.8 million and once put on the market for around $20 million, is perfectly positioned at the end of the street, affording maximum privacy and magnificent views from all sides. The traditional heavily wooded driveway winds up a hill to the colonial brick exterior of the home, emptying out into a large motor court where space abounds for cars should one be in the mood for a little entertaining.

The three-bedroom, 17,000 square-foot home is in the traditional mode, but Lili Zanuck is not. She exudes strength and confidence in her jeans and boots, a poster child for the hip that is Hollywood today. "This is a young man's business," says Zanuck, and that results in hipness to some extent. She sees the transplant culture of L.A. as imbued by a sense of adventure—seekers drifting in looking for something, anything—an analysis which largely mirrors her own experience.

In her work as a producer, which she refers to as her "craft," Mrs. Zanuck looks for unconventional manuscripts. She makes movies that she herself would like to see.

Although she maintains that it is Southern California generally rather than Hollywood specifically that influences cultures across the globe, Zanuck also says that the public doesn't necessarily know what they want to see, so Hollywood has to be forward-looking to find the next hit. "Who would have wanted to see a movie about a Jewish lady and her chauffeur before *Driving Miss Daisy* came out? Who wanted to see another film about the Titanic?"

When not producing, Lili Zanuck is active in fundraising for women's issues, AIDS causes, and Democratic politics. She points out that Hollywood's liberal bent comes from the nature of those who made it: The motion picture industry founders were all self-made men who were naturally for the underdog. "Nobody here is to the manor born."

When Lili Zanuck first came to Los Angeles, she was bothered by the lack of a center, a main focal point such as those found in Paris or New York. She now considers this to be an advantage because it enables her to "have an entirely private, private life." L.A. author Carolyn See concurs, characterizing the city as "a place where you can be very rich and no one will bug you. You can be anonymous." The L.A. spread allows well-known residents to walk down a street without meeting five of their acquaintances. Zanuck says this sort of privacy would be impossible for her in New York. She describes L.A. as loose socially, lacking a social calendar to which you must give weight as in New York.

And Hollywood is clearly the loosest socially of them all. Zanuck describes the Industry as "a factory town" where "people work very strange and long hours." "We leave for six and seven months at a time." She adds that her schedule is so unpredictable that she cannot make social commitments even two weeks in advance because she might have to leave town for a shoot. The Zanuck family projects in 2001 illustrate her point. Richard Zanuck produced *Planet of the Apes* in Los Angeles. Lili was in Ireland shooting *Reign of Fire*. Dean Zanuck, one of their two sons, was in Chicago producing *The Road to Perdition* with Tom Hanks and Paul

Newman. Their other son Harrison remains in the Beverly Hills offices of the Zanuck Co., which oversees about 10 projects at a time. The Zanuck reach resounded in the summer of 2002 as both *The Road to Perdition* and *Reign of Fire* opened on the same July weekend.

Former Music Center Chairman Andrea Van de Kamp concurs that regular volunteer activities prove difficult for Hollywooders because of the last minute scheduling so common in the Business. A good chunk of Hollywood production is now done elsewhere. In Old Hollywood days, most production was local. Almost all the stars lived in Beverly Hills and developed a certain attachment to the area. Their existence was more stable as the studios' job was to line up projects for them.

Lili Zanuck, after explaining how her day can vary depending on whether she is visiting a movie shoot or attending a meeting, is ready to leave home for her office. This woman lives and breathes Hollywood and like many in the Business, seems to talk in film metaphor and simile. "A serious book on Hollywood, hmm. We have never taken ourselves seriously in film . . . hmm . ."

Hot Property

To move up in L.A. today, you move west, explains Ruth Ryon, "Hot Property" columnist for the *L.A. Times*. You may purchase a "starter" property in the Hollywood Hills for several million dollars after your first big movie hit, as did 1998 Best Actress Helen Hunt, who bought the old Errol Flynn lot for $2 million and built a house on it for 3 million dollars. Singer Sheryl Crow also calls Hollywood Hills home after purchasing a home there for just under 2 million dollars. As you get richer, you progress to Beverly Hills or Bel-Air, and then finally to beachfront property in Malibu, where lots are being measured in beachfront **feet**. Beverly Hills realtor Jeff Hyland, co-author of *The Estates of Beverly Hills*, confirms that there has always been a drift westward toward Malibu. Richard Gere fits this pattern of Hollywood stars moving west. Gere started out in

Hollywood Hills, moved to Beverly Hills in the 1980s, and then on to Malibu in 1990. The seaside enclave of Pacific Palisades is another trendy Westside location with names such as Spielberg, Hanks and Whoopi Goldberg gracing Amalfi Drive, the new "super street" where the Reagans, the Pecks and the Joseph Cottens lived in the 1950s. Nicolas Cage sold a home in the Hollywood Hills for $1.5 million after having bought a Bel-Air home in 1998 for 7 million. Since 1990 Cage had lived in a Hollywood Hills home built in 1928 with 5½ baths, a circular library, a wine cellar and a humidor. Cage also has a place in Malibu and purchased an additional 400 acres in Malibu Canyon. Cage is clearly bullish on L.A. real estate.

The Beverly Hills Flats, an enclave between Santa Monica Blvd. and Sunset Blvd. once populated by Old Hollywood stars such as George Burns and Gene Kelly, is not considered good enough by many celebrities today, partly because it is too open to stargazers. In years gone by, in more relaxed times, stars living in the Flats might even wave at the busloads of fans. It is said that Beverly Hills culture was so open that once Jimmy Stewart, who lived across the street from Lucille Ball, took vegetables grown in his Liberty Garden to her front door, only to be told by the maid, "We don't want any." But today privacy and security are of paramount value and explain in part why so many stars wind up in Malibu, Brentwood or Pacific Palisades.

As for prestige, you can't beat East Gate Bel-Air, described as "prime, prime, prime" by one realtor, home to ultra-exclusive properties such as the former Salvatori estate. The late Henry Salvatori helped to found the Music Center, and was also one of the founders of Reagan's Kitchen Cabinet. The Salvatori estate, one of the 5 major estates in L.A. proper—a notable estate being defined by one realtor as "four prime acres surrounded by a wall"—sold for close to 20 million dollars in March 1998 amid an increasingly hot market in high-end properties. The 12,000 square-foot home sat at the end of a long private drive on four flat acres and features 33 rooms, a tennis court, pool, guesthouse and an eight-car garage. Characteristic of L.A.'s frenetic Westside real estate market, the Salvatori home's new owner tore down the house to make way for an even larger structure.

The Golden Triangle of Beverly Hills, Bel-Air and Holmby Hills is also home to most studio heads, who prefer the reasonable driving distance to the studios, and features many less sizeable properties of one and one-half acres or more of level land. Disney's Michael Eisner lives in Bel-Air, while Michael Ovitz calls Brentwood home. Most studio moguls, such as Paramount's Sherry Lansing, former Warner Bros. chiefs Bob Daly and Terry Semel, and Eisner also keep beach properties in nearby Malibu.

For the ultimate status, Holmby Hills, location of the famous South Mapleton Drive—dubbed by one realtor "the most important street west of the Mississippi"—is not far away. South Mapleton Drive has boasted names such as the late Ray Stark, onetime head of Columbia Studios; Alan Paulson; Howard and Libby Keck; Charles Wick, Reagan Kitchen Cabinet member; and the late Lita Hazen, Walter Annenberg's sister. The famous Aaron Spelling estate, "a minor major estate," graces the street, as does Hugh Hefner's Playboy mansion. South Mapleton Drive can claim Kentucky connections as well. The Paulsons owned 1996 horse of the year Cigar, the Kecks raced Kentucky Derby champion Ferdinand, and Ray Stark bred racehorses. Down the street lives Marjorie Everett, who ran Hollywood Park racetrack for many years.

L.A. Times columnist Ruth Ryon notes that most stars keep a foothold in L.A., which boasts two of the top three most expensive residential real estate markets in the country—Beverly Hills and Brentwood. Stars often buy, but should they prefer to lease, the rents can be as high as $20,000 to $30,000 per month. Homes can become so identified with their former star owners that they bear their names. Some homes boast multiple celebrity owners. An Egyptian-style house complete with moat in Benedict Canyon was home to Cher until Eddie Murphy bought it. A Beverly Hills home near the Beverly Hills Hotel once owned by Buster Keaton was later bought by Cary Grant and then by Barbara Hutton. The star-struck home was later purchased by James Mason and his actress-wife Pamela Mason. A home's pedigree carries considerable weight with potential buyers, although realtors disagree as to how much if any additional money buyers are willing to pay for the second-hand glamour of residing in a star's former home. The houses are usually quickly remodeled anyway, wiping away traces of their famous former owners.

Then there are properties whose histories include not merely celebrity owners but notoriety as well. The Knoll, a nine-acre estate in Beverly Hills now owned by Marvin and Barbara Davis, had been home to Edward Doheny, who was murdered by his secretary in what was rumored to be a gay romance gone wrong. Dino De Laurentiis and Kenny Rogers also called The Knoll home before the Davises paid Rogers just over 20 million dollars for it.

Some homes do not survive their notorious history. In 1998 O.J. Simpson's former Rockingham Drive house was demolished by the new owner. Neighbors were hopeful that the demolition would rid the street of media crews and lookey-loos, almost constant features of the location since the double murder of Nicole Brown Simpson and Ronald Goldman thrust the neighborhood into the national and even international spotlight.

Just when you think you've seen it all, you drive out to Malibu for an entirely different haute scene. The Malibu Colony is a six-mile coastal stretch of ultra-prime real estate established after a book revealed the addresses of many movie people in Beverly Hills. Some chagrined Old Hollywood stars left for the beach, forming the Malibu movie colony. Early colony residents included Bing Crosby, Gloria Swanson, Gary Cooper, Barbara Stanwyck, Jack Warner and Clara Bow. Now Tom Hanks and Rita Wilson number among the many Hollywooders who live in the Malibu colony, and the Marvin Davises rent there. Just who shows up in Malibu is as intriguing as a high stakes poker game.

The Malibu home bought in 1997 by the late Dodi Al-Fayed before he and Princess Diana became an item has a new resident. Stan Kroenke, board member of Wal-mart, co-owner of the St. Louis Rams and owner of the Kroenke Group real estate investment and development corporation, bought the house with furnishings for around $9 million. Kroenke's wife Ann is the daughter of Bud Walton, who founded Wal-mart with his brother Sam. Sam Walton was known for his frugal lifestyle reminiscent of the wealthy of the early 1800s and before. But the second generation of Walton wealth is clearly living more in a manner befitting the billionaire club.

Today the Malibu crowd, like most of the beach-oriented set from Laguna Beach and Newport Beach on down the coast, is thoroughly modern and contemporary. Malibu is L.A. style in its purest expression. Malibu is not just the stars or the movie moguls—even Ovitz, Sherry Lansing, Eisner, Streisand, Jane Seymour and Cher cannot compete with the magic of the fabled California coast itself. Just inland from the coast rest the several-acre spreads of Malibu's horsy set. The area seems to be more country than beach living. At Carbon Beach reside former Warner Brothers heads Terry Semel and Bob Daly, DreamWorks' Jeffrey Katzenberg and producer Arnon Milchan. Up the coast at Point Dume live Fred Hayman, Johnny Carson and Barbra Streisand, who paid $12.5 million for two houses on three bluff-top acres.

Real estate, Malibu-style: Take the former property of Abe Lurie opposite the Malibu pier. Lurie sold part of the land after a proposed hotel project didn't fly so he could free up some cash to buy his wife an $825,000 necklace. What a nice man. Of course, his wife's family owns King Communications, which bought "Wheel of Fortune" from Merv Griffin. The new owner built a house in the form of a horseshoe with the driveway alone costing 2 million dollars. Its unique design allows its residents to follow the sunrise in the kitchen and watch the sun pass throughout the day until viewing the sunset from the den. Realtor Jeff Hyland handled the 2 million dollar transaction for a 5% commission. Nice deal.

Malibu real estate can also get hot and nasty when the billionaires and multi-millionaires clash with plain old millionaires. SunAmerica chief Eli Broad, Haim Saban of Saban Entertainment and then L.A. Mayor Richard Riordan and wife Nancy Daly Riordan bought six parcels in Malibu and tore down the existing structures to build new homes. Broad's home was to be designed by Richard Meier, who also designed the new Getty Museum complex. Since their project would block precious beachfront views, the group made a deal with the Coastal Commission to buy another parcel down the road and preserve its ocean view. Good deal, right? The Commission thought so, voting 12-0 for the plan. Not so the homeowners near the second parcel, who flew into a tizzy at the prospect of lookey-loos coming their way. One of the discontented, legendary Hollywood agent Freddy Fields, who founded Creative Management Associates and was later President of MGM, expressed the homeowners' sentiments: "This is a ramrod job. It's totally immoral to take your problem and dump it on someone else." Lou Adler, renowned recording producer who handled The Mamas and the Papas and Carole King, concurs: " . . . And it's really rude to the people who live out here all the time, not those who just come out a few weekends a year." And so it goes in "laid back" Malibu, where the development of the tiniest parcel can cause the earth to tremble and incite wealthy residents to trade barbs.

Desirable features of high-end properties in Malibu and L.A. generally include total privacy and park-like grounds. Sound-surround theatre and wine cellars are two of the latest trends. The current preference is for a gym or office adjacent to the master suite. You may find a powder room that is truly a "rest room," sporting a canopied lounge bed beside one wall. Not a bad idea considering how tiring the party circuit can be. If one wishes, she could be at a party every night. Although by Parisian standards the parties are not late (no 2 a.m. dinners after the opera), the bewitching hour of midnight has often passed before guests head home—this in spite of the L.A. tradition of early evenings born of the Industry's 5 a.m. shootings. Some celebrities eschew the party scene altogether to get some shut-eye. Brooke Shields says she had to give up late nights when she was doing early morning shoots for her television sitcom "Suddenly Susan."

Hollywood types in particular crave rooms with specialized functions since it's a luxury for them to be alone, explains Naomi Leff, interior designer to Spielberg, Katzenberg, Geffen, Diller and Cruise. Hot Hollywood rooms include a worship room (often for devotees of various strains of Buddhism, Kaballah and other esoteric traditions), a billiard room, a gym, a playroom, and of course, a screening room. Also popular are private libraries, private sitting rooms, and individual home offices.

Then there is the simply unique—a house in Malibu with stainless steel walls. As with the middle class market, kitchens and master suites sell homes. Classical 1920s architecture can co-exist with contemporary decor, as in the Holmby Hills home of Marc and Jane Nathanson. Some owners will go to great trouble to achieve the perfect look. One Beverly Hills resident bought an Italian quarry so all the marble in his entry hall would match. Another spent millions of dollars removing earth to improve his view and to expand his grounds to the two level acres needed to make the property officially an estate.

Although elements of the upper crust have thrived on publicity since the 1920s, the drive to be seen ends at the manor's gates. This desire to be completely secluded when at home stems largely from concerns over security and a wish to avoid celebrity watchers. Some owners don't want to be in Ruth Ryon's *L.A. Times* column on high-end real estate for the same reasons—she has been called by readers angry because they found their homes mentioned in her "Hot Property" section.

Unusual reasons abound for the purchase of a high-end property, above and beyond the obvious motivation of status. You may buy to keep your wife busy and out of trouble, or you may wish to give her a "career." You may be playing the tycoon's version of keeping up with the Joneses, or you may simply crave the privacy and perfection of a multimillion-dollar home. Whatever your reasons, when you have found the mansion of your dreams on the Westside, you send your attorneys and CPAs to negotiate the deal. One more item to remember if you're thinking about movin' on up: You must, of course, pay cash.

Hotel Hollywood

Los Angeles has never been known for its fine hotels nor necessarily, it seems, as one hotelier once joked, for its illustrious guests. Upon being thanked by a guest for allowing his purebred dogs to stay with him at the hotel, the hotelier in question quipped, "That's all right—they're better bred than most of my guests." Jokes aside, places such as Paris, New York and San Francisco have always come to mind as hotel capitals. L.A. has had the noted Biltmore Hotel downtown and the now defunct Ambassador Hotel, home of the Cocoanut Grove, a famous nightclub where Merv Griffin played the piano and Fred Hayman was once the maitre d'. During the Grove's heyday you might see Howard Hughes sitting in the back with Marilyn Monroe, and Rosalind Russell throwing a party. The Ambassador became infamous in its waning days as the place where Robert Kennedy was shot during the 1968 presidential campaign.

Take the stately Regency Beverly Wilshire in Beverly Hills, the hotel with its own private street in the back and no identifying sign in front. The Beverly Wilshire's doors open onto Rodeo Drive, where the sidewalk in front of the hotel provided the backdrop for Julia Roberts' prancing about in *Pretty Woman*. Ron Howard, the hotel's official ambassador, describes the location as being "on the cusp of the shopping capital of the world." This is the hotel of dignitaries, where the princes and princesses stay, the hotel which has hosted virtually every head of state in addition to First Ladies such as Nancy Reagan and Hillary Clinton. The

Beverly Wilshire is L.A.'s version of European and New York haute elegance, complete with chandeliers and streetlights reportedly from Edinburgh Castle. Walking out its front doors is reminiscent of stays in Paris and gives one that city feeling found in only a few locales in L.A.

The Beverly Wilshire has had its share of hoopla—Elvis used to practice in a large space at the top of the hotel that was later converted into a suite for Warren Beatty. The hotel has demonstrated a rare quality in L.A.: Staying power. In a city that redefines itself every 10 years or so, the Beverly Wilshire has been around since the late 1920s. Along with the Beverly Hilton, the Beverly Wilshire continues to serve as a venue for Society events. With enduring brilliance, the hotel hosted a pre-Oscar bash in 1998 held by Elton John to benefit the Princess Diana Foundation. Today, L.A.'s haute hotels are also venues for entertainment industry press conferences. The DreamWorks team of Steven Spielberg, Jeffrey Katzenberg and David Geffen announced plans for their studio at the newer Peninsula Hotel in Beverly Hills, and Disney's Michael Eisner has used the Beverly Wilshire for press conferences.

History in Los Angeles is anything before 1960. Turn-of-the-century L.A. still had remnants of the old Spanish land grants operating as ranches. So a hotel in L.A. that actually has a history stretches the imagination. The Regency Beverly Wilshire is one such hotel. The Beverly Hills Hotel—the Pink Palace, as it has been called—is another. The Beverly Hills Hotel is what L.A. is all about. The crown jewel of L.A. hotels, the Pink Palace surpasses the ultra-exclusive Bel-Air Hotel and the upstart on the block, the Peninsula Hotel. The venerable and classic Regency Beverly Wilshire could belong to any of a number of top cities, but the Beverly Hills Hotel could only happen in L.A. If you're visiting Los Angeles and need a reminder of where you are and what the Southern California lifestyle is all about, check into the Beverly Hills Hotel and all will be made clear.

The history of the Beverly Hills Hotel is a storybook

tale in a real life Hollywood movie. Built in 1912 by Burton Green even before Beverly Hills was incorporated as a city, the hotel was a harbinger of things to come—Hollywood and so much more. It initially stood alone amidst the bean fields and hills that would one day see the most expensive residential real estate in the world. The hotel that according to comedian Milton Berle has been through more wealthy hands than Zsa Zsa Gabor must have seemed pure folly in 1912, standing alone as an haute rest area halfway between L.A. and the ocean. But with its sprawling California Mission Revival design, the Beverly Hills Hotel has always been a truly California hotel. Its refreshing twelve-acre resort atmosphere and the fact that it came to be enveloped by prime residential and not commercial property meant that the hotel has always had an un-city like and *très* L.A. feel. By comparison, the Beverly Wilshire ballroom in the 1920s displayed all the traditional European royal trappings and today, even at the foot of the ultra-glitzy Rodeo Drive, the Beverly Wilshire feels like a European hotel. Not so the Pink Palace, which was built from the start as a resort hotel. "The Beverly Hills Hotel is what out-of-towners imagine L.A. to be," explains Helen Chaplin, once the Executive Assistant Manager at the Beverly Wilshire under Hernando Courtright and later a consultant for the Beverly Hills Hotel. One way to understand L.A., which is a feel and an attitude more than a series of structures, is to lounge about the Beverly Hills Hotel and consider its history.

The history of the Beverly Hills Hotel is forever entwined with the history of Hollywood. Silent film stars Mary Pickford, Douglas Fairbanks, Charlie Chaplin, Gloria Swanson, Rudolph Valentino, Tom Mix and Will Rogers all built homes in the bean fields surrounding the hotel soon after its opening. The hotel provided a focal point for this small community of stars who would dine at each other's homes or party on Saturday night at the hotel and then attend church service set up at the hotel on Sunday morning. Will Rogers' inauguration as the first mayor of Beverly Hills took place on the hotel grounds. Despite its noteworthy start, the hotel fell on hard times during the Depression but was salvaged by banker turned hotelier Hernando Courtright and a group of Hollywooders that included Loretta Young, Irene Dunne and Harry Warner. Courtright went on to revamp the Beverly Wilshire Hotel where for decades he hosted many a head of state as well as European royalty.

With Clark Gable and Carole Lombard finding each other in the famous bungalows of the Beverly Hills Hotel before his divorce and their marriage in the late 1930s, the hotel was back in full swing under the stewardship of the Courtright group. The pendulum began to swing to fabulous new Hollywood heights. Courtright named the famous Polo Lounge in honor of the many celebrity polo players, including Darryl Zanuck and Will Rogers, who would wander in after nearby matches. The Polo Lounge became the place to be seen among the Hollywood crowd and in time a living legend where movie moguls would gather for power breakfasts. The Lounge also became known as the place women blessed with beauty but no money might catch a wealthy husband while drinking their lunch. By night the spot attracted high class hookers seeking the bonus benefits derived from a rich clientele. When the Beverly Hills Hotel temporarily closed for a 100 million-dollar renovation in the 1990s, Charlton Heston lamented, "Nobody knows where to have breakfast now." Heston had made deals for the movies *The Agony and the Ecstasy* and *Planet of the Apes* at the Polo Lounge. Today a renovated Polo Lounge operates in full swing, and the restaurant cultivates its own herb garden on the hotel grounds.

Howard Hughes took up residence in several of the hotel's famous bungalows, really private homes, in the 1940s, reserving one for his starlet wife, Jean Peters. The eccentric Hughes, who was once seen naked in the parking lot and reportedly signed away ownership of TWA while sitting *au naturel* under a light bulb, would order pineapple upside down cakes from his personal chef at 3 a.m. and retrieved roast beef sandwiches from atop a tree branch outside his bungalow so as not to be seen. A guest on and off at the hotel for decades, Hughes at one point had his Cadillac parked on Crescent Drive, the street adjacent to the hotel, for over two years without moving it. With its flat tires and sprouting greenery, the car quickly became an eyesore. But the Cadillac remained nonetheless, tropical look and all, ignored by the hotel staff and the Beverly Hills Police Department. After all, it was Howard Hughes' car.

The history of the Beverly Hills Hotel is also a history of liaisons and secret trysts, of marriages made and marriages broken. The secluded bungalows, where you can arrive without being seen, have hosted many a noted couple over the years for fun and frolic, including Elizabeth Taylor and Richard Burton, who had a standing order for two bottles of vodka with breakfast and another two with lunch. Marilyn Monroe and Yves Montand practiced in a bungalow for *Let's Make Love*, filmed at Fox studios. Norton Simon and actress Jennifer Jones spent time in a bungalow before they were married. John Lennon and Yoko Ono hid out and relaxed in post-Beatles days.

Longtime Polo Lounge maitre d' Nino Osti recalls one evening at the Lounge when he had to quickly whisk the wife of a top studio executive to one side since her husband was already dining on the other side with his mistress. The now retired Osti had to know just who was who. He would keep abreast of the new Hollywood players by reading *People* magazine and various Hollywood publications so as to recognize the fresh young faces that might appear for lunch.

Perhaps no pool is more famous than the Beverly Hills Hotel pool, where Katharine Hepburn once dove in, tennis clothes and all, after a match at the hotel's courts. Raquel Welch was discovered poolside, and the Beatles sneaked in the back way to take a swim during the Beatlemania years of the '60s. Back to the future, you think about the little playground Old Hollywood once was as you approach the pool area, complete with private cabanas and fragrant lemon trees. As you pass singer Michael Bolton you remember the celebrity-rich history of the hotel. You do not acknowledge him unless he smiles first: You do not go gaga over celebrity in L.A.—it's an unwritten rule. You may discreetly speak of a celebrity citing after he or she has safely passed at a distance. Everyone in your group acts accordingly as Bolton passes.

You recall the Oscar party attended by the *Titanic* crew at the Polo Lounge when the film won an avalanche of awards. You are on your way to lunch there when you hear that Brad Pitt had one table and the heads of Creative Artists Agency had another the other day. As you glance at a hotel guest talking on a phone poolside while being cooled off by wet towels, you wonder what movie deal starring whom is unfolding as he speaks. Billy Crystal has held pre-Oscar press conferences before near the same spot.

After lunch you look about the refurbished hotel and out at the line of tall palm trees. The lush landscape consisting of over 180 species of plants has that unmanicured look which requires an army of gardeners to maintain. The hotel's thematic garden decor, featuring the famous banana leaf motif and art depicting plants and flowers, blunts distinctions between indoors and out.

The Beverly Hills Hotel, that quintessentially L.A. spot, will be approaching its hundredth year in a city unused to counting back before 1960. You wonder if L.A. will experience some kind of mid-life crisis on the anniversary. As you leave that night, you are spellbound as you watch a gorgeous woman dressed to the nines step out of a taxi, smiling as she walks by on the red carpet leading to the hotel's main entrance. You wonder if you should turn around and stay.

PART FIVE

THE L.A.-ING OF THE WORLD

CHAPTER TEN

L.A. Hip: Melrose and the Middle Class Talk Back

The Hip L.A. Attitude

If Los Angeles were like any other city, this book would have ended here. But L.A. is not a city like any other. Its influence is now definitively global. Only in L.A. do the hip world of music and the world of outrageous street culture with its déclassé, trendy styles reverberate into the upper reaches of the upper crust. If the cravings of L.A.'s wealthiest residents for haute products influence the broad middle class, so too do déclassé chic and spectacle from the street percolate upward through Hollywood. For if the Hollywooders are Rodeo Drive and Oscar party haute in style, they are also Malibu hip. Nowhere but in L.A. does such a volatile mix of this and that and the other make up a city's top social circles. Film is forever feasting on new cultural possibilities gleaned from L.A. street culture, and Hollywood acts as a conveyor belt for these new styles. Five-inch heels, purple hair—whatever the trend of the moment—Hollywood is there to project it to a mass audience.

Before his untimely death in 1989, Steve Rubell, co-owner of Studio 54, the Manhattan nightclub rage of the late '70s, had plans to come out to Los Angeles for business opportunities. The man who threw what Society columnist Aileen "Suzie" Mehle of *W* called "The best party I ever went to in all my life," referring to the 1988 bash Rubell arranged for *Vanity Fair*, spoke about tying in to the L.A. attitude. When opening his successful Morgans Hotel in Manhattan, Rubell considered hiring a Hollywood casting director to select his staff, which had to have "a certain look." The conventional business suits of Wall Street were definitely not what Rubell had in mind. Where did this L.A. hip look and attitude come from that Rubell wanted to emulate?

While hippiedom was synonymous with San Francisco, hip grew up in Los Angeles fueled by Hollywood's need to mimic, amalgamate and create culture at the cutting edge. Until the 1960s, the music business, which goes hand in hand with pop culture, was based in New York. The media took the New York pulse to gauge the latest taste. Tastemakers came from the New York scene. Then the Beatles visited the Hollywood Bowl. The Beatles' label was Capitol, and Capitol was in Hollywood. Soon the California sounds of the Turtles, the Mamas and the Papas, Sonny and Cher and the Byrds were beaming melodic tunes to a hungry nation, and the Sunset Strip became the place to play your way into rock 'n roll history.

It is generally not known outside the music business that singers as diverse as Frank Sinatra, the Beach Boys, Michael Jackson, the Doors and Fleetwood Mac recorded many of their top hits in L.A. Los Angeles is at the forefront when it comes to first-rate recording studios and has a rich recording tradition. The fanciful Capitol Records building, which now has landmark status, was completed in 1956 at Hollywood and Vine. Its distinct structure, resembling a stack of records on a turntable, was a whimsical suggestion about the music success to follow within. But no one could have predicted that Capitol Records would be a harbinger of the incredibly vibrant L.A. music scene that ensued.

Capitol Records had been founded by singer Johnny Mercer, music store owner Glen Wallichs and Paramount movie producer Buddy De Sylva. The Capitol Records building was quickly used by the likes of Frank Sinatra and Dean Martin in the 1950s. Meanwhile, Columbia, Warner Bros, RCA, Elektra, and Decca all opened recording studios in L.A. At a happier time, Phil Spector (arrested in connection with a death of a Hollywood starlet found in his home in 2003) produced the Ronettes' 1960s hit "Be My Baby" in Hollywood. Elvis Presley recorded "Jailhouse Rock" and "All Shook Up" in L.A., and the Rolling Stones cut "Satisfaction" in Los Angeles.

Music producer Lou Adler, producer of the famous Monterey Pop Festival in 1967 that launched the careers of Janis Joplin and Jimi Hendrix among others, comments on the Sunset Strip of the 1960s, "Kids would drive by, hanging out the car windows playing tambourines." You could barely walk the sidewalks as you tried to get into the Whiskey-A-Go-Go or some other club to see the next up and coming performer. And Adler saw something else even more marvelous as a result of the rock explosion in LA in the go-go '60s: The mutual courting of Hollywood and the record industry. When the Mamas and the Papas played the Hollywood Bowl, Hollywooders such as actor Steve McQueen were in the audience. Actor Peter Fonda hung out with David Crosby of Crosby, Stills and Nash. Mia Farrow bought Mama Cass silk robes in Beverly Hills. Jack Nicholson dated Michelle Philips of the Mamas and the Papas.

L.A., almost overnight, it seems, had become a trendsetter. An L.A. entertainment juggernaut was set in full motion. Joni Mitchell's 1970 album "Ladies of the Canyon" highlighted this concentration of rock vocal and guitar power in L.A. Regular residents of Laurel Canyon, from Carole King to Joe Cocker and others too numerous but no less important to recount, were joined by a host of visiting groups: The Stones, the Beatles, the Animals and so on. A taste of the '60s canyon lifestyle: Judy Collins is introduced to Stephen Stills. They have a love affair and Stills writes "Suite: Judy Blue Eyes."

By the 1970s the Sunset Strip, once the place Hollywood stars would dine, had become the absolute center of American pop music, according to *L.A. Times* music critic Robert Hilburn. Elton John, Tom Petty and Bette Midler all had gigs on the Strip in those years. Music hip had combined with Hollywood trendy. Elton John described his engagement at the Troubadour in August 1970 when he was introduced to an American audience by singer Neil Diamond: "My whole life came alive that night, musically, emotionally... everything... I was a fan who had become accepted as a musician..." Larrabee Studio in West Hollywood was a hotbed of the disco scene with artists such as Donna Summer and The Village People. Larrabee is now heavily into Soul R&B and has hosted projects by Brandy and Monica, Montell Jordan and Will Smith.

And the beat goes on in Los Angeles. Ocean Way, one of the busiest recording studios, was used by Bonnie Raitt for "Nick of Time." Whitney Houston's "I Will Always Love You" and Natalie Cole's "Unforgettable with Love" albums came out of Ocean Way in the 1990s. Originally Douglas Fairbanks' sound stage, Ocean Way was converted in 1959 to its main use as a recording studio. Music business roots in L.A. added to the Hollywood entertainment cocktail that has catapulted Los Angeles from an also-ran to a city of culture creation.

But that is not all. As American culture played out more and more on the streets, it was L.A.'s streets to which everyone looked. The Venice boardwalk and the shops on Melrose paraded a street fashion found nowhere else on the planet. L.A. street style competed with haute trends from the top couture collections on a flourishing Rodeo Drive and influenced the ready-to-wear mass lines. In the 1990s the Sunset Strip itself came to represent an upscale version of this hip trend as cafés and trendy clothing stores abounded. Celebrities, recording industry executives and Hollywood Hills locals dine and shop on the famous street. Art, too, has felt the influence of the street, with a decidedly contemporary flavor surfacing.

L.A. is now teaming with hip, ultra-cool hotels such as the Mondrian and the Argyle that provide venues for that special L.A. mix of entertainment executives, stars, model-types, Eurofashion-aholics and rock and rollers. The Mondrian's Ian Schrager, who also owns Morgan's in New York, reflects on the hip L.A. hotel scene where hanging out has become yet another art form: "Hotels are picking up on the importance of entertainment and sex appeal." After opening yet another provocative hotel in London, Schrager announces matter-of-factly, "I am in the entertainment business." Hollywood, meaning that little touch of show biz, pops up in major social venues around the world. And L.A. is the crème de la crème of showbiz nightlife glamour: Just try getting into Sunset Boulevard's famous SkyBar after midnight if you are not a major recognizable star.

Only in L.A. has the marriage of hip and haute lifestyles flowered into its widest possible expression. L.A.'s hip side grew out of New Hollywood's irreverent attitude toward tradition and from the L.A. street culture of Melrose and Venice Beach. What is the L.A. attitude? It is the "This is where it's at" attitude, the "We walk to our own beat" attitude so that others have to try to emulate us, to catch up. The L.A. attitude may often be bizarre, but it is refreshing in its hip form. L.A. style can be fabulous but also overdrawn in its haute form. In isolation, Rodeo Drive is a caricatured L.A., an L.A. created by those who fancy only the film images of the city as real. Reflecting this cultural dichotomy, people either love or hate L.A.: Pick your poison or pick your pleasure. Paradoxically, the L.A. haute attitude was actually brought from outside by retailers, some of whom were foreign nationals and transplanted Society wannabes.

Although the emerging L.A. haute culture was initially imported, it simmers and glimmers in the L.A. sunshine (after all, everything does) and is in turn exported to America and the world via television, film and the print media. Jackie Collins' 1985 bestseller *Hollywood Wives* was conceived while she was "doing" lunch in Beverly Hills. Judith Krantz's *Scruples*, published in 1978, takes place on Rodeo Drive. Both books became made-for-television movies. But this L.A. haute culture developing in the 1970s and '80s on the Westside was superimposed on a more laid-back L.A. lifestyle, and the two co-exist today, at the dawn of the new millennium, in an uneasy, almost schizophrenic, relationship.

L.A. haute culture is somewhat disingenuous because at its ever vibrant center stands Hollywood. And Hollywood, despite being the seat of great fortunes and surrounded by the aura of the stars it creates, cannot escape its artistic side and somewhat Bohemian origins. It is as hip as it is haute. So billionaire David Geffen, dressed in jeans, meets *sans femme* with an *L.A. Times* reporter at his multimillion-dollar mansion. This is not the image of an haute couple in a New York penthouse, dressed to the nines, looking like a pair of mannequins. If you're in L.A. and you're rich enough and confident enough and happen to be gay, you don't need to go two by two and you can wear what you like. Hollywood films have been criticized as formula, but Hollywood lives are anything but formula. Arnold Schwarzenegger goes to Color Me Mine to paint pottery for his kids. Lili Zanuck does yoga.

L.A. attitude is unpredictable and takes on many hues—as imposing as a Rodeo Drive boutique, as laid back as a mid-day stop at a juice bar, or as intriguing as a movie industry power lunch. The L.A. expression is hip as in ponytails and haute as in a Bel-Air estate. Los Angeles happens outside in the streets and open spaces. Hip L.A. is everywhere: On the beaches at the Venice boardwalk, in the small clothing stores on Melrose, and throughout the Industry that generated this ultra-creative city among the writing teams and production crews of Hollywood.

L.A. style is whatever has the upper hand at the moment, for a moment's attention is all a new trend gets from a city always looking for the **next** trend. Youthful tourists and locals comb the Melrose fashion corridor searching for this next trend. Shoppers, participants and onlookers come to Melrose with hopes that they will be one of the first to wear the new must-have shoes, dress, T-shirt, sunglasses and so on.

Move up the road to the Sunset Plaza where Rodeo haute and Melrose hip mix in the open-air cafés below the Hollywood Hills, and you find L.A.'s own version of a European street scene. Sitting high above most of the L.A. basin, how could you feel anything but smug as the waitresses, mostly aspiring musicians or actresses, eye you as a potential business contact as much as a customer? Excess and pretension are unnecessary parts of the Sunset package, too. Where else in the world could this social scene exist with film and music industry people, the modern-day cultural movers and shakers, sitting side by side? If you do happen to pop in on the Sunset Plaza to seek your calling, don't forget to ask if your fresh fish is broiled or baked in an herb sauce—or it might come with a heavy egg batter uncomfortably reminiscent of that on the frozen fish your mother used to serve you as a child when you incorrectly decided you didn't like fish. California Cuisine has not yet hit the Sunset Plaza restaurants, which try too hard to be European. This topsy-turvy Sunset scene is characteristic of much of a city where real culture and excess, authenticity and mimicry, exist side by side as the modern L.A. culture rather unevenly unfolds.

Hip L.A. struts its stuff at the world renowned Art Center College of Design in Pasadena where automobile design, modern product designs, illustration and set design for the motion picture industry, and theme park designs meet. Housed in the Art Center's modernist structure are artists from all over the world who come for hands-on study with all types of visual arts professionals. David Brown, the Center's former President, sits in his open offices dressed in jeans. Cutting-edge design and daring abstract art provide the right fuel for the L.A. dream machine. If the modern culture works, it works in L.A. or it doesn't work at all.

The L.A. attitude is modernist—the old must prove its worth or be cast aside. The attitude comes with a certain conceit, but one backed up by real performance. Conceit plus performance plus action equals power. Hollywood is an industry of images, but behind the images rests the real power of money and status. Hollywood does not equal Los Angeles, but since at least the 1960s, the special flavor of L.A. has come from Hollywood and its celebrity-based image.

Hip L.A. from the street in turn influences the Business and affects the development of an L.A. upper crust. Sitting astride the top of the American social structure, Los Angeles looks New York, the previously undisputed leader, in the eye. The two upper classes look the same on the surface. If we view L.A.'s Betsy Bloomingdale and New York's former San Franciscan Nan Kempner back to back at a charity ball in L.A., they are clearly of the same class. But the origins of the two upper classes are diverse, their geographical settings dissimilar. Los Angeles simply has the geographical advantage. One cannot equate a Beverly Hills mansion with a Park Avenue penthouse. L.A. wealth is tied to a special Industry that has a corporate counter-culture streaking up its back. And that Industry is riding an unprecedented appetite for its product as part of a worldwide explosion of the entertainment market.

L.A. Culture Goes Global

The Hollywood structure is fed by scores of writers and technicians who are more hip than haute. For a time there were more men with ponytails on L.A.'s Westside per capita than anywhere else. The Hollywood complex, although a seedbed of great fortunes, has always had a somewhat anti-corporate attitude. The ponytail at a long lunch says, "I am not tied down to an 8 to 5 job; I am not homogenized or sanitized—I am not packaged. I am unique." Producer Lili Zanuck can be found at her Beverly Hills offices in Armani or in jeans. Even the writers, agents and production types who may be bit players on the Hollywood scene carry more social distinction than their counterparts on the corporate ladder in other industries. There is no dress code on the set, and young people often make key decisions. This is why the Peter Pan phenomenon of older men trying to look hip or younger surfaces so much in Hollywood.

Former Universal Chief Executive Frank Biondi, Jr. and Universal President Ron Meyer were pictured in a 1996 *L. A. Times* article with Biondi in the traditional corporate attire of suit and tie while Meyer wore khaki pants with a white button-down shirt sans tie. What major corporation allows one of its chief executives to work without a tie? The only exceptions may be in the West Coast-based computer industry. The pair hardly looked like co-executives of a major company.

At lunch in the executive commissary, Biondi ate the traditional fare of a turkey sandwich with fries and a diet Coke, while Meyer ate an L.A.-style Cobb salad with bottled water. Yet even Biondi had been touched by the L.A. hip style, as his colorful tie would have been deemed outrageous at IBM. Elsewhere in corporate America, Biondi undoubtedly would have been admonished for his excessive taste with the message, "This is not the image of security and stability we wish to project to our clients." No "dress for success" look here—at least not the kind IBM would recognize.

The late Nancy Vreeland, one-time owner of her own fashion company and daughter-in-law of the late *Vogue* editor Diana Vreeland, observed that although a certain fashion elegance still comes from New York and Paris, street fashion such as weekend wear and athletic wear starts in L.A. Both she and Caroline Ahmanson have pointed out that the fashion industry per se is bigger in Los Angeles than in New York. "Body conscious dressing emanated from this coast," explained Vreeland. In large part this results from what Mrs. Ahmanson calls "the physical culture of L.A.": Angelenos have access to fresh fruits and vegetables and sunshine all year, so people are more health-conscious. "People here dress to be seen," notes one fashion insider. Unlike the Midwest, where people want to blend in, Angelenos want to be noticed when they step into a room. Historically, L.A. has paved the way for "the casual, comfortable look, the honest wearing of pants," recalls Ahmanson. The display of sensuality, being provocative, athleticism—"What the stars wear and how they wear it has tremendously influenced what designers are designing." "More fashion trends emanate from this city," concluded Vreeland.

When you look as if you are trying to make an L.A. fashion statement, when it's noticeable, you have gone over the top. The L.A. look is above all cool, and cool is not over the top. The real L.A. is more focused on doing and creating than on show, display, or simply play—this in spite of the city's status as a vacation Mecca. The authentic L.A. is truly in the American tradition coming from the Puritans up through colonial times that values work over leisure. It was never quite as fashionable to be simply a "gentleman" by profession in America as it was in Europe. In Hollywood the first question asked is, "What project are you working on now?" Studio heads are automatically in the top L.A. social circles since they are automatically doers—the ultimate dealmakers.

The L.A. upper crust is a strange mélange of charities and socialites, Rodeo Drive, transplanted wealth and the hometown Hollywood creative establishment—of disparate ingredients that never come together fully. Perhaps Malibu is Hollywood's real image to itself. Weekend hideaway of the stars, the elegant seaside enclave moves to an easy tempo, evoking a relaxed distinction. As Parisians spend weekdays in Paris but prefer the country on weekends, and wealthy New Yorkers remove to Connecticut estates or the Hamptons on Long Island, so Hollywooders make their escape to Malibu. The Parisian notion that the world must pass through Paris has been appropriated by L.A. as its motto. If it's happening, it must happen in L.A. first. And if it hasn't happened in L.A., it can't be genuine. Captivated by that elusive but seemingly accessible L.A. style, vacationers come from around the world to validate this creed.

In some ways Los Angeles is better understood abroad, says Caroline Ahmanson, for years an unofficial ambassador to China. L.A. is the place foreigners look at to understand the United States. They sense the power of the city that harbors Hollywood and its central place on the world stage. Ahmanson reports that in China, L.A. means Disneyland and Hollywood, and 90% of all taped and printed material comes from the L.A. area. Globally, Los Angeles is in the cultural lead.

From one Hollywood producer's point of view,

Southern California is incredibly influential in American culture as well. Lili Zanuck cites skateboarding and skateboarding fashion, alternative anything and holistic medicine as just a few cultural trends emanating from the L.A. scene. And the movie industry must be on the pulse of street culture or their movies will bomb, explains L.A. author Carolyn See. Producer Brian Grazer, who runs Imagine entertainment with Ron Howard, goes so far as to walk down Melrose and poke around the shops, asking passersby why they like a particular star and in general tuning in on the latest trends. "It's about coolness," he says.

The L.A./Hollywood now hip, then haute style can become America's ultimate rejection of Old World aristocracy and pretense, the final revolution against the more distasteful elements of Tradition. L.A.'s attitude toward culture—irreverent and modernist—is redefining taste in America. Elsie de Wolfe, one of the nation's first interior designers who adorned the palaces of the robber barons, offered a traditional view of beauty and taste that has been shattered by the L.A. upper crust. "The principles of beauty do not change," she stated. "Form, proportion, light, air, prospect, purpose—these are the values with which they are concerned." L.A. has no proportion in art, architecture or culture, continually creating itself as it goes. An *L. A. Times* architectural critic writes that in Los Angeles, architecture is "where anything goes, where individual self-expression is among the most prized values. The abstracted Mediterranean style of Irving Gill, the textile block houses of Frank Lloyd Wright, the Modernist masterpieces of Richard Neutra, Rudolf Schindler and Charles and Ray Eames, the recent experiments of Frank Gehry, Frank Israel and Eric Owen Moss—together they add up to one of the great repositories of architectural experimentation."

Propelled by Hollywood and bolstered by hip circles scattered throughout the city, the L.A. upper crust is leading a social change that the New Yorkers never had the courage nor inclination to pull off. In art and architecture, the most logical expression of the L.A. lifestyle is modernity. In food it is nouvelle, nouvelle, nouvelle. In style, it is fresh, sometimes daring but never gaudy. L.A. creates its own cadence. In social expression, it is laid back, cool. "All I want to do is have some fun—I've got a feeling I'm not the only one," sings Sheryl Crow in her ode to L.A., "All I Wanna Do." In a few lines she captures the coolness of L.A., its still innocent frivolity. It's clear why her single became a national hit: Everyone just wants to "have some fun, until the sun comes up over Santa Monica Boulevard." L.A. hip is an attitude, and L.A. haute is a lifestyle and ultimately an idea about living, not just a collection of objects to display.

But the L.A. style risks becoming excessive. At its extreme, the L.A. attitude becomes haughty and loses the natural American penchant for openness and innovation. Rodeo Drive haute and Melrose hip represent the two sides of the L.A. predicament, with Malibu's laid-back haute combining aspects of the two extremes. The attitudes are on a seesaw as the real face of the L.A. upper crust, of this infant turned adolescent, slowly emerges.

Middle Class Stories

The flip side of L.A. haute consumption, of the mania for success and validation, is the need to keep up with the Beverly Hills Joneses. This need creates a large degree of insecurity in L.A. living that cuts across class lines, and through Hollywood's films, projects materialism and fear across the nation and the world. Los Angeles is not insecure so much because of the constant threat of earthquakes or fires, but because of the daunting social task of managing the modern culture. Tradition has been blown to bits in L.A., but what culture and lifestyle are to take its place? The string of 1990s L.A. *noir* books contend that if the modern culture does not work, it will certainly not work in L.A. Instead of glamour, the *noir*ists look at maxed-out credit cards; instead of cultural power, they look at discontent—and it does exist in the land of sunshine. But if L.A. ultimately doesn't work, if multiculturalism and modernism fail in L.A., then not the city but the entire modern media culture must be questioned. Scenes from L.A.'s valleys provide a snapshot of the tension in the broader culture that often plays out in the city today.

Scene One:

You and your wife combine for a six-figure income. You are "making it," or at least you are supposed to be making it. You were a star at your high school reunion driving there in your Mercedes. Your wife got to wear her special $1,200 Versace gown she bought on Rodeo Drive, relieved to escape the monotony of the business suits she wears for her consulting work. You have just gotten back from a trip to the Bahamas, and you live in one of the choice neighborhoods in the San Fernando Valley.

Your house is enormous, much bigger than you will ever need, with every new gadget on the market. You show off your new big screen television on Super Bowl day. Of course you have a pool and a large backyard. Houseguests are invited to use your indoor Jacuzzi. You have a part-time maid. Your wife never tires of complaining to friends that there is still so much work to do. Your two children attend private schools, although the public schools in your upper income area are quite good.

You and your wife work out daily at the gym. But you stopped that recently when you read that the really rich people in Beverly Hills have their own trainer come to their homes. Anyway, you noticed that some of the people at the gym were pretty ordinary.

When you drive to work, you always use your cell phone even though you don't really need one. You usually carry your cell phone as you walk around the Beverly Hills commercial district. You compare yourself to the Parisian businessmen you noticed on your vacation in France while walking on the Ave. St. Honoré. You are dressed in your standard business suit, but you took time to buy your power tie at Giorgio Armani.

When you get to work you decide to call your broker to check on your small portfolio of stocks. You have always scolded your wife for not saving any money (you have less than $10,000 in the bank), and you are proud that your stocks have steadily climbed in value. But that was before the Dot Com bust, and of course you were heavily invested in tech stocks. It bothers you that your net worth is now a mere $125,000. You will soon be forty, and now is the time to be making your fortune.

You need to take the next step, but as you glance nervously around the office, smiling at your secretary, you grimace. You feel stuck. You have lost some of the optimism you felt when you were twenty-five and on the rise. You were to be rich by forty.

Now you feel that you have nowhere to go in the next twenty years and where you are is not enough. You are not rich and you know you are not rich. You are admired in your circle of friends, but what your friends think is not that important. In American society at large you are still a part of the broad middle class. Every day as you drive to your West L.A. office in your Mercedes with your cell phone in hand, with your power tie in place, you look up at the hills above Sunset Blvd. and wonder just what it would take to get there.

You smile as you think of the exquisite meal you had at that Melrose restaurant the other night. The white chocolate ice cream with raspberry sauce was almost as good as sex. You were dining with the best! You wonder what the valet thought when you pulled up in your Mercedes. Did he jump to open the door! But now you are back at your job. You hate to call it a job since you are a manager. You get to dine at the executive commissary. One day you sat at the same table as the chairman of the company. You sat silently as all managers do, nodding your agreement whenever appropriate. Your wife enjoyed talking it up to her friends.

But now you will have to wait another year for your next three weeks of vacation. You grimace because you read in the newspaper that ordinary workers in France and Germany get five. Somehow lunch at the executive commissary does not seem like the two-hour power lunches taking place down the street among the Hollywood crowd.

You wonder whether you are working in the right industry. You felt irritated sitting at the Melrose restaurant the other night when you saw that longhaired man in a group of Hollywooders talking about the Business. You and your friends talked about vacations and new cars, not work. You wonder if you are living in the wrong town. You could be big somewhere else, but you shudder to think about living anywhere but Southern California.

If only the investment you and your partners made in that special lens for sunglasses had paid off. You would be managing your own company. While you lost $40,000, you just read that someone else now runs a new 30 million-dollar company producing designer sunglasses.

You will be working sixty-hour weeks until Christmas. You may get an inheritance soon, but it won't be enough. Your portion will be about $100,000. You still can't buy an important piece of art for your home. You can't change your zip code to 90210. As you leave your Mercedes in your driveway, you notice that the wax job seems to have lost some of its luster. But deep inside you know that the car is not the real problem. The driveway is what bothers you. It is not in that special part of town on L.A.'s Westside where all the cars seem to shine just a little bit more.

Your wife is getting involved in the charity for the private school your kids attend. The fundraiser will be a black tie affair. But the *L.A. Times* will not cover the event for its Society section. There will be no movie stars to brighten the proceedings. Scenes from the dinner will not appear on the Society pages of *Beverly Hills 213* magazine. The event takes place in a social vacuum. Your parents are proud of your efforts as they sit at your table, but pleasing them has not been the measure of your success since you left college. Your honor and glory seem to be packaged in an airtight container, unable to spread out around you into society. Like you in your job, they are circumscribed and made trivial.

You dabbled in Philosophy at UCLA, unlike the other business majors at the fraternity, and even though you have never read the French existentialist Jean-Paul Sartre, you feel existential despair. The brief social superiority you felt at the frat in college days has given way to social isolation. Your social shout is but a whimper. You seek recognition, but feel none. You want to make a mark on society and be seen and heard, but you never escape the social din of your class.

You consume well beyond the level of your parents, whose memory includes the Great Depression and who would not understand your malaise. They have lived at the same address in the Valley for 25 years. Your mom has changed her sofa only once in all that time. Your parents have never spent more than 30 dollars for a meal, and their faces would redden if you told them about your $200 dinner on Melrose the other night. Your dad has always driven a Ford and does his own car repair. Your parents usually vacationed in the national parks where they camped out to save money. You remember the days. They would bring the extra food back from a relative's birthday party. They still don't get cable.

Yet despite your six-figure income, you know that you may never save as much money as your parents have put away even though your mom didn't work and your wife does. You don't understand their contentment. They feel so in tune with the American Dream. They have a home. They raised a family. Their kids are productive citizens. They don't understand you. But they don't have your frame of reference. They weren't bombarded by the images of haute consumption every day in the media as you were. They didn't see the top of society as you do daily. Oh, they knew it existed, but it wasn't part of their social framework. You glance at the book by a scholar who says that Americans are better off now than before materially since everyone now has gadgets such as DVD players and cell phones that they didn't have in the glory days of the 1960s. You decide not to buy the book. You did not study Sociology, but you are sure of one thing: You are measuring yourself in relation to your own society today.

You know that what your parents have is an existence in a stew of mass consumption. You know it because you have lived in it and you have tasted better. Perhaps you know it because you did **not** study Sociology. Your dad was a proud mechanic, never ashamed of getting his hands greasy. Your own job is a means to an end. Your goal is to live and consume with the best. You also want to "keep up with the Joneses," but your Joneses don't live across the street in the Valley but in Beverly Hills. And where you live and what you consume tells who you are in American society. The type of work you do, your job, is not important. You would be happy buying and selling copper futures, in effect contributing absolutely no value to the American economy, if it would put you up there on the hill.

The social peak you strive for seems to rise ever higher, and the more you try to reach it, the more your feet seem to sink into the ground as if trapped in quicksand within a social labyrinth. As you leave the fundraiser for your children's private school, you feel you are driving the wrong way home, and an empty feeling creeps into your stomach. Monday you will be back at work.

Scene Two:

When you married a doctor instead of going to college, you thought you were set for life. But it didn't work out that way. The divorce settlement didn't take you very far, and your parents, themselves fallen on hard times, couldn't help. It all seemed such a long way away from the half-million dollar house you grew up in, your mother's furs and diamonds.

But you made it through college and have since been able to secure several sales positions. Even so, your rent in Irvine—planned community par excellence of the affluent Orange County, California—is a stretch and would be impossible if not for your credit cards.

After your divorce you treated yourself to a BMW with part of the settlement. Your wounded ego saw the pricey, status-oriented car as an antidote to your low self-esteem. The high it gave you lasted less than a year, but the payments kept coming due. These days you find that driving the generic company car is your only real option. Although you enjoy your job, the money just never seems to be enough.

Your apartment is in the most upscale section of Irvine, yet almost next door in Newport Beach, pinnacle of Orange County, you see Big Canyon, a private world of multimillion-dollar estates. Its aura of exclusivity seems to beckon you each day as you drive past the gate-guarded entrance on your way to work. You are fast losing hope of ever living such a lifestyle—the lifestyle you know you deserve.

Just a few years ago you still firmly believed you could "make it" on your own. You still decry your bad luck at investing in that movie company that never saw the light of day. You risked everything for a long shot, and you lost. Luckily you were able to declare bankruptcy and wipe most of the debt off the credit cards you had tapped to the max for your once-in-a-lifetime chance at fortune.

And then there's your love life. You will be forty this year and no man is in sight. Yes, you date, but somehow that ticket to Big Canyon or even, you had hoped, to Beverly Hills, eludes you. You are stylish and appear younger than you are, but you are increasingly fearful that you are permanently on your own.

Your parents raised you in the traditional manner to be a wife and mother. Although your family was not wealthy, you became accustomed to upscale products. With all your credit card bills and the $120 you pay to the Sports Club each month, you feel more and more squeezed. You have champagne taste on a beer budget.

As you watch T.V. and look at the glossy magazines, you sense that everyone has what you want—except you. All the women appear rich and part of a happy couple. You know those shots are touched up big-time, but even so, the women all look so radiant, so young. Yet many of the stars pictured are older than you. But when you look in the mirror these days, you see the onset of age: The slightly altered jaw line, the cheeks beginning to sag, and tiny crows' feet around your eyes. Your breasts have lost the fullness they once had, and your thighs could benefit from liposuction if only you could afford the procedure.

Looking back, you wonder how it all happened. You are still beautiful, but that doesn't seem to be enough anymore. The pictures in *Vanity Fair* and *Vogue* exude perfection, and you don't measure up, workouts or not. Somehow the fact that you are the best looking among your friends doesn't make you feel any better. You feel pressured from every direction to look perfect, to dress perfectly, to consume perfectly.

Your good looks seem hollow as the media's constant parade of perfect women makes you feel plain and old. You bring in $80,000 a year, but when you see the rich and famous on T.V. or drive by the gilded gates of Bel-Air, you feel poor. In spite of your exquisite taste, you cannot consume at the top. The world seems to be at a party to which you have not been invited.

Scene Three:

You live in the Valley in one of the many neighborhoods that epitomize the middle class. Your tract home is nondescript like all the others in your neighborhood. Like most of your neighbors, you have the family camper parked in the gravel driveway, whose many cracks have let the weeds come up. The house next door needs painting badly. Your own twenty-year-old house needs a new roof, and your yard needs a lot of work. The kids' toys are scattered here and there.

You take pride in the family room you added where you and your friends watch the new big screen digital T.V. The big screen was a hit on Super Bowl Day. You bought your $5,000 toy on credit, and the first payment is not due for another six months. You do not stop to think that you are unable to make payments on the credit you already owe. You took out a second mortgage five years ago to build your family room and pay off the credit cards with high interest rates. The family room is complete, but you and your wife have again run up the credit cards. You say to yourself that you will pay off the one at 20% interest since you just received a new card with a credit line of $6,000 that charges only 15% interest.

Your oldest child is now thirteen and you still have no savings for her to go to college. You had to use her college education money when you were laid off from work seven years ago. After nine months you finally took a job with less pay; you needed the benefits since your wife was pregnant at the time. When you got married your wife didn't work, but she now works a part-time job at Target and makes hand-made dolls to sell for Christmas. You haven't bought a new car for eight years, and both of your cars have more than 100,000 miles on them. You dropped the comprehensive portion of your car insurance when you were unemployed.

You look across the street at your neighbors' house with the Lexus and Bronco in their driveway. You wondered how they did it. They have had the truck for three years now, having bought it new. Yet they are only now expecting their first child. You know that they have also flown off to several expensive vacations. Then you found out that they both went through personal bankruptcies and that the down payment for their home came from the wife's parents, whose names are on the deed to the house.

You are proud of your son, who is a star on the local little league team. You regret that you and your wife could not spend the time with him as you had with your daughter. His grades have never been high at school as he has difficulty reading. The teacher suggested he be placed in a private reading program for additional help. But since you took that part-time janitorial job, you haven't had the time to look into it. Besides, you know that you can't afford it.

You are proud of yourself for being an assistant coach for your son's baseball team. You are also active at church, always taking a lead in the barbeque fundraisers. You have even taught Sunday school, and once you took a group of kids camping. Each year you load up your own kids and the camper and take off with another family for a week at the beach. You bring plenty of hot dogs and beer and Hamburger Helper along. For recreation at home, you and your family rent movies twice a week and munch on popcorn. There are always birthday parties to go to between your and your wife's side of the family. Now and then you get into your discount suit and go to a wedding.

You go to the Price Club once a month to buy your groceries in bulk. Your wife clips coupons the rest of the time to save money. You are still mad at her because she insisted on new furniture. You are now paying for it on the 20% interest credit card. You are glad that she has been working for five years now, but you wish she had started sooner. You had used credit cards for almost three years just to pay bills even though your $40,000 a year salary was at the national average for families. You understood that she wanted to stay home for the kids, but you are suffering financially now as a result. Your mom did not work as you grew up, and you remember her reading to you nightly. You think of your son again who has trouble reading.

Someday you will inherit your parents' house in another part of the Valley, but there will be three other children who will have their share also. Your parents did help you with the down payment for your house, and you feel bad that their equity was diminished when you took out an equity line of credit. When you bought the home, you did not know that plumbers cost forty dollars an hour and heating repair men sixty dollars an hour. Your own hourly pay is slightly less than half of that. You now wish you did not have a pool. To repair the crack in it cost $3,000, and you can no longer afford the pool's upkeep.

You had not counted on the endless visits to the dentist for the kids, your daughter's eyeglasses, the cost of putting in a new sprinkler system, the cost of a new transmission for your car, and the cost of the endless birthday presents for relatives. You used to love Christmas, but now you dread what it will do to your credit card debt.

You figure you are still paying for the Christmas of three years ago at 18% interest. You used to love to read history, but now you compare yourself to a serf on a feudal estate who pays a tithe each year to the lord. Instead of a tithe, you pay interest year after year to credit card companies as the balance stays the same or climbs higher. Someone has a permanent title to part of your income, and it is not the U.S. government.

While you have your big screen T.V. and your wife has her new furniture, you have long since given up any notion of becoming rich. You have less than $2,000 cash in the bank, no stocks or bonds, and you now owe almost $30,000 on credit cards that charge high rates. Only the rising value of your home prevents you from having a negative worth. You have let your life insurance policy lapse. You have even cut down on your weekly contributions at church.

You wonder if you will ever have anything to pass on to your children. But most of the time, you are just trying to make ends meet. Your kids never stop with their demands to have the things that their friends have or that they see on T.V. You still don't have a computer for them. You refuse to buy a $75 pair of Nike tennis shoes for your son, but he does have a new bike. A trip to Disneyland just cost you $250. You almost never eat out except at a fast-food restaurant. Your neighborhood, which looked so stable a few years back, now has a graffiti problem. You have heard there is gang activity not too far away. You worry about your daughter entering middle school. A shooting occurred near the school the other day.

You take pride in your work and your kids. You are proud of the contributions you make to your church. You are living the American Dream of your parents, but it does not feel the same. You feel engulfed in a financial storm that has arisen from nowhere with no beginning and no end. You look around your neighborhood and do not feel the warmth and optimistic spirit of the 1960s when you grew up in another part of the Valley. You think of what your kids will have to face—the local gang activity, the cost of a college education—and you know something is amiss. You listen to the politicians, but their sweet words do not describe your reality. You go to work six days a week and do your job well, but you are not making it.

Scene Four:

When you were growing up near Disneyland, you dreamed of one day raising a family in a Newport Beach home with a view of Catalina Island. Now as you sit in your Harbor View home taking in that coveted Catalina vista, you feel satisfied that your childhood dreams have become reality.

Your husband is a successful Newport Beach attorney, and your children are academic stars at their neighborhood elementary school. You have been able to continue dabbling in your accounting career while devoting most of your time to your children's activities. And even without working full-time, you are able to afford all the trappings of affluence. Your husband finally bought his new E-class Mercedes last year, and you feel powerful behind the wheel of your BMW 740IL. You and your husband belong to The Spa, working out there at a cost of $300 per month. You are thinking about buying a boat and perhaps even joining the Bahia Yacht Club. Your home, decorated in an upscale nautical theme, garners compliments from all of your friends.

As you watch the setting sun, you remind yourself that you have everything you could possibly want—a lovely home, a happy marriage, and promising children—but still there seems to be something missing. The other day as you drove by Pelican Hill on your favorite route to artsy Laguna Beach, you stared in awe at the recent construction of Orange County palaces, some upwards of 21,000 square feet. You can't figure out where these people get their money. Your house seems small and ordinary by comparison.

Your husband has recently developed some professional connections in the Beverly Hills area, and this has further aggravated your malaise. When you were growing up in Anaheim near Disneyland, places such as Bel-Air and Beverly Hills hardly existed for you. Orange County was its own little universe, a perfect place to live and raise a family. Your parents were proud to be Anaheim residents in spite of their sense that they were the only Democrats in Orange County.

Now, though, you have begun to taste the haute L.A. scene, and you know that even Newport Beach cannot compete, despite the fact that millionaires are in residence and that billionaire real estate developer Donald Bren makes Newport his home. The few business functions you have attended in Beverly Hills have made it painfully clear that you are not on the social map. For the real movers and shakers, you do not exist. You tell yourself that you have what really counts, that the opulence of the Westside does not guarantee happiness. Still, that opulence makes you feel decidedly and permanently middle class.

Your parents were happy being middle class. Bob's Big Boy provided their weekly restaurant treat, and cross-country car trips punctuated by overnight stays in motels with pools satisfied the family vacation needs. But as you sit in a local restaurant watching your husband happily devouring his favorite steak and fries, you remember that special night you feasted at Spago in the heart of Beverly Hills. Regardless of his affluence, your husband has no greater appreciation of haute cuisine than he did as a student years ago. Since the super chefs are fifty miles away on L.A.'s Westside, there is little chance you will ever make their delectable creations a regular dining experience.

You know it's pointless and even ridiculous to feel dissatisfied because you are not at the top. You will never own a Bel-Air or even a Pelican Hill estate, and you will never be invited to the White House for a state dinner. You consider yourself to be practical and commonsense, but you don't know how to fight this nagging feeling of smallness. You will always be more than comfortable, but you will never be known in the highest circles. And while you are more than proud of your children, somehow basking in their accomplishments is not enough to satisfy your inner thirst for acknowledgement. You feel guilty for having these thoughts, but you know your longing is genuine as its small voice tells you that you are still so full of life, with a zest waiting to be unleashed, almost desperate for a social outlet in which to be displayed.

CHAPTER ELEVEN

L.A. Haute Culture and the Renewal of American Values

Competing for Social Distinction: The Historical Basis of the L.A. Predicament

The once powerful "old" wealth of New York that was really only new wealth all along now dances with the new wealth of Los Angeles to form the counter-pillars of the American upper crust and American society in general. The social life of the nation owes its tempo to the dual cadence of this L.A.-New York upper class lifestyle. Mass-produced, homogenized goods are out; designer products bought at specialty stores are in. Today, the bookkeeper in Atlanta not only knows about the high fashion of Armani and Versace— of the world's top designers whose creations glisten in the stores on Rodeo Drive in Beverly Hills. If she had the money, she would buy couture. She knows the difference between shopping at J.C. Penney and Armani, and more importantly, **she knows the social significance of this difference**.

In the generations immediately following World War Two, the bookkeeper would neither have known much about the symbols of upper crust distinction nor would she have cared. American culture was then far more disparate. The mass media had yet to weave vast tentacles into every nook and cranny of middle America, had yet to fabricate all of the small, often localized cultures into one great mass culture. And the upper class, still reeling from the Great Depression and World War Two, had lost much of its luster and was in no position to lead the social nation. The great new fortunes soon to be made from selling to the emerging mass market and from buying and developing real estate were still in an embryonic stage. A new generation of wealthy had yet to splash their dollars in glorious consumption, bursting into the upper class and establishing haute taste as the national ideal.

The two great cultures—the emerging culture of the broad middle class and the then dormant culture of the upper class—coexisted as if in separate worlds. America's social throne remained vacant, the social arena localized.

By the 1970s, the owners of the newly created fortunes generated by the post-World War Two economy entered high society. The upper class enlarged and spread geographically throughout the nation. As the emerging channels of the media created one great social marketplace, the upper crust became more immediate. Their opulent lifestyle became more tangible to a middle class increasingly influenced by media images. The gradual weakening of the social glue in locales large and small, along with the suburban spread facilitated by the expanding highway system, left T.V. and Hollywood as the primary cultural links. The contest for social distinction and honor reemerged on a grander scale with consumption as its basis.

A social structure in which success and recognition are based on haute consumption must follow the lead of the social grouping that consumes at the highest level. The baby boomers-turned-yuppies sought to make their own way into the upper reaches of American society. These educated college graduates from middle America set their sights to the measure of their abilities: They aimed for the top. They began to understand that social distinction no longer rested on the consumption of homogenized, machine-made, mass-produced goods owned by their proud middle class parents. 1950s and '60s middle class suburbia was a predictable Hoover vacuum—it was ordinary and therefore, in the long run, wanting. What really mattered was carefully hand-crafted goods, items of quality stamped with excellence. The social scene that really counted was high society, not the local Lions Club. By the 1980s, harmonized by the Reagan presidency, the upper crust had been revived as the nation's social arbiter.

The younger generations of the middle class, "yuppies" as they were often called derogatorily, understood that the top of American society hovered far above the plateau that embodied the American Dream. This supposed pinnacle of the social ladder, epitomized in middle class terms by the family home containing an abundance of mass-produced goods, was but a barren desert in the face of the new display of consumption of haute products by the upper crust. Unlike the hippies of the 1960s who rejected the "Establishment" for its crass materialism, the problem for the yuppies was that the middle class did not have **enough** style and quality goods. Middle class taste had been debased by the sheer gross quantity of material goods that surrounded it, goods without definition, without distinction.

To the yuppies, the blandness and homogeneity of middle America reflected this lack of social distinction. "Yuk," they cried at the tract home, at the hot dog with mustard, at the family camper. French philosopher Simone de Beauvoir commented on this homogeneity in her travels to America decades before the yuppie phenomenon when she wrote, "Hundreds of cities and a hundred times the same city. One can travel day after day in the same bus, across the same plain, and arrive each night at the same city which only carries with it a different name." The yuppies wanted more out of life—sameness wouldn't do. The mass market's response to the yuppies' aspirations was a polarization into "upscale" and "downscale" modes, aiming at the growing disparity in middle class consumption patterns and lifestyle attitudes. Consumption values from the 1950s co-existed with those of the 1980s, often in the same family. While a mother shopped at Sears, her daughter would pop in at a Rodeo Drive boutique.

The yuppies' yearning promised to do something daring and original: The yoke of mass consumption around the middle class would be broken in the name of quality. Designer furniture and caffé latte would take their places in the middle class market alongside Wal-mart. But the yuppie ship was wrought with hazard as it rode the 1980s wave of haute consumption, since many haute products are products the vast majority of Americans cannot afford. Even the more affluent members of the middle class can feel the upscale pinch, as an L.A. couple found out when they agreed to pay $690,000 for a modest Brentwood home, only to have the house snatched from them by someone willing to pay $40,000 more than the asking price—and this before the price increases of the last few years.

The cutting edge of haute consumption brings not only the sweet spoils of success to middle class neighborhoods, but also a longing for the unattainable. One status-conscious middle class woman from Orange County quickly found herself with $20,000 in credit card debt as she tried to emulate the lifestyle she saw around her: "I didn't care how much it cost . . . It looks like everybody lives like this. I can be a real person. I do not want to die without having lived [spent] at all." Acting out of euphoria, as if blindfolded, the yuppies find themselves resembling Tantalus, doomed to stand in water that recedes when they try to drink and under branches of fruit they can never reach.

The yuppies plunged into an American arena where the consumption of products largely beyond one's reach has become the ultimate pleasure, as the satisfaction once derived from honest work fades into the shadows and middle class avenues of social expression atrophy. The middle class predicament recalls Sisyphus's rolling the rock up the hill to escape oblivion, only to see its inevitable plunge to the bottom. As the rock descends, credit card balances rise. The L.A. upper crust did not create this consumption juggernaut, though it does augment the trend. But paradoxically, L.A. is the city that can find a way out. Can freewheeling consumption be anchored for the pure pleasure it promises? Is there a way out of the consumption conundrum? There is, in fact, and an unlikely Hollywood holds the answer.

Sears vs. Chanel: The Mass Market and Haute Products

The American upper class has always had an uneasy relationship to mass production, which tends to undermine the distinctive quality of goods. The upper class has clung to the notion of the artisan who produces the unique item that is difficult to reproduce. Its rarity guarantees a high price if not always high quality. Couture clothing is dominated by the Italians and the French because the level of workmanship and embroidery that distinguishes haute couture and the couture collections, setting them apart from mass-produced ready-to-wear clothing, cannot be replicated in the United States due to lack of qualified labor. The highly specialized labor of a Parisian company that does nothing but make feathers for couture clothing does not exist in the United States.

The upper crust has escaped the monotony of mass consumption through designer products. The chair in a Beverly Hills mansion is not just a chair: It is a work of art. It has designer quality, is usually one of a kind, and cannot be bought at department stores such as J.C. Penney or Sears. The owner of the chair does not have a license plate frame proclaiming, "I'd rather be shopping at Nordstrom" or "A woman's place is in the mall." Goods in upper crust homes tend to be superior in materials, craftsmanship and design to middle class goods found in mall department stores. These haute products are purchased only at specialty stores. The upper crust is the only social grouping in America to have escaped the mall syndrome which dots the consumer horizon with an oppressive sterility.

The upper crust lives mainly in an haute world, though now and then it must bow to mass society. When they do not have a corporate plane or a private jet, the wealthy must fly to Europe on commercial airlines like everyone else. With television sets and cars and a multitude of non-descript devices in their homes, the upper crust has maintained a veil of exclusivity in part by demanding that the retailers and entrepreneurs who provide them services be absolutely top drawer. People who sell to the upper crust better be at the high end of excellent. Beverly Hills realtor Jeff Hyland, John Martens of Neiman Marcus Beverly Hills and Fred Hayman, who sold couture clothing on Rodeo Drive, are retailers who have their own style, flair and the cool necessary to deal with the L.A. super rich.

Goods for the middle class have always to varying degrees been patterned after the high-end quality goods of the upper class. But after World War Two, new attitudes toward consumption surfaced. The throwaway mentality meant that a middle class family replaced their car every year, not because it didn't work but because it no longer looked right. And the surge in the mass production of goods from the 1950s to 1970s lost almost all pretext of quality. Bigger was better. More was better. Tail-finned Cadillacs and quarter-pounders were the order of the day. In the 1960s, the hippies rejected blind consumerism and viewed their parents' middle class lifestyle as crass materialism devoid of the rich individual and social values that make for a satisfying life. They challenged their seemingly content parents who, coming from humble origins, now basked in "a mountain of things," as Tracy Chapman would later sing. The hippies' contribution was to point out that this upward spiraling of commodities did not necessarily guarantee personal fulfillment.

During the 1970s and '80s, floods of middle class university graduates were hobnobbing with young adults from the upper class and being acculturated to alternative patterns of consumption. Many visited Europe, experiencing an artisan culture and consuming refined products. To them, the American Dream of a standardized home in the suburbs and the fast-food mentality could only be a wasteland. But unlike the hippies, whose denial of materialism was absolute, the yuppies understood that human beings have wants and use the things around them to enrich their lives. Humans live in a material world upon which they act. Madonna was at least partly right when she extolled the "Material Girl."

With the growth of communications in the 1980s, of the media as the great amalgamator of culture, images of the very rich popped up on the screen with regularity. Shows such as "Dallas" and "Dynasty" mirrored images of haute lifestyles in the glitzy magazines that found their way into middle class living rooms. As the media beamed images of incredible wealth and power across America, the middle class realized they were light years away from the new American Dream, a sort of Horatio Alger story recast in Hollywood glitz. And while rags-to-riches might still occasionally apply to dogs lucky enough to come into an animal shelter from a run-down South-Central L.A. street and leave in a Rolls Royce bound for a new home in Beverly Hills, you knew that the human version of upward mobility was increasingly elusive. It was hard to measure up to the relentless stream of images on the screen.

But there is more than one version of the American Dream. The Horatio Alger rags-to-riches variety, a key part of the cachet that draws people to the United States from around the world, historically has not been the Dream on which most Americans set their sights. The middle class paradise of the late '40s, '50s, and '60s offered a more attainable Dream. If you had a few children, preferably at least three as in "My Three Sons," owned a home in the suburbs which boasted a yard for the kids to play in, and maybe even had the proverbial white picket fence and a dog, you had achieved the American Dream. You were not rich, not even close, but you were considered successful. You felt appreciated.

But already by the 1980s the middle class had significant sections that identified more with haute culture than with the culture of their middle class origins. The yuppies' goal, like that of the upper class, was to obtain the best in products and services. Consumption was viewed as an act of the individual that could either affirm or debase him, rather than a purely animal pursuit for the displacement of a need. "I consume food because I am hungry" became "I consume food that is fresh and beautiful and that stimulates my palate. I experience food." The difference between feeding and dining was clear as eating became an art form, and consumption as artistic expression provided the latest trend.

The equation of quantity with prosperity commonplace to American thought since colonial times had been abandoned long before by the upper class, and was now rejected by the yuppies as well. With "prosperity" as quantity permeating the culture, the more-is-better philosophy—lived out in everything from a closet full of bargain dresses to a plate overflowing with spaghetti topped with Ragu—held no attraction for those hoping to live above the fray. Quantity and quality were now irreparable enemies. They might have been raised on all-you-can-eat buffets, but the yuppies now dined, to the fullest extent of their wallets, on the haute (read: small portions) cuisine of the celebrity chefs.

The yuppies de-masked the notion that $100,000 a year for a couple is rich. They challenged the American Dream for being inauthentic. But they also found themselves stuck on the corporate ladder in a faux existence of their own. They were making six figure incomes, but they did not have major stakes in their companies, their net worth was minimal, and they worked long hours in corporate corridors burdened with the very uniformity they had vowed to escape. They often were no closer to haute culture than their parents. Worse still, in spite of "Millionaire in Training" bumper stickers, they knew this was the case. The yuppies had mistaken the hill for the peak of the mountain, and haute consumption lay far beyond what they had imagined. They had bought into the corporate world only to find that the real players cavorted far above and apart from the corporate structure. Refusing to be consoled by the myth that the rich aren't happy anyway, they felt existential despair. A little bit of haute consumption is bliss; too much, addiction.

The middle class too often risks any present security for the all but irresistible call of lavish consumption, much as Odysseus longed for the sirens' sweet song above the treacherous shore where he would surely meet his death. Have the yuppies become prisoners of their determination to escape consumer oblivion, their siren the sweet but perilous credit card that has ravaged many a household budget? One 27-year-old mortgage broker was trying to answer the call on his $100,000 annual income until his company closed. Within four months he filed for bankruptcy because of his

$30,000 credit card debt and gave up his Acura, the payments on which he could no longer afford. His $2,000-a-month restaurant dining ceased, and he was forced to sell most of his possessions and move in with his parents.

"I Owe, I Owe, So Off to Work I Go"

Bumper stickers can reveal much about the culture that creates them, and so it should come as no surprise that in the face of consumption mania, the savings rate in American households is among the lowest in the industrialized world, at about 3.5% of income in 1997. According to the Federal Reserve, consumer debt rose 19% in 1995, to over 440 billion dollars. By mid-1999, in another year of a robust economy, consumer spending was increasing faster than growth in personal incomes—actually producing a negative savings rate. This rampant spending is not surprising since credit card companies send out a now record 3.5 billion solicitations for new business each year, often with quick promises of lines of credit up to $100,000. Tear up one of the applications and another one is on its way *toute suite*. Many credit applications require only a phone call to get the process in motion. While some consumers borrow in the classical sense, to escape a financial squeeze, many American consumers are spending discretionary income and then some instead of saving for a rainy day. It is alarming that 2/3 of households with incomes from $50,000 to $100,000 have credit card debt. Old-fashioned middle class savers have become historical relics as the memory of the Great Depression becomes cast as a part of some prehistoric time. How quickly the collective social memory fades. Instead, taking place is what economist Robert H. Frank calls in his book *Luxury Fever* "competitive spending," spending to keep up with those at the top.

75% of Americans with credit cards pay only the minimum payment each month, according to American Bankers Association figures. Credit card debt now accounts for 40% of all consumer debt, up from 14% in 1977.

Personal bankruptcies, most of which stem from unmanageable credit card debt, are at a record-breaking high, up 350% from 1980 levels. Astonishingly, 15% of the 1.3 million bankruptcies in 1997 were filed by families making more than $50,000 a year. Perhaps one shopper summed up the situation best: "Every day is Christmas."

At least some of the meteoric rise in consumer debt in the 1980s and '90s can be attributed to the drive to emulate upper crust haute consumption. One Orange County executive laments his frustration with keeping a check on his family's wants and spending habits: "It's a poison . . . [that] comes from the vast multiple sources of media that we see as a family. I'm outnumbered by television . . . We're trying to be conscious [of spending], but we can't always win."

The modern culture Los Angeles has embraced is an unabashedly consumerist culture, and with it comes the consumption conundrum. Your neighbors' Mercedes which you know they can't afford, vacations put on credit cards, the new wardrobe that replaces the other new wardrobe, the better new truck to replace the other new truck—this restless and almost obsessive middle class consumption aims not only at gratification. It seeks to replace what it cannot: The satisfaction of productive activity, of social recognition, of glory, of belonging.

A Positive Role for Haute Consumption: Can Hollywood Lead the Way?

Los Angeles has been a city that nobody really noticed. Of course everyone knows that L.A. is the land of smog, earthquakes and fires. Films such as *L.A. Confidential* and *Chinatown* point to the city's seedy politics. People have heard of all that. L.A. has immigration problems, sweatshops, traffic jams and water issues. All you have to do is watch the news. L.A. has no history—or so it seems. And tourists can't seem to find the city even as they stand in it. "Where is it?" they ask. The one cultural link a tourist will notice is the ubiquitous automobile. "You and your car culture," a Green Party member from France admonished as she passed through the city. All can agree that L.A. is the home of Hollywood. But after a walk along Hollywood Blvd., the ever-complaining tourist will remark, "Is that it? Where are all the movie stars?" The reaction brings to mind Creative Artists Agency's Bob Bookman's view that "Hollywood is a state of mind, not a place." People look at L.A., but do they really see it?

What you see at first glance is not what you get. Not in L.A., not here. For many who refuse to believe, Los Angeles is still the epitome of the slimy, the defeated, the vulgar. Whatever people hate about the modern culture they blame on L.A. Everyone has a reason not to like Los Angeles. One reporter for the *New York Daily News* at the 2000 Democratic National Convention held in Los Angeles wrote that L.A. "is the most glaring example in America of the increasing gap between rich and poor," a "once solidly middle-class city" that has begun to look "like a post-colonial Third World outpost, with an upper crust of wealth sheltering inside guarded, gated communities and an economy seemingly based on valet parking." One wonders what the writer sees when he looks at New York. Does he use the same yardstick to measure his own city? A reporter from the *Pittsburgh Post-Gazette* wrote during the convention about South-Central L.A.: "It's mile after flat, trashy mile of liquor stores, crack houses, chicken joints, taco stands and low-end doughnut franchises. It's a long way from Spago (and the Westside)." Yes, there are poor people in L.A.—the city and the modern culture distribute the fruits of labor unequally. A worthy topic. But does inequality exist only in or especially in L.A.? Is there no reality to the California Dream?

While everyone complains about the city, on another level they are fascinated by it because what happens in L.A. tends to happen elsewhere too. In Japan, women are wearing platform shoes. In a French village, two men fight over a near car accident using kickboxing techniques eerily similar to film renditions. The swimsuits in an Iowa public pool look surprisingly like those in Newport Beach. Global culture is media-driven, and an inordinate number of those images come from the L.A. lifestyle. You can't help but see bits and pieces of L.A. around the world, because Los Angeles represents the modern culture. The L.A. of influence, of social power, is the real L.A. story. People experience this real L.A., but still pay attention to its *noir* shadow of earthquakes and fires and social inequality as if that were the only reality. Earthquakes and fires are permanent, but if the issues of inequality, multiculturalism and the like can be resolved anywhere, why not in Los Angeles, the land of Hollywood?

The real L.A. is a new phenomenon and its possibilities are endless. Los Angeles "is less than most cities a prisoner of its past," explains CAA's Bob Bookman. L.A. social power has developed over the last four decades. Before 1960, there was no discernible L.A. street culture and no formidable upper crust. Beach life was Bohemian at best. Melrose was an ordinary street. Rodeo Drive had the name but not the glitz. Hollywood was still an enclave in a city without veritable cultural institutions. There was no L.A. hip and little L.A. haute. Los Angeles was decidedly provincial. L.A. culture was quaintly Midwestern. All that has changed.

If transplanted wealth from around the world didn't change the city, if the music industry didn't alter its essence, the enormous development of Hollywood certainly did. Suddenly, L.A. was becoming more and more the image of Hollywood. How could it be otherwise, when the whole world was becoming more and more media-driven? The world looked to and needed Hollywood. The French and Italians forever rail against Hollywood movies but attend them in record numbers. The media is more and more overt in people's lives. The movie *EDTV*, with a camera following someone in his daily life while everybody watches, no longer seems farfetched. Reality T.V. mocks us all. How do you turn off the camera's lights? Where do the image and the reality begin and end? What is really worth noticing? The modern society has as yet no answer. Can Los Angeles find the answer as the world watches?

The modern world needs validation. Hollywood is in the spotlight because Hollywood is the social realm in the modern world. Hollywood's taste becomes the world's taste. Hollywood consumption defines excellence. But can social avenues other than consumption be honored? Can the modern culture embrace other values as well? Haute Hollywood and hip Hollywood are the twin beams of a cultural realignment. Hollywood and L.A. may hold the key to the way out of modern culture's excesses and insecurities. Los Angeles must deal with these dilemmas if it is to become the city of the new millennium.

The current L.A. upper crust, dominated by a new Hollywood, has developed a radically modern, hip strand that in art, architecture, food, dress, demeanor and attitude represents a completely new life approach, a new step on the social dance floor. As Gagosian's Robert Shapazian aptly puts it, "This city's not about Greek temples—it's about avant-garde; it's about Frank Gehry." The culture of haute consumption takes its cue not from the penthouses of Manhattan but from the mansions of L.A.'s Westside. As the new cultural leader, the L.A. upper crust takes center stage either to push this social opening and create a new haute culture, or to slip back into the class-based, class-dominated, insular culture of aristocratic patterns of style and taste.

L.A. haute culture offers a cure to the consumption malady it helps to create. While consumption is not a noble act per se, it is a gratifying life experience when it takes a balanced position in daily life alongside work. The pursuit of excellent products is a positive sign after the weary, dreary years of mass produced goods of the 1950s and 1960s. The pursuit of excellence can also re-invigorate production values and elevate the quality of work. Haute consumption can lead to a rebirth of individualism in consumption habits. Consumption can then become the secondary individual avenue of self-expression alongside the natural primary expression of purposeful work.

The L.A. upper crust, at the head of the social nation,

can create a new and healthy balance of excellence and individual style, of elegance without pretension, of "sleek sophistication," in the words of one Beverly Hills retailer. The L.A. upper crust alone is in a position to expand this social space. As Westside realtor Jeff Hyland affirms, the L.A. free spirit allows you to do anything and everything you want to do: "We are now Ellis Island."

The Industry above all industries can re-cast production values as a central part of the happening L.A. lifestyle beamed across the nation and the world. Because of its relative newness and the Industry that dominates it, the L.A. upper crust holds work and merit in much higher esteem than do the more traditional upper classes of New York and Europe. These are values Hollywood players themselves live every day. All Hollywood needs to do is look at itself in its daily life. For as Oscar-winning producer Lili Zanuck explains, Hollywood is preeminently a work culture: "Everybody's working . . . everybody is attempting something. You've never met anybody in our business who retired and moved to Florida." And people don't have to leave town in August as in New York or Paris.

The L.A. work ethic from Hollywood and first generation wealth is infectious. Reagan supporter Earle Jorgensen, who in 1998 celebrated his 100th birthday at the L.A. Country Club under a tent set up on the lawn, reportedly still went into his office at Jorgensen Steel until his death in 1999. Billionaire Marvin Davis is up at 7 a.m. heading for his offices even after attending a top social event the night before. Davis reportedly tried retirement one time "for about three hours." Retirement is also a disease for News Corp. owner Rupert Murdoch, who "can't imagine what I would do with myself in retirement." 90-year-old agent Phil Gersh, who has handled stars such as Humphrey Bogart and David Niven, still goes to his Beverly Hills office. Gersh states bluntly, "I'm not retiring." "People don't stop," adds L.A. author Carolyn See, pointing to the many older Hollywood players with trophy wives. The late Universal chief Lew Wasserman, who died in 2002 at age

89, worked 60-hour weeks well into his eighties, getting up at 5 a.m. to call the East Coast. Events involving Wasserman served dinner promptly at 7 p.m., and any speaking was done before 10 p.m. since "Nobody listens to anything serious in L.A. after 10 p.m." Tomorrow is always a workday.

The Los Angeles upper crust eases onto the scene, a natural star as Hollywood broadcasts its real-life images of haute consumption to the nation and the world. In modern mass society, the style of consumption is the ultimate measure of social standing. Production values based on work recede into the background. What you have becomes more important than what you do. The proud American work ethic plays second fiddle to the glory of consumption. The tail wags the dog. Yet ironically, this is not so in real-life Hollywood, where you can be worth $20 million and upward but if you are not working and the phone isn't ringing, you are hurting. Haute living Hollywood-style, because of the mania to keep working and creating, stands contrary to the trend. While haute consumption is the sweet fruit of the money tree, labor gives it meaning. In Hollywood, if you are not working, even your Oscar looks lonely and tarnished on the shelf.

Hollywood's own actors and players in their own real life L.A. drama can take the lead in extolling a solid work ethic and new attitude of confidence as they shed any remains of aristocratic purport for the democracy of modernism. Hollywood's products can create a new standard of culture instead of the debased culture that its films and television have come too often to display. Its corporate culture can serve as a new model for business success, freeing workers and managers in corporate America locked in the business suit mode.

The Los Angeles upper crust can say yes to the new attitude that defines itself as it goes, that can change direction in mid-stream, that can try and fail and try again until it feels right. Culture, fashion, social attitude, responsibility, work demeanor, values—these are all aspects of American life that need renewal. The L.A. upper crust can say no to the temptation of the class-based culture of aristocracy, to the mimicry of the charlatans who cultivate the Old World. It can be a catalyst for a genuine American haute culture, anchored in production values, that spreads it allure throughout the nation and the world, paving the way for a rich individualism. Haute Hollywood can help to re-create an authentic high society in which not merely consumption, but accomplishment and benevolence attract recognition and public honor. Hollywood's hip side coupled with the pursuit of excellence can lead to a renewal of values for America and a new cultural step for the world.

Interviews

The authors have been privileged to have the input of the following people:

Caroline Ahmanson is the *grande dame* of L.A. Society. She and her late husband, Howard Ahmanson, were major donors in the early days of the Music Center. The Ahmanson Theater is named after the family. Mrs. Ahmanson is one of the largest stockholders in the Walt Disney Co. She has often functioned as an unofficial ambassador to China, and has served on the Federal Reserve Board.

Wolfgang Puck is L.A.'s super chef who started the original Spago restaurant, a hot spot for Hollywooders and site of many an Oscar party. Puck's current Spago Beverly Hills is the premier restaurant for Hollywood and L.A. Society. Puck was a key figure in the development of California Cuisine.

Lee Minnelli is a noted Hollywood hostess, wife of Oscar-winning director Vincente Minnelli, and stepmother of Liza Minnelli. Mrs. Minnelli has hosted parties attended by Hollywood royalty such as the Kirk Douglases and the Gregory Pecks.

Alan Ladd, Jr. is the son of classic western star Alan Ladd. Alan Ladd, Jr. has worked in Hollywood for four decades. Oscar-winning producer for *Braveheart*, once an agent for Robert Redford, and a former studio head at 20th Century Fox, Ladd then completed a six-picture contract for Paramount.

Lili Fini Zanuck is a major Hollywood producer along with her husband Richard Zanuck. The couple won an Oscar for *Driving Miss Daisy* and produced the 2000 Oscar telecast. Richard Zanuck is the son of legendary producer Darryl F. Zanuck.

Thomas Schumacher is the producer of the animated feature film *Lion King*. While head of animation at Walt Disney Co., Schumacher was also instrumental in the successful Broadway production of *Lion King*. Schumacher presided over the releases of *Toy Story 2* and *Dinosaur*.

Bob Bookman is an agent for Steven Spielberg at Creative Artists Agency, the biggest talent agency in Hollywood. Mr. Bookman is also past president of Fraternity of Friends, a men's support group for the Music Center. He has co-chaired an entertainment industry fundraising drive for the Music Center.

Dale Olson is a Hollywood publicist and Academy member who works on the Public Relations Coordinating Committee for the Oscars. Olson spearheaded the DreamWorks Oscar marketing campaign for *American Beauty*. A former executive at Rogers and Cowan, Olson's clients have included Steve McQueen, Gene Kelly, Shirley MacLaine and Diana Rigg.

Tim Vreeland is Professor of Architecture at UCLA, son of the late *Vogue* editor Diana Vreeland and frequenter of Society functions.

Nancy Vreeland was a major L.A. Society doer who co-chaired the 125th year salute to the Los Angeles Public Library.

Jody Jacobs was Society editor for the *L. A. Times* for fifteen years. Ms. Jacobs is highly regarded throughout the city in all the top social circles.

Andrea Van de Kamp is past CEO of the Music Center and West Coast President of Sotheby's. She is chairperson emeritus of the Music Center. Her husband, John Van de Kamp, is a former Attorney General of California.

Joni Smith is past President of the Music Center's Blue Ribbon, the top women's group in Los Angeles.

Terry Stanfill is an author and former hostess of studio parties with her husband Dennis when Dennis Stanfill was Chairman of 20th Century Fox. Mrs. Stanfill is on the board of the L.A. Opera, is a West Coast International Representative for Christie's, and writes fiction. Her novel, *The Blood Remembers,* was a finalist in general fiction for the Independent Publisher's Award.

Michele Lamy created Les Deux Cafés, the trendy French hideaway in the middle of Hollywood that quickly became part of the must-see, must-do L.A. restaurant scene.

Ruth Ryon writes the high-end "Hot Property" section of the *L.A. Times*.

Jeff Hyland is head of a top Westside real estate firm with partner Rick Hilton, and co-author of the book *The Estates of Beverly Hills*.

Joan Quinn is former Society editor for the *Los Angeles Herald-Examiner*. Mrs. Quinn is a photographer and writer for *Inside Events* magazine and has made several appearances on "Hard Copy." She was an early collector of contemporary L.A. art, and her collection is shown throughout the country.

Jane Nathanson is a top collector of contemporary art. Mrs. Nathanson organized with Lee Radziwill the 1988 reception for the Armani fashion show in L.A. She is a board member of the Museum of Contemporary Art and attended the 1998 White House reception for British Prime Minister Tony Blair. Her husband, Marc Nathanson, founded Falcon Cable TV.

Alyce de Roulet Williamson is married to Warren B. Williamson who, as a member of the Chandler family, sits on the L.A. Times Mirror Board. Mrs. Williamson is a board member of L.A.'s First Families, a Trustee of the Art Center College of Design and a past president of the Hollywood Bowl Patroness Committee.

Lenore Greenberg was an early collector of contemporary art in Los Angeles. Mrs. Greenberg is a past president of the Museum of Contemporary Art and a Blue Ribbon member.

Joan Hotchkis is President of the Blue Ribbon. Mrs. Hotchkis is also active in the Colleagues, another prominent L.A. social group. She chaired the 30th anniversary celebration of the Blue Ribbon.

311

John Bruce Nelson is head of his own top real estate firm and a long-time Beverly Hills resident. Nelson's clients have included Helen Hunt, the Sultan of Brunei, George Harrison, Elvis, and Steven Spielberg.

Carolyn See is the author of *Dreaming: Hard Luck and Good Times in America,* a portrayal her family wrought by alcohol and drugs in the context of pursuing the American Dream in the L.A. of the 1950s and '60s. See is a professor of American literature at UCLA and an accomplished novelist.

Alan Berliner is the photographer of choice for L.A. Society and Hollywood. Mr. Berliner has photographed a Who's Who of Hollywood including Tom Cruise and Nicole Kidman, Demi Moore and Bruce Willis, Dustin Hoffman, Frank Sinatra, Sly Stallone, Sharon Stone and many others. Betsy Bloomingdale, Marion Jorgensen and Barbara Davis are also regular clients.

John Martens is General Manager of Neiman Marcus Beverly Hills and active on the L.A. social circuit.

Robert Shapazian is head of the Gagosian Gallery in Beverly Hills.

David Brown is past President of the Art Center College of Design in Pasadena.

Helen Wolford was the first president of the Music Center's Blue Ribbon.

LaVetta Forbes is the owner/editor of *Beverly Hills 90212* magazine.

Helen Chaplin has served in executive and consulting positions at the Beverly Wilshire Hotel and the Beverly Hills Hotel. She arranged for high-level staff to answer our questions at both the Beverly Wilshire and the Beverly Hills Hotel.